ROONEY'S GOLD

ROONEY'S GOLD

JOHN SWEENEY

First published in Great Britain i

Biteback Publishing Ltd

Heal House

375 Kennington Lane

London

SE11 5QY

ISBN 978-1-84954-054-4

10 9 8 7 6 5 4 3 2 1

A CIP catalogue record for this book is available from the British Library.

Set in Kepler and Myriad
Printed and bound in Great Britain by TJ International Ltd, Padstow, Cornwall

To Tomiko

Without her constant mockery and unstinting criticism, I wouldn't have had to prove to her that this book would one day exist.

CONTENTS

ACKNOWLEDGEMENTS

No Wayne, no book, so thanks to Big Wayne and Jeanette Rooney for bringing him into the world. No Wayne, no great stories; no Coleen, no romance, so thanks to them too.

In London, thanks to half of Fleet Street for stimulating, entertaining and, only occasionally, revolting copy on the Crocky Cyclone. Thanks, in particular, to his ghost, Hunter Davies, and to tabloid sleuth Graham Johnson.

In Liverpool and Birkenhead, thanks to a string of people and a grand selection of pubs, including the Wezzy.

In Manchester, thanks to those who wear green and gold.

In Russia, thanks to the staff of *Novaya Gazeta* and the friends of the late Yuri Shchekochikhin, whose poisoners, one day, will be brought to justice.

Having a glass of wine with my agent, Caroline Michel, was one of the best things I have done in my career. Thanks to Iain Dale at Biteback, who is steady under fire.

Thanks to a slew of characters at my day job, who know who they are, in particular the Chelsea fan, the Spurs fan, the Swindon Town fan, the West Ham fan, the Wycombe fan; also, fans of Tranmere everywhere and the Leeds scum.

Special thanks to Sam, Molly, my mother, Barbara, and to the memory of my father, Leonard, who didn't drink in the Western Approaches but fought there.

London
May 2010

INTRODUCTION

The English like their lions rough, not smooth. This is the story of the rise and fall and rise again of Wayne Rooney, a boy from the mean streets of broken Britain – few streets meaner than Croxteth in Liverpool – who lifted himself out of poverty by his footballing genius to play for Manchester United and England.

On the pitch, most of the time, a hero. Off it, the centrepiece, with his wife Coleen, of perhaps the most vacuous media soap opera of modern times.

Wayne Rooney was a tabloid angel who became a demon overnight when it came out that he'd been having sex with a PVC-clad grannie called the Auld Slapper. (There's no serious evidence that ever happened, but on Planet Rooney the truth is stranger than the headlines.)

He shrugged off the abuse and carried on scoring goals. Lots of them. He can be bad tempered and foul mouthed, but there's no doubting his passion for the beautiful game – and a basic, street-level sense of fair play. He was sent off in the 2006 World Cup for doing the cha-cha-cha on the testicles of a Portuguese player, but it was his arch-rival 'Roonaldo' who seemed to play dirty, Rooney who emerged the victim, whose disgrace seemed unfair.

Rough, working-class, surrounded by an unlikely crew – including a dodgy agent, a crooked lawyer, tarts and gangsters – Rooney is a very lumpy hero. *Rooney's Gold* looks at the characters who have been attracted to the fabulous money he gets for kicking a pig's bladder around a field. Some of them have tainted his gold. Some of them will not enjoy reading this book. One of them – his agent Paul Stretford – did his best to stop it. Later, he was fined £300,000 and banned for nine months by the Football Association.

Oh dear.

Others have tried to do their best by Rooney. They include some of the brightest lights of modern football, including David Beckham and Sir Alex Ferguson. Of all the contenders to be captain of England at this summer's World Cup, it is Rooney who has become the model husband and father, Rooney who changes the electricity of a game the moment he walks on the pitch, Rooney who scores the most goals, Rooney who fights the hardest.

This book is no hagiography. (That's fancy talk – from the ancient Greek meaning the story of a saint – for arse-licking.) Where Wayne Rooney has behaved badly, he gets his arse kicked. It's also about others who may have behaved badly – including women who get paid for sleeping with men and men who get paid for chopping up other men. And, funnily enough for a book about a footballer, it's about something bigger than a game of two halves. 'The battleline between good and evil runs through the heart of every man,' wrote the great Russian writer Alexander Solzhenitsyn, who never played for Tranmere, let alone Man United. Perhaps more than any male celebrity in the modern age, Wayne Rooney has been surrounded from the word go with the demons of temptation. To begin with, the demons were winning, big time. But not now. Other members of the England team are getting all the wrong headlines.

Not Rooney.

Above all, this is the story of a boy who, despite all the forces pulling him down, rose up to become a hero.

Cynics might say this is a book about an angry potato by an exploding tomato. The cynics would be dead right. My own personal brush with 1′37″ of fame – if you don't know what I am blethering on about, look me up on YouTube – has perhaps helped me understand and empathise in some small way with the pressures on real celebrities. It said in the papers that I said: 'Don't make me angry. You won't like it if you make me angry.' I never said that. It doesn't matter. If you're in the papers, they control you. You don't control them. Is that unfair? Yes. Can you do much about it? No, not much. Is free speech more important than embarrassing stories – even if they may sometimes be horribly unfair – for celebrities and those who wield power? Yes. If you disagree, go to North Korea. Pyongyang rocks, some say.

One of the themes of *Rooney's Gold* is that we should not judge the man unless and until we have taken a good look at the context, at the story behind the story, at his circle, at our society, at our world and the Big Money that makes it go round and round.

Why does a man with a genius for computing how a ball arcs through a parabola in space-time faster than seven billion people make a king's ransom for himself? Well, that's a consequence of our moral idiocy. That's not his fault.

The life and times of Wayne Rooney make, perhaps, *the* dysfunctional fairy story of our time – Beauty and the Beast meets Alien v. Predator meets Cinderella-in-Football Boots, not forgetting the Curse of the Black Thong. Perhaps more than any other pantomime nonsense from the beginning of the twenty-first century, it shines a light on our moronic celebrity culture. He and his circle often appear to have been the victim of creatures that creep on the face of the earth – hedge-fund managers, whores, newspaper barons, thugs, reporters, gangsters – in no easy order of virtue.

That's not his fault, either.

Brand Rooney may be a living symbol of a world that has lost its marbles. In our new age of austerity with the country up to its eyes in debt and millions on the dole, he is paid £4.68 million a year to kick a football and £1.5 million a year to allow his image to grace household-name products – for example, for a teeth-rotting-fat-bulging-belch-inducing-hyper-making-super-sugary carbonated water which rhymes with 'poke'.

But Wayne Rooney is a great athlete and, not just by the standards of the grim place he hails from, not a bad man. He has come a very, very long way from Croxteth: holidays in the Caribbean with a butler thrown in, now a pad of his own in Barbados, a gin-palace off the south of France, a whole Vroom-Vroom of motor cars, enough to make Jeremy Clarkson, TV's anti-pope of global warming, snot green with envy, a new-build mansionette in Cheshire – albeit one that brings to mind the architecture of a gas showroom – a good woman as his wife, a son and, maybe this summer, a fair shot at the World Cup.

Like muck to a farmer's boots, dirt sticks to Rooney's gold. One cannot hope to understand the full majesty of the fairy story – Boy becomes footballing star at the age of seven, the myth of Auld Slapper, The Dodgy Agent, the Gangster and his Friend who kept his .45 Magnum underneath his Mother's Flowerpot and the Leg in the Lay-By – without getting a little bit mucky. After he left Everton and scarpered down the East Lancs Road for a Manchester United shirt and a barrel load of cash, the Toffees had their revenge. The Everton fans chanted:

> He's fat,
> He's round,
> He'll shag your nan for £40.
> Rooney!

Stop there. There is not a shred of reliable evidence that Wayne Rooney ever slept with the PVC-clad prostitute baptised by the tabloids as the Auld Slapper. She is one of a number of people in this narrative who emerge, not perhaps brilliantly, but less badly than some of the people poking their fingers and crying 'Shame!' So does Wayne Rooney.

True, as a teenager, pumped full of adrenalin and cash, he did have sex with consenting adults for money. For the record, he paid them. That was foolish but it's not the worst thing you can do in your life, by a long chalk. Some of the others in this story – a senior police officer whose mind froze at the worst possible moment, a whole slew of newspaper bosses, a thuggery of gangsters and an agent on whose word a criminal court could not rely – come out much, much worse than the Boy Wonder himself. Some people preyed on the young and silly superstar.

That's not his fault.

For the moment, Rooney appears to be the best striker and also the best money-generator of Manchester United, one of the richest sporting clubs in the world, and also one of the most heavily borrowed against. If the amount of money paid to Rooney seems bonkers, then one should also consider the financial genius of former Florida trailer-park entrepreneur Malcolm Glazer, whose family business bought the club in the mid-noughties by borrowing roughly half a billion quid. The interest on that loan cost the Glazers a reported £60 million a year, so they have at the start of 2010 issued a £500 million bond. This is all fancy money talk. In plain English? Well, the Burnley fans did chant about United's finances while Rooney put one in the back of their net in January 2010: 'We've got more money than you have . . .'

You can make a lot of money out of taxing passion – and in the modern world the passion engendered by the most famous team on the planet is a very profitable passion indeed. Perhaps that's why, since the Glazers took over, seat prices at Old Trafford have gone up, critics say, more than 40 per cent. Perhaps that's why Manchester United's corporate bond bid wasn't based in Manchester at all, but 180 miles south in London's ever-so-posh clubland, Pall Mall. The man in charge of the corporate side is that modern folk devil, a banker. To anyone who believes in the truth rather than the fairy story of the beautiful game, perhaps Manchester United should more appropriately be named Pall Mall Rovers. That probably won't be happening any time soon.

But a whole new set of wannabe owners have ridden into the glen, garbed in green and gold – harking back to the club colours of Newton Heath, the old name of the Reds. The Manchester United Supporters Trust, MUST, have little time for what they say is the mountain of debt built up by the Glazers. They want the Glazers out. At the time of writing, MUST has 150,000 fans signed up to its website and on away days the Man United end is awash with green and gold. But wanting something is not the same as having it. Enter the Red Knights, led by United hardcore fan and Goldman Sachs chief economist Jim O'Neill. Bankers? He knows buckets of them. If MUST and the Red Knights are all they are cracked up to be, this could mark a moment of revolution in British football – the time when the fans stood up to Big Money and shouted them down. If football's number one fashionista is a guide, then when AC Milan played United, David Beckham looked very fetching in his green and gold scarf.

This space will be watched. For their part, the Glazers' spokesman has said: 'Manchester United is the most profitable club in the world.' The £500 million bond issue was subscribed twice over. The Glazers have said, loud and clear, that Man United is not for sale.

As far as the man himself is concerned, Rooney's genius on the pitch used to be cast into shadow by his genius at getting into pitch off it. The verdict of one woman he paid to have sex with when he was seventeen before he started dating Coleen – he signed a note, graciously thanking her for the shag – that he can't write properly and didn't seem all that bright, was, back then, hard to refute.

He's changed. The tabloids are still after his head. Or, better, his dick. He's given them next to nothing to go on – off the pitch – for years. That's a signal achievement – and one that other members of the present England team might care to copy.

Rooney is a multimillionaire because he has something amazing inside his head which enables him to get the better of, let us hope, a player named after the bloke in the toga who invaded Britain in 54 BC, Júlio César Soares de Espíndola, who is, of course, Brazil's goalkeeper.

That, too, is not his fault.

In our society, his skill is rewarded massively more than people who face the battle of the classroom every morning, who look after the old, the sick and the dying, who save people's lives, who arrest the nasty bastards, who risk their lives fighting wars started by other people, who put out fires.

That's wrong but not his fault.

A lot of mush has been written about Rooney and Coleen, some of it even, allegedly, by themselves, and hopefully this book won't add to it. Wayne and Coleen's lifestyle choices may sometimes appear like a crude satire on the banality of materialism. The bling – the rocks and frocks and motor cars (some that all but triple the speed limit in Britain) – they spend their money on seems proof, if proof were needed, of Alexander

Pope's sally: 'One can tell the contempt God holds for riches by the people whom he chooses to give them to.'

Rooney's Gold casts a critical eye on all and everyone whose stories have entered Wayne's World, from a top police officer who told a terrible lie to the Director of Public Prosecutions to a psychotic gangster who chopped body parts up and dumped them across the Home Counties in matching luggage, to Britain's most crooked lawyer, to a whole gallery of soccer players.

As I have mentioned already, Rooney's agent Paul Stretford comes in for a measure of criticism in this book. He did charm the socks off Wayne's mum and dad when he met them in 2002, while Wayne was still contracted to another agent. In that year Wayne Rooney signed a footballing contract with Proactive – the agency Stretford set up – while still contracted to the other agent. That is against the rules of the Football Association.

To make matters worse the Rooneys ended up getting independent legal advice to look over the paperwork from Kevin Dooley. Once upon a time, Dooley had been the lawyer of choice for Liverpool FC's stars. He was a character, a fixture at Anfield and a legend in his own lunchtime. But by the turn of the twenty-first century, Kevin Dooley was a very bent lawyer in a hurry, under investigation by the authorities for his part in a well-publicised scandal involving other people's money disappearing into the hands of a conman known as 'Long John Silver'.

Dooley & Co. had been raided in 2000, then shut down for good by the authorities in 2002. Although Dooley's firm had been closed down, he still had a solicitor's ticket and he moved to another firm, albeit working under a cloud. In July 2002 he was tried by the Solicitors' Disciplinary Tribunal for his role in the Long John Silver scam and while awaiting the verdict, in August, Dooley advised the Rooneys. In September, the bent lawyer was struck off for good. And who introduced the Rooneys to Dooley, one of the most crooked lawyers in Britain? That, according to Stretford on oath, was either him or a colleague at Proactive. Stretford has made it clear he had no idea that Dooley was in deep trouble when the lawyer was introduced to the Rooneys.

Later, Stretford, suspected of muscling in on Rooney, became prey to threats of violence. He sat down at a meeting with people who wanted to take Rooney away from him or get a slice of the Roo action. Also present was a very nasty London gangster indeed. A while later, a large ex-boxer Scouser, accompanied by two Australian cage fighters, burst into a meeting and frightened the life out of Stretford. Whatever you may think about the agent, he didn't deserve that. You cannot read a description of the boxer-cum-cage-fighters-incident without feeling sorry for the agent. A blackmail trial followed with Stretford as the Crown's star witness. But the trial collapsed after Stretford gave evidence on the stand which did not stack up. The prosecution told the court they could no longer rely on his word. He continues to deny he had misled the court, blaming the prosecution for bungling his evidence. The Football Association investigated and found that Stretford had given 'false and/or misleading evidence' to the police and 'false and/or misleading testimony' in eight instances at the trial, including his denial that he had 'muscled in' on the previous agent. Stretford appealed and lost and ultimately accepted a £300,000 fine and a nine-month ban. Late on in 2008, after the FA's Disciplinary Committee had poured a bucket of the brown stuff over Stretford, he and Proactive – now part of Formation Group PLC – parted company.

The posh blokes with wigs on their bonces – they call themselves lawyers – are, at the time of writing, still arguing about the consequences in cash for the Rooneys of that split between Stretford and Proactive/ Formation. Wayne Rooney still trusts Stretford and the whole family sticks by him. In the flesh, Stretford appears like a northern clone of Arthur Daley, the entrepreneur in ITV's *Minder* – a wheeler-dealer played by George Cole.

To sum up Stretford in four words: easy patter, dodgy charm.

He has an eye out for the main chance, he looks after his own interests, but in the shark-infested world of British football Paul Stretford, just like Arthur Daley, is, on the sliding scale of sharkishness, not so much a Great Killer White, more a dogfish.

The world of Wayne Rooney can be mucky and messy and the money is silly. But let's note that in Christmas 2009 Wayne and Coleen dumped their fancy holiday plans and stayed at home to visit Coleen's adopted invalid sister, seriously ill in hospital. Two months later his mum, Jeanette, and dad, Wayne Senior, went in to bat for him in court surrounded by an unease of pin-striped lawyers and, by their lights, they did their boy proud. When Jeanette was invited by a learned friend to leaf through one of the bundles – an enormous ring-binder containing a yawn of legal documents – and it exploded, bursting out its contents, Jeanette started to giggle like a schoolgirl, a refreshing moment of humanity in the bleak courtroom. Wayne Senior and Jeanette and the rest of the Rooney clan may have left finishing school a term too early but on the essential things of life – looking after your family and friends – they're not bad people. Coleen is gracious and good for him. And Wayne? If your house was on fire and he was passing, you could rely on him to kick the door down, rescue your loved ones and do the right thing. He's rough as rough can be, but he's still a hero.

A word about Liverpool because the city, too, is a character in this book. Overseen by the two Liver Birds – the female bird looking out to sea, checking to see whether there are any handsome sailors coming in to port, the male bird looking over the city, waiting for the pubs to open – Liverpool comes in for a fair amount of stick in this book. It can be too big for its boots. Take the Mersey ferry on a sunny winter's day. Observe the quick brown slosh of the river chopping against the ferry's bow. To the north, Liverpool Bay and beyond that the Irish Sea and the Atlantic. To the south, Stanlow oil refinery. To the west Tranmere oil refinery, an old U-boat and the empty sheds of the great Cammell Laird shipyard. To the east, Liverpool, the Pier Head dominated by a snazzy new-fangled ferry terminal, and behind that the Chicago mobster era architecture of the Liver Building, empty docks, canyons of brick and concrete and rows of terraced houses. The commentary from the ferry's tannoy booms: 'Liverpool's Maritime Mercantile City has been named as a UNESCO World Heritage Site, along with the Taj Mahal.' In Liverpool, you're never five minutes from something that makes you howl with laughter.

Some of the stories in this book might give you the idea that Liverpool is populated only by unsaintly football players and gangsters and prostitutes – I didn't make them up – but that wider impression is not fair and not true. I know that because the Mersey runs in my blood, er, so to speak. My mother was born in Liverpool. Her mother, Edith Owen, was a theatrical landlady with a wicked sense of humour. She looked after young actors at the Liverpool Rep like Richard Briers and the lady who played Mavis in *Coronation Street.* On a film set once doing a story, I bumped into Briers and he instantly remembered my gran: 'Oh, of course, Mrs Owen. She cooked our wedding breakfast.' My father was born on the west bank of the Mersey in Birkenhead, and grew up to become a ship's engineer in the Battle of the Atlantic. I learnt the arguments why Everton was the best team in the world from my uncles, why Liverpool was the best from my Auntie Jean and why Tranmere Rovers was the best from my dad. For some reason I cannot explain, I follow my dad's team.

True, Liverpool was once an imperial city through which, in the early part of the nineteenth century, passed 40 per cent of the world's trade – including profits from the slave ships. Those days are long gone. In living memory, Liverpool did its bit in the Second World War, the base from which Britain fought Hitler's U-boats. In those days the Mersey was full of ships and, come midnight on New Year's Eve, the whole city would echo with the sound of the ship's foghorns. The ships have gone too, and the old docks, and for a while it was a city that seemed to be dying.

But the Liverpool I know is full of life and fun. I remember visiting my gran, who lived in Page Moss, not far from the Eagle and Child pub, when I was a schoolboy, and sitting on a bus when a bread van cut in ahead of us, causing the bus driver to stamp on the brakes. Quick as a flash, the bus driver yelled through his open window: 'Use your loaf!' I remember visiting Knowsley Safari Park in Auntie Jean's Mini, and the monkeys ate the windscreen wipers. If New York never sleeps, then Liverpool never bores.

The former Conservative leader Michael Howard, born in Wales but a long-time Liverpool fan, is a very different kettle of fish from Wayne Rooney. He once said that the difference between Liverpool and London is that when you step into a lift in London, when you arrive at the ground floor everybody gets out unsmiling; in Liverpool, everybody gets out laughing.

The ethos of this book is contained in the old Swahili proverb: 'The higher the monkey climbs the tree, the more you can see its bottom.' My favourite philosopher is not Wayne Rooney but Diogenes the Cynic (410–320 BC), who lived in a tub, was rude to the ruler of the known world and once wandered around Athens with a lamp in the middle of the day 'looking for an honest man'. Both the Swahili wit and Diogenes would have gone 'ooh' and 'ahh' at Rooney's play; both would have gone 'no!' at some of the things he's done.

Rooney's Gold pokes fun at Brand Rooney and Wayne Rooney. But it also recognises that celebrities, however moronic they can sometimes be, are human, too. It's hard to imagine the pressure on someone like Wayne Rooney. If you're in the public eye, you shouldn't lose your temper – not several times, not even once. He loses his temper too often and that is his fault. But he is still a great footballer and football is a great thing: it converts the passions and hatreds of tribe, war and battle into a game, which sometimes can be beautiful. And if you lose, no one dies. The challenge for Wayne Rooney has been for him to unlock the genius but lock up the anger inside him.

That way we can be proud of him, all of the time.

But we know he's only human.

That's how we like our lions.

1

THE TRUTH ABOUT THE CROCKY BOY WONDER

It's the morning of Halloween night in Crocky and yellow-and-blue police scene-of-crime tape flutters in the breeze outside the Wezzy. Deep purple storm clouds pile up over the Welsh hills and billow eastwards towards Liverpool, bearing with them the certainty of rain.

The police tape is not a pre-Halloween stunt. Gangsters shot someone, a seventeen-year-old, in the leg, just behind 'the Wezzy' – the Western Approaches public house – the previous night. The pub boasts a fine sign of a steamship ploughing bravely through the grey Atlantic. It gets its name from the patch of ocean to the left of the British Isles where our brave merchant seamen brought home the bacon while Hitler's U-boats lurked in the depths intent on murder and mayhem, just like, critics might say, the regulars today. Drinkers in the Wezzy treat strangers to their pub with a circumspection that can be chilling. I've been to Chechnya twice and the Wezzy twice and, to be frank, I can't recommend a weekend break in either.

Welcome to Planet Rooney.

It feels rather too much like a war zone. If you don't believe me, go there, buy a pint and just clock the hostility of the faces clocking you, with a thousand-mile stare that the Khmer Rouge would have thought a bit over the top. I wasn't wearing a sequinned hot-pink ensemble, I didn't squeal 'Can I have a banana daiquiri?' in a falsetto, and I didn't have a tarantula on my nose, but I might as well have done. If you're an outsider, the Wezzy is a contender for being the least friendly pub in the western hemisphere.

Bleak isn't the word for Crocky, Liverpool 11. Bleak doesn't begin to describe the too-wide avenues and the dogshitty grass and the razor-wire fences and the shutters on the front of every shop – even the public library – and the hunch-shouldered not-much-hopery of the smudge-faced people walking to the bus stop so that they can get into the city and a bit of life.

You only go to Crocky if you turn off the East Lancs Road by mistake. The taxi driver was apologetic: 'There's not much, the pub, a few shops, a bookie's,' and he was so guilty of over-selling he ought to retrain as an estate agent. The place where Wayne Rooney was born and bred is an alien environment, somewhere you drive through in a hurry with the car doors on lockdown. Croxteth, to give it the name only people in uniforms call it, is not an inner-city slum but somehow something worse, more depressing, an edge-of-city slum, a modern, state-of-the-art dystopia, a £2 bus ride from anything civic worth shaking a stick at; spaced out, not crowded in but no less deprived, circles of asphalt and concrete, swathes of grass, banished to the eastern rim of England's poorest big city. Crocky was built postwar on farmland, first to house people from the Scotland Road area of Liverpool (where my mother was born) made homeless by Hitler's bombs. A second wave of council houses were built to replace the slum clearance made necessary by the second Mersey tunnel.

The suburb's greatest export was raised inside a small grid just to the south of the East Lancs Road, and this is where you can find most of Roo's extended family and his infants', junior and secondary schools, all within a few hundred yards of each other. It is where he first snogged Coleen McLoughlin, his teenage sweetheart who, the snotty used to say, was the Crowned Queen of Chavs.

Trying to make sense of what Wayne and Coleen have done with the celebrity (and the bucketloads of cash) that have been thrust at them requires getting to know a little bit about Crocky. The East Lancs Road – the main artery between Liverpool and Manchester, before the motorways were built – runs west to east. To the north is the sewage works. Turn to the south, down Lower House Lane, and you pass on your left the drive-in McDonald's where the staff called Rooney all sorts of names after he quit Everton for the fool's gold – they would say – of Manchester United; and then a long grey wall, and behind that a lot of greenery. Before you get too excited by the rural idyll, closer inspection reveals gravestone after gravestone. West Derby cemetery is the most restful part of Crocky, though some say a few of its inhabitants still collect their benefit. Of course people fiddle the system here – and why not? – because you can't help thinking the system has screwed them. Poverty, deprivation, long-term unemployment, children forcibly removed from 'abusive' families, high crime, bad diet, vandalism, more than half the children at school claiming free school meals, high premature death rates: this place ticks nearly every box of the 'you don't want to live here' checklist.

The Wezzy – a formidable brick two-storey monument to 1940s utility architecture – stands on the corner of Lower House Lane and Storrington Avenue. Inside, the clientele sport trackies, have ruby-veined noses and sccm lost in their alcohol.

They drink to remember.

They drink to forget.

They drink because there is nothing else to do.

Turn right into Storrington Avenue, past the parked police cars and the scene-of-crime officers investigating the previous night's shooting, and there is a newsagent's-cum-post office and a bookie's, boasting anti-ram-raid shutters which will come down the moment the shop shuts at the end of the day. I don't think I saw a single shop in the whole Liverpool 11 area without these tell-tale metal defences from their own customers. Crocky is Shutter City.

Storrington Avenue is the bottom of the grid, running parallel to the East Lancs Road. Immediately to the west lies Norris Green, which is as rough as Crocky but doesn't quite sound it. The amenities stick out like a sore thumb. If, for whatever reason, you don't fancy the Wezzy, you could go and drink at Wayne's dad's old local of choice, the Dog and Gun. The local joke had it that it was unwise to step past the threshold of the Dog and Gun unless you had a gun and a dog. On my visit, it had been boarded up and closed down, according to the taxi driver because of police pressure: 'There were too many guns and not enough dogs.'

Hang a left just past the derelict Dog and Gun and you're on Stonebridge Lane, running north towards the East Lancs Road. Halfway down Stonebridge Lane is the old Rooney family home. A giant poster stuck to the door sports a vomit-green-faced Frankenstein monster beneath Gothic letters in blood proclaiming 'Happy Halloween'. The monster's eyes flash off and on, off and on.

It's Halloween night every night in Crocky.

Ordinary people do extraordinary things. Many – most – in Croxteth are decent souls, trying to get by and get a little extra for their loved ones without doing anything very wicked to anyone else. The professionals help, during the day. And then they go away. For example, at Wayne's old school, De La Salle Comprehensive, at midday I counted about thirty cars neatly parked in the car park behind automatic gates and a security fence so high that I had last seen something like it surrounding a Royal Ulster Constabulary post in South Armagh. You get the feeling that if a tough teacher known to discipline left his car out on the street, the tyres wouldn't last very long. Or the engine block. Or the chassis. And by five o'clock there were about five cars left behind the security fence. Everybody else had commuted out and gone home to somewhere, pretty much anywhere, nicer. Money, the middle classes, the ambitious or self-starting working classes have so drained away from areas like Croxteth that all you have left is a hard-core sump of deprived families. A few individuals may stand up for community values and stay in Crocky, but not enough to keep the place from giving off a sense of long-term neglect and defeat. Worse, the decay feels continuing, remorseless, unopposed.

The neighbourhood has gone further down the nick since Roo left, after the soccer money started flooding through his letter box, and that's not that many years ago. The gunplay at the back of the Wezzy in October

2006 was part of a tit-for-tat chain of shootings which started before the murder of Liam 'Smigger' Smith, aged nineteen, and ended in something much, much worse. Smigger was shot in the head outside Altcourse prison in August 2006.

Imagine contempt for the forces of law and order so profound that you are willing to whack a rival outside a nick.

Smigger's killing was one episode of a long turf war between two gangs of scrotes, his Nogga Dogs or Nogzy Soldiers or the Strand Crew from Norris Green and the Crocky Crew from Croxteth, just on the other side of the dog dirt.

What happened was that Smigger, while seeing a friend in the prison's visiting hall, was spotted by a prisoner from the rival Crocky Crew, Ryan Lloyd, who was in the visiting hall chatting to his sisters. Lloyd ran out of the visiting hall back into the prison wing shouting: 'Quick, quick, give us the phone, I'll get the boys up here to pop them.' Lloyd got a contraband phone and made a call. Smigger left the prison within an hour. He was shot in the head by a sawn-off shotgun fired from five yards away.

After Smigger's death, the pathologist dug out old shotgun pellets from his body, dating back to a previous shooting months before the one that killed him. Immediately before his funeral, the Nogga Dogs redecorated eighteen premises in the small parade of shops in Norris Green with graffiti proclaiming 'Smigger RIP'. The teenage gangsters ordered that the shops and pubs shut down for the day of the funeral 'as a mark of respect'. Or else their businesses would be torched. The taxi driver told me the gangsters went round telling the shopkeepers that if they didn't do as they were told, they would be firebombed. Taxi-driver talk? *The Times* reported exactly the same thing, adding that the Merseyside Police took this warning seriously enough to urge shopkeepers and publicans to comply.

And shut down the shops did.

Some parents kept their children off school. Smigger had a proper mobster's funeral, even though he died still a teenager. Black-suited mourners and, de rigueur for all the gangsters who go to stick up the Pearly Gates, a horse-drawn hearse. You're not honoured unless you go to your grave – or the crem – in the transport of choice before the internal combustion engine was invented. The only off-notes were the cortège of hoodies in trackies immediately behind the hearse, a score of dayglo policemen, backed up by mobile video vans watching and identifying the hoodies, and a gang of council workmen who began washing away the 'Smigger RIP' graffiti immediately the mourning hoodies had passed by. The floral tributes remained.

One cannot but sympathise with a family that has lost a son before he is twenty. But the Nogga Dogs are a different matter. Being able to enforce public grief – or else your shop gets torched – is evidence that the gangstereens in this part of Liverpool have got too much power. Gang law rules in Liverpool 11. The *Liverpool Echo* and the local worthies gave good 'the violence must stop' quotes. Local West Derby MP Bob Wareing compared the scene to Chicago in the 1920s: 'I am absolutely appalled by the idea of ordinary, decent people running businesses and shoppers being intimidated in this way. We have to put an end to this. We cannot have part of a city run by gangsters. What they do between themselves is one thing but to make the lives of hundreds of ordinary, decent people miserable is something we cannot accept.'

Merseyside Police seemed rather embarrassed about this display of submission to teen gangsterdom and pulled their finger out. After the murder of Smigger, they had a bit of a crackdown and seized mobile phones and came up with a battery of not-so-happy 'happy snaps'. One shows a victim, blood pouring from gunshot wounds in his face, posing for the camera; a second, a hooded youngster brandishing a shotgun, careful to avoid getting fingerprints on the stock and barrel; a third, a loaded handgun; a fourth, two fighting dogs ripping at each other, urged on by their owners; a fifth, a cache of weapons and ammunition laid out for the camera; a sixth, huge knives displayed on the wall of a gang member's home; a seventh, a wheel-spinning Ferrari in a car park, thought to be that stolen from Everton FC's Andy Van der Meyde; and the eighth, a dog ripping at the trouser leg of a young girl.

Young Wayne is sometimes compared to one of the Bash Street Kids, from the comic strip in *The Beano*. The sad thing is that Bash Street is less depressing and more life-enriching than the real thing. It's certainly safer. The sequence of events in the mid-noughties – a series of shootings ending in a shotgun assassination outside a prison – can be seen as a depressing confirmation that the gangs noted the official displeasure and the heightened police activity, and decided they have more important things to do, like continuing to try to kill each other.

Because the police crackdown in Crocky in 2006 did not change much. That October I saw the police scene-of-crime tapes at the back of the Wezzy with my own eyes. The gunplay hadn't stopped. Worst of all, one August evening in 2007, a year after Smigger was shot dead, Sean Mercer of the Crocky Crew took out his gun by the Fir Tree pub – fifteen minutes' walk from the Wezzy – and went 'bang-bang-bang'. One of the bullets blasted Rhys Jones, a wholly innocent bystander, who was going home after a game of soccer. The bullet entered through Rhys's shoulder blade and exited through his neck, killing him. Rhys was eleven. The murder of a schoolboy caused outrage across the world, but for weeks many of Mercer's gang members and his mother kept silent. Mercer was convicted of murder with a recommendation that he serve twenty-two years. (While in prison Mercer used a pair of tweezers to stab Jake Fahri, who killed altar boy Jimmy Mizen in a bakery shop in London.) Mercer's mum got three years for keeping back evidence that would have helped the police catch her son.

This is what has become of home sweet Crocky home for Wayne Rooney. Many of his 'rellies' – Scouse for relatives, extended family – still live there, including his uncles, aunties and cousins. The Rooney family, rough as a brick outhouse though they may be, are by no means the roughest customers in Crocky. On the contrary, for that part of the world, you use the words 'respectable' and 'Rooneys' in the same breath.

To some, Wayne Rooney was a monstrous sign of our time, an out-of-control, gum-chewing, bad-mannered, whore-mongering, ill-tempered thug who earns multiples of money on the soccer pitch for kicking a ball around, apart from the last World Cup, when he disgraced our nation by kicking the balls of a Portuguese player. For his critics, Rooney is the emblem of our national malaise: a yob with feet of gold. But, to be fair, it's not Rooney's fault if we throw money at his form of genius. It's not his fault that his education wasn't of the best. A man's life is dyed with the colour of his own imagination, said Marcus Aurelius – not a Lazio fullback but the last of the great Roman emperors – suggesting, perhaps, that every man is a prisoner of his own mind, framed by home, family and circumstance.

Before condemning Rooney out of hand, it would be necessary, or at least polite, to ask two questions: first, was it the little monster (Rooney) or was it the swamp (Crocky)? Second, was the monster or the swamp to blame for the extreme Darwinian nature of football, or, for that matter, many other parts of our national life today – crazy riches if you are a winner, a cup of cold sick if you are a loser?

The petrol-head Voltaire of our day, Jeremy Clarkson, summed up Rooney's autobiography in four phrases: 'Wayne gets born, grows big ears, kicks a football, shags a grandmother.'

I'm not so sure he did shag a grandmother but I defy anyone to spend five minutes in Liverpool 11 without beginning to have at least a sneaking admiration for someone from Crocky who gets out of the place. Here, Wayne Rooney feels like a hero.

Wayne Mark Rooney was born on 24 October 1985, at Fazakerley Hospital, Liverpool, just down the road from Crocky, the first-born son of Thomas Wayne 'Big Wayne' Rooney, unemployed hod-carrier and labourer, and Jeanette Rooney, née Morrey, dinner lady and part-time cleaner. The couple lived at 28 Armill Road, Croxteth.

If you seek this address, you find a stretch of razor fencing, with a red-and-white plastic bag twisting poignantly – plastic bags never twist any other way – in the wind. Roo's first house has been demolished and is now the car park of a community centre. The street is otherwise wholly unremarkable.

But he was *conceived* in the middle of an eighteen-game unbeaten run that swept Everton to the 1984–5 title, and that's much more important than his birthdate. The Rooneys and the Morreys were Blues, lifelong Everton fans. Time was when religious bigotry cut across Liverpool as it does, even today, across Northern Ireland. In 1958 Cardinal Heenan was stoned while visiting a sick woman who lived close to an Orange Lodge. People say that Liverpool was the mainly Protestant team, Everton for Catholics, but those old religious divides have faded.

But if you live on the east bank of the Mersey, you're either Liverpool or Everton. There is no doubt that young Rooney's family home in Crocky was a shrine to the other Liverpool club. What Everton lacks in money and trophies, it makes up for in character, graft and that special loyalty people have for the underdogs. They call Everton 'the Toffees', some say after Mother Noblett's toffee shop, which was close by.

You can get some idea of Everton from what happens when the team walks out on to the pitch at Goodison Park: the Toffees rise and sing the theme from *Z Cars*, the black-and-white TV cop show from the 1960s set in Merseyside, which made a feature of panda cars, Scouse wit and storylines with working-class grit. No one in *Z Cars* died in the library, having been killed by a candlestick wielded by Professor Plum. It could be said that it is a sign of Everton's lowly status in the football fashion food chain that its theme tune was first heard in 1962 and belongs to a long-dead TV show featuring the late Inspector Barlow and the late Sergeant Watt. And yet it's a bloody good tune to mass-hum – and the beauty of supporting Everton is that the Toffees don't give a damn.

Little Wayne's immersion in the family cult was total. He said: 'All I ever wanted to do was walk out at Goodison Park with our theme tune, *Z Cars*, playing in the background. I wanted it so much . . . As a kid, I used to get shivers down my spine when I heard it and still do today.' Later on, a combination of pressures – big money, a claimed unhappiness with the manager, a hunger to win the big competitions – gobbled up Roo's loyalty to Everton and spat it out. For the moment, the future Evertonian was safe enough in his pram.

Wayne Rooney opens his autobiography, *My Story So Far*, with the shocking admission 'I was nearly called Adrian'. *My Story So Far* was typed up by Rooney's genial moustachioed ghostwriter, Hunter Davies, who knows a thing or two about very silly first names. Cynics might add that those first five words alone probably cost the publisher, HarperSport, around £500 and that's the best bit of the whole book, but that would be unfair. Adrian Rooney would have been a cursèd name for the headline writers. Adrian sounds like somebody who lives in Guildford, wears slippers and lives with his mum. Adrian would never have been sent off in a World Cup, although he might have made a cup of cocoa for the linesman.

'Wayne' is working-class, rough, tough and can be turned into the tabloid-friendly 'Wazza', which rhymes with Gazza and carries with it the instant suggestion of an unguided missile, 'rogue genius' quality that Fleet Street's in-house self-taught shrinks believe is shared by England's two most charismatic soccer heroes. Apart from the name of some Roman bloke who built a wall in Northumberland, nothing rhymes with Adrian.

It was Big Wayne who fancied calling his son Adrian, after an Everton player of yesteryear, Adrian Heath. Mum Jeanette, who talks loudly and carries a big stick, won the argument and the baby was named after his dad.

The huge plus for the newspapers is that you can manufacture an awful lot of puns out of 'Wayne Rooney' – 'Wayne's World' just for starters. You can even cut the whole thing down to three letters – ROO – which is always useful on a newspaper front page, and then build it up again: so we've got Roomania, Roonaldo – better, more British than Ronaldo – Rooling the Roost, Kanga-Roo, Roo-ful, blah blah blah. If you're a football supporter, you can chant the two syllables beautifully: 'Roo-ney, Roo-ney'.

'Wayne Rooney' is the perfect name for a street footballer. It's almost as if Baby Rooney was a made-to-order construct by the tabloids at the moment his parents signed his birth certificate. The rest was just kicking a ball around.

The Big Wayne/Little Wayne thing has its comic side. Little Wayne, now at five ten, stands some four inches taller than Big Wayne, his dad, who is two inches smaller than his wife. But you wouldn't want to mess with Big Wayne. He was a ferocious lightweight boxer in his day, representing first Liverpool, then the north-west counties. He fought and won against the navy and even went to Finland for a European competition, where he won silver and gold. Big Wayne could have been a contender, but somehow he never made it to the big time. His brothers Ritchie, John, Eugene and Alan all won in the ring, but Wayne says in the autobiography that his dad was the best of them all. There is a photograph from 1981 of young Big Wayne, with a towel around his shoulders, holding a boxing cup in one big glove while patting an opponent's glove with the other: when you study the photo, you think, 'He looks very much like his son' and 'I wouldn't like to mess with him'.

One of Rooney Senior's opponents in the ring was the young John Hyland, now a colourful Liverpool boxing promoter who re-entered the Rooney saga in 2003, when, attended by two cage fighters, he scared the living daylights out of Little Wayne's dodgy agent, Paul Stretford. It all ended messily in a blackmail case, but we are letting the narrative get ahead of itself.

The Rooneys were of poor Liverpool Irish stock, Roman Catholic enough to put 'RC' down on official documents and have a fight about the infallibility of His Holiness the Pope if any Protestant daft enough wanted one. Young Rooney was never going to be an altar boy. There has only ever been one famous Rooney before, Mickey Rooney, the pint-sized American actor with eight marriages to his name. He and Wayne are, sadly, not related.

Wayne Senior is one of eight children, five brothers and three sisters, most of whom still knock around the Croxteth area. He left school at sixteen, got a job as a butcher's boy for two years, and then the shop shut, so he became a labourer, ready to turn his hand to anything manual. He worked off and on throughout Little Wayne's childhood. The family never had much money and he never learnt a trade. Jeanette Morrey appears, to outsiders at least, to be the one who wears the trousers in the relationship. She seems to be sharper, more outgoing than her husband, to have more drive. The family name is French, according to Roo's official autobiography, but Scottish if you look it up on one genealogical website. Jeanette was one of nine children, and also Catholic. Her mother's dad, William Morrey, had been a professional footballer for Southport and two of her brothers – young Wayne's uncles – had also played the beautiful game. Uncle Billie had appeared for Marine, a non-league club from

Crosby, Liverpool, before he emigrated to Australia where he turned out for Green Gully, and Uncle Vinnie got one schoolboy under-15 cap for England. The Morrey side of the family claim another sporting relative up their sleeve: Bob 'Gentleman Ruby' Fitzsimmons, crowned Heavyweight Champion of the World in 1897.

Big Wayne and Jeanette decided to get married when Roo was seventeen months old. They had a local register office ceremony and, because they were living off Big Wayne's £120-a-week pay as a labourer, there was no honeymoon. The couple had two more children, both boys, Graeme and John. As soon as she was able, Jeanette went back to work, holding down two jobs: a dinner lady at the all-boys Catholic comprehensive De La Salle – where Little Wayne ended up going – in the day, and a cleaner in the evenings at the all-girls Catholic St John Bosco's, which was Coleen's secondary school.

The relative that young Wayne seemed to cherish the most was Granny Mavis, his dad's mum. 'GRAN WAS MY ROCK . . . I'M SO SO SAD SHE DIDN'T LIVE TO SEE ME PLAYING FOR ENGLAND' was the headline to the World Exclusive for the paper that got Rooney's story first. The young player went on to describe how he learnt his football in his granny's backyard: 'I'd play with my cousins in the garden but we'd kick the ball against the wall and the pebbledash would drop off. She used to go mad with me and give me a clip around the ear. But I was very close to my nan.'

Stop. Stop. Stop. *World Exclusive?* Wayne Rooney hates the media. In *My Story So Far*, he is straightforward about the worst thing in the life of a professional footballer: press intrusion into his private life. His aversion to journalists is so great that he has canalised the entire history of his (not very long) life and early footballing career into an official autobiography – and woe betide any friend or member of his big extended family who spills the Rooney beans to any paper or journalist writing outside that deal. Five million quid – the rumoured money for the autobiography deal stretching over five books – buys a fair amount of respect, even today, even for a celebrity in Britain, but the underlying purpose of speaking his heart out in *My Story So Far* – if speak his heart out he does – may not be just money but editorial control, to tell his story the way he and his advisers want it told. The autobiography came out in 2006, but there was one journalist working for one particular newspaper who got in there first, in 2004, and succeeded in interviewing Wayne Rooney, Coleen McLoughlin and their families and close friends. Her name is Sue Evison – who went on to write Roo's first biography, *England's Hero* – and she works for *The Sun* and her World Exclusive deserves a round of applause.

Clap with one hand.

It was a scoop, of sorts. Money came into the deal – a reported £250,000, which to Wayne, in 2004, when he was still playing at Everton, before he had hit the big, big time, would have seemed tempting. But that's not the whole story of Evison's scoop.

The full history behind the getting of the *Sun* World Exclusive tells you something about the true nature of what it is like to be a celebrity. The money that can be made out of A-listers and their stories buckles lives. The Big Money that stages the show gives a percentage, a cut to the celebs, and that money buys bling, buys things – lots of things – and that blinds people, the celebrities most of all, to what is really going on with their lives. Take Rooney's motors. In *My Story So Far*, he admits that he has developed a passion for cars. Since his sponsored Ford Ka – a runtish-looking, snub-nosed motor some people claimed he didn't like very much – he says that he and Coleen have had a few but 'nothing too extravagant'. He then lists them: a brace of BMW X5s, a Mercedes 4x4 and a Mercedes SLK. When Coleen started earning 'decent' money she bought herself a new Range Rover, and just before the England squad left for Germany in 2006 she bought him an Aston Martin Vanquish as a surprise early birthday present. Over the years, he has run a Cadillac Escalade, a Bentley Continental GT, top speed 195mph, and a Lamborghini Gallardo, top speed 193mph.

Nothing too extravagant? My arse.

The dream couldn't get any better, you might think. But the flipside of the dream is the nightmare of constant intrusion. Big Money can buy any and every detail of your life. If the price is right, you go along – and why not? And one day you wake up and realise that you don't have control of your life any more. You are something that is traded, a pet in a gilded cage in a market full of pets in gilded cages. And all the Lamborghini Gallardos in east Lancashire can't make up for that.

Once you have 'celebrity' stamped on your forehead, any aspect of your life is up for sale, available at the right market price, even something as seemingly innocent as a family's memories of a kid's first kick against his granny's pebbledash wall. Nothing is quite what it seems in the celebrity pet cage. You have lost control over much of your life, and that includes your past. And remember, you may only be getting a percentage, a cut. Down the years, the Big Money gets to keep the lion's share because it is the lion and the celeb is the snack. And there's always another tabloid football sensation or reality TV star to snack on, if you are happy to wait five minutes.

To understand what has become of the Wayne Rooney franchise, we need to go back to something terrible, an event that scarred his home city for ever when he was just three and a half years old.

When the wind soughed in from the Irish Sea, thousands upon thousands of cellophane-wrapped wreaths crowding the Kop's goalmouth at Anfield whispered. It was all the more eerie for being such a slight, dry, thin sound. To the eye, the cellophane shrine was curiously gaily coloured, in its reds and blues and whites more like a Hindu temple or a Buddhist shrine than a (kind of) Christian place of mourning. When the sun shone, the light bounced off the cellophane like an inland sea. The paintbox colours were given the lie, however, by the faces shattered in grief, the thickset, tough-necked Scousers clutching yet another wreath to add to the whispering. It smelt like a giant florist's shop.

A taxi driver took me to the shrine, played tough, moaned that Radio City, the local pop station, hadn't played good, lively music for three days after the disaster. It was a reasonably convincing display of callousness which lasted a while. And then he said: 'I've got a shop, you know, and I've probably lost about eight customers from a mile radius. I haven't bothered to find out. I can't bear to.' The crumpling of the tough-guy act was, for me, a stranger, almost unbearably moving.

An FA Cup semi-final between Liverpool and Nottingham Forest at Sheffield Wednesday's Hillsborough ground had, in April 1989, ended up with ninety-six Liverpool fans crushed to death – and I had been sent to report on the cellophane shrine for my old paper, *The Observer*.

The Sun handled the story somewhat differently. Editor Kelvin MacKenzie stuck the boot in with the front-page screamer 'THE TRUTH', and beneath it three sub-headlines: 'SOME FANS PICKED POCKETS OF VICTIMS', 'SOME FANS URINATED ON THE BRAVE COPS', 'SOME FANS BEAT UP PC GIVING KISS OF LIFE'.

The Sun's story went on to claim that 'drunken Liverpool fans viciously attacked rescue workers as they tried to revive victims' and 'police officers, firemen and ambulance crew were punched, kicked and urinated upon'. A quote, attributed to an unnamed policeman, claimed that a dead girl had been abused and that Liverpool fans 'were openly urinating on us and the bodies of the dead'.

'THE TRUTH' was, as it happens, not true.

Newspapers are always on dodgy ground when they claim to be telling the gospel truth because they are bound to get something wrong, but in this case 'THE TRUTH' was the opposite of what *The Sun* said. Not only did no one ever substantiate any of the appalling claims made on the front page against the fans – they did not steal from the victims, they did not deliberately urinate on the police or anyone else, they did not beat up a copper giving the kiss of life – the opposite was the case. Liverpool fans are not angels, but human beings. They had realised the nature and the scale of the tragedy before anyone else. It was, after all, happening to their mates. Some fans helped others climb out of the crush, creating human ladders. Others ripped down advertisement hoardings to use as stretchers. They didn't act out the cliché of mindless hooligans pissing on the cops or robbing the dead, full stop. That fantasy was running in the mind of Kelvin MacKenzie.

The Sun had turned black into white. The paper blamed the fans and championed the police. The judge who subsequently investigated the tragedy came to the opposite conclusion. The main reason for the tragedy was not the behaviour of the fans but the failure of police control. As the time of the 3 p.m. kick-off neared, it became obvious that there was a big bottleneck at the Leppings Lane end of Sheffield Wednesday's ground, which had been assigned to the Liverpool fans. Roadworks on the trans-Pennine motorway had delayed many of them from arriving in good time. Hillsborough's turnstiles were antiquated and there were too few of them, so pressure built up as fans, impatient not to miss the start of the match, milled around. Police estimated 5,000 fans were trying to get through those few turnstiles, and things looked bad. To ease pressure, the police officer in charge that day, Chief Superintendent David Duckenfield, decided to open a set of exit gates, Gate C. The order was given, the gates swung open and a mass of fans, several hundred strong, entered the ground at the same point, and at the same time. The decision to open Gate C did not ease the mass of humanity trying to get to see the game but had a far worse effect: concentrating that mass into a blocked channel. A wave of human pressure poured into a narrow tunnel at the rear of the terrace. Police and stewards should have been there to direct the fans away from this tunnel, to other parts of the stand, but they were not there in any numbers. It helps to visualise exactly where the fans were trapped: in the tunnel underneath the stand. They couldn't move forwards and they couldn't go back.

The fans in the tunnel were trying to see the game, and they were fighting for space and air in the tightly packed closed space. Imagine a bad day at Oxford Circus in the narrow tunnel between the Victoria and the Central Line, but all you have to do is push a little bit, and then you can get some air . . . The fans began to panic and pushed the people in front of them. They didn't know – because they couldn't see in the crush – that the two pens ahead of them, the ones they were moving towards, were already dangerously crowded, and the people at the very front were being crushed to death.

The only person in a position to identify and attack the problem and prevent the tragedy was the police commander. Individual police officers could see the crush at the front, where people were being squeezed against fences erected to prevent pitch invasions. A few fans did scream in terror as they felt themselves being squeezed, but the majority of the crush victims made little sound: they went white, stopped breathing and lost consciousness. It is hard to imagine a crueller death. Individual police officers could see the problem at the back, thousands of fans milling around, trying to get in and see the game. The police had radios, they could even use other tunnels, where the fans should have been directed, and walk round and see the cause of the crush themselves. Individual police officers did heroic things that day to save lives, but that is not true of their leader.

Duckenfield's mind froze. He had never been in charge of a big game before. The officer who knew how to run a game had been moved to Barnsley. Sitting in his control box, Duckenfield appeared to labour under the false assumption that what was happening was a pitch invasion. A pitch invasion is a classic tactic by fans who fear their side is about to lose, to get relegated, to blow their chance of winning the cup. That all happens at the end of a game, in, say, the last ten minutes of a match. A deliberate, malicious pitch invasion before the very start of a match makes no sense at all. Something else must have been going wrong – but this screamingly obvious conclusion eluded the Chief Superintendent. He did nothing to ease the crush. He did nothing very much at all.

The strongest witnesses against Duckenfield were his own constables. Some of their original witness statements for South Yorkshire Police were subsequently and selectively edited, including cutting back criticisms made of their own police command. Eventually, after a lot of digging by journalists and MPs from Liverpool and campaigners for justice for the ninety-six and, it has to be said, learned judges, the whole truth came out. The airbrushed evidence turned out to be the most damning of all: PC William Holmes had made a statement saying: 'There seemed to be a total lack of contact with police control or at least a senior officer who could have informed us as to what action was required.' This sentence was deleted. Another officer, PC Desmond Brophy, had said: 'My single most strongest observation that I would make was that for a significant period of time there appeared to be a lack of radio guidance from control.' This too was deleted. PC Kevin Bennett had criticised the way the police herded supporters into an already dangerously overcrowded stand: 'No senior officers at this stage appeared to be in command of the situation.' This, also, was deleted.

In the absence of effective police command, everyone kept working on Duckenfield's assumed pitch invasion: keep the fans off the pitch. And that made everything worse. The Chief Superintendent could have stopped the game, allowed people on to the pitch, made a personal plea over the public address. Instead, the game went ahead, while lungs were being so compressed that people could no longer breathe. When too many people are crushed together in a frenzied mass, they panic. Some scream because they can, some piss themselves – as one doctor told the inquest, that's what people do when they are afraid – and some, the worst affected, the ones being crushed to death, faint and lose control of their bodily functions. The last thing you do before you die is urinate.

Others are so desperate to escape the crush that they will fight to get out of it – lashing out limbs, fighting to breathe. That is a wholly human response. So part of what *The Sun* alleged was not wrong – people pissing uncontrollably, fans panicking, lashing out for air – but the paper ascribed malevolent, thuggish intent to natural human responses to crush injuries. What MacKenzie did was take some accurate, first-hand descriptions of mass death by crushing, confuse those reports with the true cause of the crush, blame the victims and exonerate those responsible, in particular the man by whose inaction so many died.

When some fans did manage to get on to the pitch, to escape being crushed to death, the police tried to stop them 'invading the pitch' and attempted to force them back.

Liverpool goalie Bruce Grobbelaar, who could see the agony happening a few feet behind him, gained the attention of the referee, and the game was halted at 3.06 p.m. Ten minutes later, Graham Kelly, chief executive of the Football Association, went to the police control box, where he was told by Duckenfield that Liverpool fans had rushed the gate into the ground, creating the fatal crush in pens three and four. That was wholly untrue: it was Duckenfield who had given the order to his officers and they had opened the gate to relieve the original bottleneck at the turnstiles. At 4.15 p.m., Kelly was interviewed by the BBC, and he told his interviewer what the police had implied to him – that the gates had been opened without authority. The story flashed around the world that drunken Liverpool fans had forced the gates open, and it was splashed all over the newspapers the following morning.

Duckenfield's conduct that day – and since – suggests that he was incapable of seizing the scale of the problem and acting to save lives. When immediately called to account for his actions, he lied. This was his first day in charge of a major public event, in which ninety-six people were killed and more than seven hundred injured. Lord Justice Taylor's official inquiry into the disaster did not blame the fans at all. The judge pulled no punches: 'The real cause of the Hillsborough disaster was overcrowding, the main reason for the disaster was the failure of police control.' In 1997 Jack Straw, the Home Secretary, asked for a second judicial inquiry, this time by Lord Justice Stuart-Smith. Straw later told the House of Commons: 'Lord Justice Stuart-Smith repeated Lord Taylor's conclusion in the most strident terms. Indeed, he stated that Chief Superintendent Duckenfield had uttered a "disgraceful lie" about Gate C being opened by fans, and he quoted with approval Lord Taylor's "stinging rebuke" of South Yorkshire Police for failing to concede that they were in any respect at fault.'

Duckenfield's conduct never merited any charge or official sanction worth writing home about. He had gone on sick pay, and took early retirement from the South Yorkshire Police.

Liverpool, as a community, took this badly. The word on the street was that this was a case of the Establishment looking after its own. However, in 1990, the Director of Public Prosecutions, Allan Green, concluded that there was insufficient evidence upon which a prosecution could be brought for any criminal offence.

Tragedies, disasters, wars: getting to the bottom of what happened on a terrible day is always difficult, because emotions run high, and powerful back eddies run contrary to the main flow of the story. The game was on Saturday. But by Monday night, before the presses rolled with Tuesday's *Sun* splash and Kelvin's version of events – he hadn't been there, the fans had – enough of the doubts about the police command were emerging to make 'THE TRUTH' a reckless and unjustifiable attempt to blame a tragedy on the dead, the surviving victims and their pals who had tried to save them.

The true story was beginning to come out and *The Sun* had got it utterly wrong. 'THE TRUTH' was that the deaths of ninety-six people were wholly preventable, and were caused by other factors entirely, including the stupidity of a police chief. In their compelling and often hilariously entertaining book *Stick It Up Your Punter! The Rise and Fall of* The Sun, Peter Chippindale and Chris Horrie describe the scene in *The Sun*'s bleak Wapping office as the editor worked on his Hillsborough splash.

> As MacKenzie's layout was seen by more and more people, a collective shudder ran through the office [but] MacKenzie's dominance was so total there was nobody left in the organisation who could rein him in except Murdoch. [Everyone] seemed paralysed, 'looking like rabbits in the headlights', as one hack described them. The error staring them in the face was too glaring. It obviously wasn't a silly mistake; nor was it a simple oversight. Nobody really had any comment on it – they just took one look and went away shaking their heads in wonder at the enormity of it. It was a 'classic smear'.

The tragedy for Wayne Rooney is that he, not the editor, ended up paying for MacKenzie's terrible mistake fifteen years on. Rooney and MacKenzie are, in their own ways both creatures of instinct, both beasts driven by primitive urges. Of the two, MacKenzie – the beast in the double-breasted suit – is the more terrifying. He certainly was, in his pomp, the more powerful. Chippindale and Horrie refer to an event in 1986, three years before 'THE TRUTH', when Kelvin turned up at the 'Currant Bun' one day, saying: ''Ere, you'll never believe this. Some fat cunt was sitting outside my house last night. What an arsehole!'

I was that fat cunt.

The Tatler, then edited by the late, great Marc Boxer, had commissioned me to doorstep MacKenzie, and so I did. Kelvin was then and is now a bully, and, back in the mid-1980s, a terrifying force for bad. It was an honour to give him a taste of his own medicine. I had turned up at his home in suburban Kent at 6.40 one bright summer morning in 1986 with photographer Mark Tillie and found an ugly rhomboid tetrahedron of brown slate and whitewashed brick, part of a newish housing estate whiffing strongly of polish for fake brass knockers, estate agents' hype and cheap money. In the middle of the front garden I remember a mini thatched roof over a false wishing well hiding a manhole for a sewer drain. Very classy.

'Ding-dong' went the doorbell.

'Hello. Who's that?' The voice was sleepy, unsurprisingly surprised.

'Hello, Mr MacKenzie.' A tousled head of blondish hair popped out of a bedroom window, saw Mark's camera and, before he could get a shot, popped back inside the house, just like the weasel in the nursery rhyme.

'Who's that?' This from behind a tightly drawn curtain.

'Hello, Mr MacKenzie, I was wondering whether we can have a word with you.'

'Who are you?'

'We've come to enquire about your soul. Do you believe in God?'

'Pardon?'

'Do you believe in God?'

'Where you from?'

'Well, let's say we are doing a profile of you for a high society magazine. It's a lovely morning and I am sorry to disturb you. I was wondering whether I could have a chat with you, face to face?'

'I'm too busy.' It was now nineteen minutes to seven. 'Give me a call at the office.'

'Well, I've done that in the past and it has always come to no avail so we thought we'd catch you on the way to work.'

'I don't want to talk to you.'

'Perhaps some of your reporters have been in exactly this situation. It would make it easier if you came out, Mr MacKenzie.'

At this there was a good-humoured but demonic chuckle.

We gave our quarry some time to get dressed – a courtesy not normally observed by *The Sun* – and took in the creature's habitat. The house number was advertised in fussy cast ironmongery, and a dinky little lamp with smoked glass dangled in the porch. At half past seven we returned.

Ding-dong.

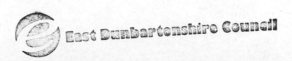

'Hello, Mr MacKenzie, sorry to disturb you.'

A disembodied voice sounded from the other side of the letter box: 'I've told you to call me at the office.'

'All we want is a picture.'

'I'll send you a picture.'

'It's always nice to talk face to face though, isn't it, Mr MacKenzie?' Kelvin remained hidden behind his stout front door, but the diabolic chuckle sounded again. There was nothing to be lost from building on this slender rapport, so I played priest to his sinner, using the letter box as a confessional screen.

'I would like to ask you the John Mortimer question first of all.'

'What?'

'Do you believe in God?' (I have no idea why I asked that, maybe some intuitive inkling that he, in his blackest moments, fears being licked by the never-ending flames of Hell.)

Puzzled silence.

'Do you believe in God?'

More puzzled silence.

'And what about your eternal soul, Mr MacKenzie?'

The sinner had tired of the joke, so we once more withdrew. A famous workaholic, he had to go to work sometime. All we had to do was wait. Minutes passed. An attractive blonde was glimpsed briefly at the window. That had to be Mrs MacKenzie, née Jacqui Holland. At twelve minutes to eight we were back on the doorbell.

'We were wondering, Mr MacKenzie, as we were standing outside, if we could have a truce or something and have a cup of tea. The other thing I am worried about is your milk. It's just standing here on the doorstep. It might be going sour. Come on, let's be friends. Let's all have a nice cup of tea.'

No response.

Unbeknown to me, MacKenzie was panicking and had even phoned his faithful news editor, Tom Petrie, to ask for help. Chippindale and Horrie report that Petrie advised his boss to 'try a reverse ferret', but no rodent-like creature going backwards appeared. At a quarter past eight things curdled a little when the front door opened and photographer Tillie sprang into action. But it was not the man himself, but his young boy, fetching in the three MacKenzie pintas. The lad was wearing a blue tracksuit and a bargain-basement scowl, which he treated us with, royally. Tillie and I pulled back, appalled at this unsporting play. We weren't interested in tiddlers, Kelvin.

Then the chauffeur arrived in a gleaming blue-grey 4.2 XJ6, clearly disturbed by our loafing presence on the pavement. The driver disappeared into the house and re-emerged alone a few minutes later, driving off with a flourish of gravel under the wheels. If this was a ruse, it was a bad one. We stayed put.

More birdsong. Time slowly slid by. And then the Jag reappeared, the dummy run an abject failure.

Suddenly the house front door opened, the chauffeur reversed the car down the drive and out our quarry popped. Medium height, sandy hair managed à la Bobby Charlton to hide a growing bald patch, trim build, tight suit – in a word: natty. His abrupt appearance after such a long wait was like a scene from the nature programme *Badger Watch*, but there was one last opportunity to enquire after the great editor's soul before the chauffeur zoomed off to Wapping.

'Mr MacKenzie, do you believe in God?'

Doors slammed and the chauffeur gunned the Jag. As it left Kelvin indulged us with a big raffish smile, acknowledging our cheek. But before the car took him entirely out of view Kelvin's expression changed: as his limousine headed for central London he looked like a man who had just had his face rubbed in dog poo. The man who has ordered more paparazzi stake-outs of pregnant princesses and bereaved relatives than most of us have had toad-in-the-hole did not, it seemed, appreciate the piquancy of our dawn door-stepping. The thing about Kelvin is that, like the enemies of Corporal Jones in *Dad's Army*, he doesn't like it up him.

So what happened next, after *The Sun*'s version of 'THE TRUTH' about the Hillsborough tragedy appeared, was bad news for him. The reaction of the city of Liverpool – Liverpool and Everton fans alike – was to stop buying the newspaper. Chippindale and Horrie report that the paper's sales before the disaster in the Liverpool area were 524,000 copies a day and fell to 320,000 after, a drop of 200,000 or nearly 40 per cent. One Scouse friend finds it hard to believe that even 320,000 were bought. Liverpool had been falsely accused, and Liverpool's answer was to give the false accuser a bloody nose. Fifteen years on, the paper's sales were still down in the Liverpool area.

How best then to bury the memory of Kelvin MacKenzie's great mistake and win back the hearts and minds of Merseyside tabloid readers? In July 2004, for a reported £250,000, *The Sun* bought up Wayne Rooney's life story and that's how Sue Evison got her scoop – as part of the paper's strategy to recover readers in Liverpool after accusing fans of pissing on the cops and robbing the Hillsborough dead. When news of *The Sun*'s buy-up of Rooney broke in the *Liverpool Echo*, one fan said on a website that Wayne had 'signed his soul away to the devil', another that he has 'accepted 30 pieces of silver'.

It's possible that in selling his story to *The Sun* Rooney did more harm to his image in his home city than benefit to his bank balance.

The Sun's front-page story on the day the paper ran Sue Evison's 'World Exclusive' interview of Wazza gave the corporate game away. The front page didn't mention the interview at all and wasn't really about Wayne Rooney, the player, or his career so far, but about how Liverpool fans were angry with him for getting into bed with *The Sun*: 'BACKLASH! FANS TURN ON ROONEY'.

The piece was illustrated with a picture of Wayne and Coleen holding a copy of *The Sun*, with Wayne sporting a T-shirt emblazoned with the legend 'Love and Hate', perhaps to help readers out with their emotions. The story intoned breathlessly that 'Soccer hero Wayne Rooney has been hurt by a hate campaign launched against him in his home city over his link-up with *The Sun*'. A whole page was given over to a leader, illustrated by a picture of Wazza in his Three Lions shirt, running towards the camera, proclaiming in big type: '15 years ago *The Sun* made a mistake over Hillsborough, for which we are truly sorry. But it is wrong to visit our past sins on Wayne Rooney.' In the body of the leader proper, *The Sun* said: 'Wayne Rooney was just three years old at the time of Hillsborough.

He and his fiancée Coleen are devastated by this unfair backlash. He should not be punished in 2004 for a mistake *The Sun* made in 1989.'

That was on 7 July. Nineteen days later, on 26 July, *The Sun* splashed: 'ROONEY AND COLEEN SPLIT : SHE SLAPS HIM AND LEAVES OVER HOOKER', so, cynics might say, he did get punished after all, and, in part, by the very newspaper that asked its readers to cherish him. To be fair, it was not *The Sun* but the *Sunday Mirror* that broke the first story – it was soon to become a tidal wave of sleaze – about Rooney's taste for prozzies, but more of that later. The point is, who has control here? The celebrity who got the cash? Or the paper, *The Sun,* that bought him up, used his good name to try to clean up theirs – 'it is wrong to visit our past sins on Wayne Rooney' – and then joined in trashing him nineteen days later?

And what, in the great scheme of things, is worse: paying not very much money for sex with consenting adults or telling lies about the facts of a disaster that killed ninety-six innocent people?

No wonder Rooney says in his autobiography that he hates press intrusion more than anything else in his life. But he might reflect that his teaming up with *The Sun* in 2004 was probably the most ill-considered celebrity endorsement ever. He sold his life story, at that time all eighteen and a half years of it, to a newspaper that was, as far as his home city was concerned, the Devil.

And then the Devil turned round and bit him on the arse.

2

A GENIUS WITH A GOB ON HIM
IS BORN

Read Wayne Rooney's ghosted autobiography *My Story So Far* and weep.

The ghost-writer, Hunter – pronounced 'Hoonter' – Davies, may have written the seemingly definitive account, but too often his book smacks of the hoovered version. All the interesting bits about Rooney have been cut back or left out, a 'no-warts-at-all' kind of book. Davies's classic inside account of the Beatles is a wholly different work, revealing that, far from being little angels, the Fab Four were, in their early years, every bit as raw, womanising and drug-abusing as the Rolling Stones. His book on Gazza's destructive genius is compelling and brutally honest about the man who Bobby Robson once said was 'daft as a brush'. But Hunteroo – a kind of Jekyll and Hyde composite character of ghostwriter and player – on Wayne Rooney can be ditchwater dull.

One dreary example is when Roo goes to Cousin James's eighteenth-birthday party, on the eve of his debut for Everton. Hunteroo records that Rooney went along, but only stayed ten minutes and just sipped a Coke. Naturally, he was on extra-special goody-goody behaviour because he wanted his debut to go well. I'm not suggesting for a moment that that story is not true – any professional athlete has to be pretty careful about what he or she might drink on the eve of the start of their career – but of all the Wazza drinking anecdotes possible, the selection of one, the highlight of which is he 'just sipped a Coke', is boring with a capital B.

There is very little in Hunteroo's *My Story So Far* that would upset anybody, particularly Coleen, his hapless agent Paul Stretford or any of his other advisers. The gangsters and the prozzies hardly get a mention.

Contrariwise, we learn that he gets some stick in the Manchester United dressing room because he often turns up in slippers. He has two pairs, just soft ordinary slippers. We also learn that he has quite a few suits but he only really wears them for certain occasions and events. *My Story So Far* performs the strange trick of turning England's greatest hope, our roughest, toughest, hardest footballing star, into someone who might be welcome to give a talk about the offside rule to the Lymeswold branch of the Women's Institute: 'Well, ladies, it works like this. . .'

It's too easy to scoff, but it might be appropriate here to write a word or two about stories and books, authorised, semi-authorised and this one, the not-bloody-likely-authorised version. There is a simple trade-off in journalism and publishing alike: the more access the source allows you, the more control he or she can place on you. So you can have perfect access, but not enough freedom to write as you find; some areas can be marked off limits and you end up writing stuff that is so bland it's not worth getting out of bed for: 'I have two pairs, just soft ordinary slippers. . .'

You get exactly the same problem if you embed with the British Army or the US Marine Corps in Iraq or the Russian Army in Chechnya: you can go to places no free-wheeling journalist can travel to, in safety, but you end up writing about our valiant boys winning hearts and minds, blah blah blah. And you don't often get to see things they don't want you to see. In Jeremy Bowen's superb book *War Stories*, he quotes an American journo comparing being embedded with the US military in Iraq with being the second dog in a dog team: you follow where the top dog takes you. I remember being in Sadr City, Baghdad, in 2003 when it was still relatively safe to wander around Iraq on your own, with only a very funny fat tub of a Welsh ex-SAS man called Taff to watch over us, and seeing a US Army Humvee go past a crowded market full of Shias, and thinking that for most Iraqis this was a drive-by occupation. If you're embedded, you don't see the full picture.

And then there is the exact nature of the access deal. Did the publishers of *My Story So Far* give Roo, Coleen or Stretford, his agent, full editorial control? With a deal like that you could end up with an official autobiography with stories about slippers and suits and sipping the odd Coke, and very little about slappers and gangsters and sipping the odd vat of booze. And that's why, in Iraq or Chechnya or Crocky, I prefer to leave the embedding lark to others. Sometimes, you don't have any choice. I don't want to get into bed with Wayne Rooney, but, to be fair, I suspect the feeling's mutual.

There is a third book on Roo, called *Wayne Rooney: 'Simply Red'*, by Frank Worrall. Published in 2005, it takes up Roo's story from when he started playing at Manchester United. It's less devotional than Hunteroo and Evison, and more of a punter's breathless blow-by-blow account of Roo's life on the pitch.

Roo loved his gran. For a shy and, back then, not very communicative lad who left school with zero qualifications, he is surprisingly articulate. It's one of the rare moments in his life story that Rooney goes into detail about his feelings. To *The Sun* he admits that he used to play pranks on her too, like putting salt and pepper in her tea, but he was close to her. He'd make her a cuppa and together they'd watch *Prisoner: Cell Block H*, her favourite programme. Young Rooney helped look after his ailing gran. He would help her do the shopping at the local budget supermarket, Kwik Save. Then they would get a cab back and he'd help with the vacuum cleaning and the washing up. When she died just before he hit the big time, he was, he wrote, 'devastated'. At the funeral he was going to help carry her coffin – an easy tribute for a strong lad like Wayne – but instead he read out an appreciation of his nan to everyone. Everyone agrees that young Wayne was very shy so reading aloud would have been much harder – a huge gesture for his much-loved nan.

In the context of what happened nineteen days later, the interview with *The Sun* which leads with Roo's love for his grandmother reads like a hollow exercise in getting the most out of a celeb while he's talking.

That's not, of course, Rooney's fault, nor does it make anything he says insincere. It just gives the reader a taste of what it must be like to be a celebrity in England, now. The rest of the interview reveals Wayne and Coleen as boringly, shockingly normal for a couple who have got out of Liverpool 11.

Back to Little Wayne, still only a little boy at infant school by the turn of the decade into the 1990s. Somewhere along the line the genius that would rocket him out of Crocky began to show. True genius, wrote the philosopher Immanuel Kant, comes out of nothing or out of total darkness. Wayne Rooney's sporting genius is real, wherever it comes from. It is to his parents' credit that they spotted it first and they believed in their son's extraordinary gift. The young boy may have had the face of a King Edward potato but he had the mind of a soccer Einstein.

The boy prodigy could play.

Depth, width, height and time: it was as though he could predict how the ball would fall with superhuman accuracy. Best had it. Gazza had it. And Rooney, even though he was in short trousers, was the new *it*. All the rest of the world had to do was find him.

We can recognise genius when we see it – Gazza, Wazza – or hear it – the music of Mozart, the wit of Dr Samuel 'Dictionary' Johnson – or try (and fail) to think our way through it – the mathematics of Alan Turing – but we still don't know the mechanism, how genius works. There must be something about a mind stripped bare of clutter, about being able to get to the crux of a problem ahead of the field: to solve a three-dimensional topographical puzzle like football; or to phrase and rephrase a musical theme, over and over again; or to light up the nooks and alleyways of the English language; or to see the weaknesses in a seemingly unbreakable cipher, as Turing, the inventor of the modern computer, did when he cracked the Nazi Enigma codes during the Second World War. Mozart, Dr Johnson, Turing, Gazza and Rooney have all shown genius at what they do.

Some smarty-pants may scoff, but they don't know how Mozart, Dr Johnson and Turing did their magic. All I am suggesting is that a football genius, a musical genius, a dictionary genius and a code-breaking mathematical genius may all share the same kind of brain, even if the problem that mind is applied to differs. All five have something in common: a wide appreciation of their genius, and the fact that they were or are a little bit odd. The relationship between genius, mathematics and some kind of mental irregularity is still not properly understood by science, but they are related.

Gazza is a classic weird wired genius. In 1998 *The Observer* sent me on a mission to understand what was eating at Paul Gascoigne, the self-destructive and sometime England soccer star who appeared to be drinking himself to oblivion. In one binge before he disappeared from public view into a drying-out clinic that year, he downed twenty Hooches (alcopop lemonade), twenty double Archers (peach schnapps) and two Mind-Blowers, a concoction of Pernod, Baileys, tequila, Galliano and sambuca.

His drinking was insane, and his antics too. Clad in a fabulously expensive salmon-pink suit in the worst possible taste, he had starred in an epic exercise in self-destruction at a do held by the Scottish Sports Writers in 1996. Said one Gazza-watcher:

> Gazza had been voted Scottish Footballer of the Year by the journalists and the players and sat as guest of honour next to the host of the event, Lord Macfarlane, an eminent judge. But it was obvious the moment he swayed in, this vision in pink, that he was well gone. Word went round the room that he had thrown up over Lord Macfarlane's shoes and that was before he got the award. Then he stood up and gave his thank-you speech. He cried, he laughed, he spoke utter gibberish, he thanked everybody. Then he sat down and fell asleep. He woke up and carried on, thanking everybody all over again. It was hilarious and it was sad, both at the same time.

The same could be said of the novel competition held between Gazza and Jimmy 'Five Bellies' Gardner – the Geordie footballer's best friend, a motherly man-mountain – at Gazza's chalet in the grounds of the chichi Cameron House Hotel, Loch Lomond. The story was told by someone who knows Gazza's circle very well. 'Jimmy and Gazza got into drinking a crate of Buckfast, the fortified wine. It causes flatulence. The two of them started letting rip, louder and louder.'

Five Bellies and Gazza are famous for the extreme rigour of their competitions. Once, Gazza bet Five Bellies a grand that he couldn't hold a burning cigarette stub to his nose for a minute. Five Bellies held a lighter to his nose for two minutes, which is why he boasts a large burn scar on his hooter. At the climax of the farting competition, Gazza got carried away, says the storyteller, 'and, as it were, followed through'.

The most gifted footballer of his generation was seen swinging his flamingo-pink trousers wildly above his head outside a chalet in Loch Lomond's most expensive hotel, intoning his despair at the accident: 'I've shat me pants, I've shat me pants.' The denouement of the story is pure Gazza. 'A few days later he turned up at the designer shop in Glasgow where he had bought the suit for several thousand pounds and complained that he couldn't get the stain out of his trousers.'

Was Gascoigne just sad, or was he mad, too? I'd read *Gazza Agonistes*, for my money quite the best football biography ever written. The poet Ian Hamilton describes Paul Gascoigne's genius with the ball, his twitches and yelpings and his weird take on the world with a real affection. He writes: 'We'd seen him twitch and blink, pull faces, gulp. If we'd been close enough, we might have heard him bark.' Hamilton touches on the speculation that Gazza might be suffering from a form of Tourette's syndrome. Victims of this illness, which has been related to astonishing acts of mathematical genius, display 'an excess of nervous energy, and a great production of strange motions and notions: tics, jerks, mannerisms, grimaces, noises, curses, involuntary imitations and compulsions of all sorts, with an odd elfin humour, and a tendency to antic and outlandish kinds of play'. They also show 'a capacity for inspired improvisation'.

Gazza's extraordinary behaviour could fill the back end of a book. The book it fills the back end of is called *Gazza: My Story*, ghostwritten, again, by Hunter Davies, but this time Davies does – or is allowed to do – a brilliant job, capturing the former Newcastle, Tottenham Hotspur and Lazio player to a T. Among other daftnesses, Gazza, on the eve of a Norway–England tie, was asked for his message to the Norwegian people, and replied: 'Fuck off, Norway.' On a trip to London, he stopped the car, got out and went over to a road-digger who was pounding the pavement with a pneumatic drill and demanded 'a go' – and got one, to the amazement of shoppers passing by. Asked for a comment on a game just played at Lazio, he lurched towards the TV microphone and gave an almighty burp. He booked a series of sunbed appointments for his Newcastle teammate, Tony Cunningham, who is, of course, black. He walked into the Middlesbrough canteen wearing nothing but his training socks and ordered lunch. He offered his friend Five Bellies a mince pie after he'd scooped out the filling and replaced it with his own excrement. He recorded a video message for a corporate party, signing off with a festive: 'Happy Christmas, you fucking wankers.' He once told an interviewer that he was so superstitious about the number thirteen that he couldn't even bear to see the numbers four and nine together. He also took a documentary team to a beautiful Scottish cottage which he informed them was his new place, pretended he'd forgotten his keys and knocked instead. When the door opened, he told the confused housewife inside he was doing a telly advert and wanted to know if she preferred Daz or Persil.

Gazza, it is worth pointing out, also scored some quite extraordinary goals.

Genius alarms people with its oddness. One gloomy October day over two hundred years ago, people were astonished to see an elderly man go out into pouring rain in the busy marketplace of Uttoxeter, remove his hat and wig and stand, stock-still, for an hour. Perhaps he was a tramp or a lunatic – no, he was the first man to draw up a great dictionary of the English language, Sam Johnson. He didn't play football but he did have many of the same symptoms exhibited by Gazza two centuries on. In Andrew Billen's brilliantly short book *Sam Johnson* we learn that Hogarth, a famous painter of his day, observed 'a man shaking his head and rolling his body about in "a most ridiculous manner". Hogarth concluded he was an idiot.' It was the Great Doctor.

James Boswell, his great friend, reported that Dr Johnson 'made sounds like a cow chewing the cud. Sometimes he clicked his tongue against the roof of his mouth, clucking like a hen. When he had finished expressing a thought, he used to "blow out his breath like a whale".'

And genius and authority don't get on. It might comfort Rooney to realise that an absence of discipline and a blind contempt for bourgeois concepts of 'good form' and 'doing the right thing' is a frequent hallmark of genius. Turing was a marvel at cracking complex mathematics, a homosexual when it was illegal, an unsung national hero and a roaring fruitcake, detested by the authorities almost all the way up to – but, thankfully, not including – Winston Churchill. Turing helped win the Battle of the Atlantic celebrated in The Wezzy's pub sign, both through the working of his amazing mind and his contempt for the bureaucracy that slowed the code-cracking down. He, too, was spectacularly odd. According to his biographer Andrew Hodges, in his terrific book *Alan Turing: The Enigma of Intelligence*, 'there was his voice, liable to stall in mid-sentence with a tense, high-pitched "Ah-ah-ah-ah-ah" while he fished, his brain almost visibly labouring away for the right expression.' He had a machine-gun laugh and, noted Malcolm Muggeridge on a visit to Bletchley Park, could be prone to 'sucking air noisily into his nose between words'.

Turing was fascinated by the appearance in nature of the Fibonacci numbers, the series beginning 0, 1, 1, 2, 3, 5, 8, 13, 21 . . . and so on, in which each figure is the sum of the previous two. They occur in daisies and fir cones, and Turing spent many happy hours wandering around the fields near Bletchley Park, 'watching the daisies grow'. A spy-conscious citizen observed him examining the wild flowers near the hush-hush War Office establishment and called the police. The coppers were embarrassed to discover that the sinister weirdo was, in some ways, the single-handed saviour of His Majesty's Royal Navy. After the war Turing was sidelined, his genius neglected, his eccentricity disliked by the authorities. He was prosecuted for gross sexual indecency and, ashamed, killed himself. When he died, none of the obituaries could do justice to his great service during the war, because it was all top secret.

Brain scientist Ashley Grossman, who is a professor of neuro-endocrinology at St Bartholomew's Hospital, London, told me in 1998:

> Gazza is a fool, but he's also a genius. It's as though one part of his brain is so over-developed that everything else has gone to pot. You find it in some autistic children who are extraordinarily able in one way, but a mess in every other. It's like a totally alien insert into his brain which gives him an extraordinary ability. Not a musical one like, say, Mozart, but supreme motor skills, an extraordinary mathematical ability to solve equations in mid-air. But it is very difficult to deal with genius. It can burn you up and leave you broken.

Could Wazza end up the same way?

Wazza, thus far, has shown that he can fail when his red mist comes down and real anger erupts, but he hasn't indicated that he is a creature of the extreme highs and lows that did for Gazza. But it's said that both players have footballing genius, that their presence alone on the field can change the outcome of a game. In Euro 2004 and the World Cup in 2006, the whole England team seemed to lose its bottle the moment Wayne Rooney left the pitch.

What I am trying to get at is that the expression 'footballing genius' may not be just figurative but literally true: that something goes on inside Rooney's head, as it did in Gazza's when he was in his pomp – some snap, crackle and pop of synapses, some fizz of brain chemistry, that is inherently different, better, faster than the thought processes of all the other players on the pitch. What the two players have in common is that their extraordinary gift appears to have been implanted into a yob – no, that's wrong, a young working-class lad with no or very little social grooming who in a bad light could be mistaken for a yob – and it appears to have come out of nowhere.

Some day science may be able to fit some kind of cap with brain sensors on a player like Rooney when he is on the pitch playing for England, and firing off in anger and in genius, and we will be able physically to see the difference between what goes on inside his head and what goes on inside those of other, lesser footballers. In the meantime, I would look for some symptoms of genius in the young Rooney: that his ability at football was innate, that he had a natural aptitude for maths and that he was out of the ordinary, unusual, mentally. I don't mean backward or disturbed or mentally ill, but maybe prone to unusual behaviour – the odd oddity.

For example, Dr Johnson, standing in the rain, hatless and wigless, in the centre of Uttoxeter for an hour, being jeered at by passers-by, was exhibiting a classic sign of autism, and that can also be a hallmark of genius. Autism is a psychiatric condition which, at its most extreme, results in a child almost completely cutting himself off from the outside world. But there is a wide 'waveband' of autistic traits, signalled by a lack of social interaction, an urge to order events, to number things, to control and 'box in' the outside world, to do crazy or odd things repetitively, bringing the chaos of the world into some kind of order.

So what observations did people make about Wazza as a small boy? Uncle Vinnie says in *England's Hero* that being good at soccer in Rooney's extended family was nothing exceptional. And that led people to miss the point: that young Roo was special. The uncle said that Roo's mum and dad were 'convinced he was going to be a great player'. He could remember everyone talking about how brilliant he was – and the blushes of a shy young lad whose genius had become the talking point at family get-togethers.

In *My Story So Far*, Hunteroo reports that Jeanette can clearly remember Little Wayne entering for every race at Stonebridge Lane Infants School, long and short, with and without egg and spoon, and him winning every one. His report from the same school is humdrum apart from two areas: physical education, 'very keen and agile in PE', and maths, 'very good in all areas'.

Pressing fast-forward with the chronology, we get to his maths report at Our Lady and St Swithin's Roman Catholic Primary School when he is ten years old: 'Wayne is quick and confident in Mathematics . . . if he can be persuaded to "slow down" and check his work, his progress will be even better.' In *My Story So Far*, Hunteroo comments: 'I always did like maths.' Young Wayne never expressed any real enthusiasm for any other subject, besides football.

What about signs of oddness? Gazza's symptoms were legion and legendary. In *Gazza: My Story*, he writes:

> Along with the twitches I developed various obsessions. I became obsessed by the number five, and had to touch certain objects five times, put the light on and off five times, or open and close the door five times. I had to have everything lined up at a certain angle, whether it was plates on a table or my clothes. I insisted on keeping the light on at night and still do. Even today I can't sleep unless there is a light on.

And Wazza? In *My Story So Far* he reveals that as a little boy he got it into his head that he shared his bedroom with a yellow-and-green ghost. Some people count sheep, others read a book, perhaps like this one, but the best way of sending Wayne Rooney off to Bedfordshire is to switch the hoover on and leave it running, and even better with the TV and light on. This is a lifelong habit that drives Coleen mad. It started when he was a little boy and his mum would go upstairs and find little Wayne away with the fairies and the hoover booming away. The downside is, every now and then, he burns out said hoover, hairdryer or fan, or any other sort of droning utility that's left on.

There is a word in the English language for this kind of behaviour: odd.

Rooney is the first person to 'fess up that he isn't much of a reader, but he does say in his autobiography that he's read about Gazza's strange habits, the twitches and superstitions of the former soccer star, and goes on to admit that he's had a few of those himself. For example, he had a superstition that it was really important for the door to be closed when he was in the room – he hated it if it was left open. 'It was the click, that's what I had to hear.'

At his extraordinary best, Wazza can be mentioned in the same breath as Gazza – on the pitch, but not on the psychologist's couch. Yes, but what about burning out hairdryers? This kind of insight can be mocked as 'cereal-packet psychology'. Fair enough. But it seems clear from the evidence that Dr Johnson, Gazza and Wazza have something in common:

genius on the pitch or in conversation in that throne of human happiness that is a tavern chair; a ragbag of twitches, shouts and neuroses; childhood terrors, some at least continuing to haunt them through to adulthood. Of the three geniuses, Wazza is the least afflicted, but he isn't quite, well, normal.

Teammates make good witnesses of strange behaviour. Rooney's Manchester United teammate Gary Neville raised one peculiar thing that Rooney does before every game. The Crocky Boy talks about it in his autobiography. What happens is, he puts his kit on in exactly the same order, in exactly the same way, for every game, and he does it like this: first, he puts on his warm-up top, slip and shorts, and then wanders off somewhere else to put on his socks and boots.

Billionaire Howard Hughes was a genius who made a fortune from oil and aeroplanes – he built one that was the biggest aircraft ever flown, years ahead of its time – and then went stark staring crazy, thanks to his obsessive-compulsive disorder. He developed a fear of having his hair washed and his nails clipped, and so, with his extraordinary wealth insulating him from the world and the mockery of good friends and family, his hair got filthy and his nails grew absurdly long. He died in filth with nails inches long.

No one around Gazza or Wazza is going to let them do the full Howard Hughes, but it is extremely difficult to tell a genius to curb his ways, to tell them to stop being silly about needing to put the hoover on at night.

The two footballers have something else in common too: fighting. Gazza records in his autobiography: 'My first school was Brighton Junior Mixed. I got into quite a few fights there because the other kids called me names.'

Wazza, in *My Story So Far*, says that he had a couple of playground fights while he was at St Swithin's.

Genius, without also the will to win, doesn't go anywhere, do anything. It's like a train and a track but no locomotive to pull the train along. In *Gazza Agonistes* Hamilton cites a story in Oliver Sacks's book *The Man Who Mistook His Wife for a Hat*. Sacks describes the case of Ray, a Tourette's sufferer who had been fired from a dozen jobs because of his condition. His marriage was in trouble, and his friends, although they liked him, could not help but laugh. It was not just the facial tics that had antagonised employers: there were also the problems of his impatience, his pugnacity and his 'coarse chutzpah'. Ray was given to 'involuntary cries of "Fuck!" "Shit!"' when he became excited. At games, though, 'he excelled, partly in consequence of his abnormal quickness of reflex and reaction, but especially, again, because of "improvisations", "very sudden, nervous, frivolous shots" (in his own words), which were so unexpected and startling as to be virtually unanswerable.'

Sacks cured Ray with drug treatment so that he now enjoys a new life, but he has lost his special gift. Sacks writes:

> He no longer feels 'that urgent killer instinct, the instinct to win, to beat the other man'; he is less competitive, then, also less playful; and he has lost the impulse, or the knack, of sudden 'frivolous' moves which take everyone by surprise. He has lost his obscenities, his coarse chutzpah, his spunk. He has come to feel, increasingly, that something is missing.

This is a terrifying description of genius lost.

Gazza and Dr Johnson were weird, and Wazza's habit of burning out hairdryers is markedly unusual, but it would be a bad day for English football if Wayne Rooney lost the killer instinct he first showed when he was in infants' school.

Little Wayne's gift for football – rather than any other sport or activity – was honed because, apart from a life of crime, there were few alternatives in Crocky. People in Liverpool 11 knew that one of the very, very few ways out to the good life that didn't involve carrying a gun and a placky (plastic) bag full of heroin was football. But Roo played it with a passion and a commitment that marked him out. He had instinctive genius and a will to apply it. He says in *England's Hero* that he remembers the first time he kicked a ball around the garden at five years old – and he always wanted to play ever since.

Rooney and his friends played football with an almost religious intensity. If it rained, they would play and get wet. If the rain fell unremittingly – he remembers a holiday in a caravan park in Wales – they would find a garage and play. Nothing would stop them. 'We used to put our coats out and pretend to be our heroes. I would always be Gazza, Alan Shearer or Duncan Ferguson,' he adds.

And very slowly the outside world beyond Liverpool 11 began to hear word and take notice of a talent that would one day eclipse all three.

3

EVERTON'S PUPPY OF WAR

Wayne Rooney's sixth birthday fell on 24 October 1991. He celebrated it, as usual, with his mum doing her son the honours with a sit-down tea, tablecloth, place names – they do that at Buckingham Palace too but somehow it feels classier in Crocky – ice cream and jelly, Jaffa Cakes and games. Afterwards there would be a knockabout with his cousins and mates in the back streets of Crocky. That month, in a different part of the forest – 200 miles down the M6, to be precise – a silly man had done something silly. His name was Sir Allan Green, he was Her Majesty's Director of Public Prosecutions – the man who had decided that no one had been criminally irresponsible when ninety-six people died at Hillsborough – and he had been caught kerb-crawling for prostitutes in King's Cross, London.

Private Eye, Britain's journal of record of Establishment folly, came out on Little Wayne's birthday and gave the lowdown in its 'Street of Shame' column on how Fleet Street had reacted to Sir Allan's fall from grace. The *Eye* reported that the morning after Sir Allan's resignation, *The Sun*'s front page had a huge headline: 'I'M THE TART'. A 23-year-old prostitute calling herself 'Samantha of King's Cross' told the newspaper, 'I lost the ******* Director of Public Prosecutions his job!' (Their asterisks.) The *Eye* went on to report that on the front page of the *Daily Mail* the same day, the headline was 'SIR ALLAN AND ME, BY THE VICE GIRL'. Nicola Evans, twenty-one, claimed that *she* was the tart that Sir Allan had propositioned. Clearly, the *Eye* noted, one of these stories was badly wrong – and then *Sun* editor Kelvin MacKenzie soon discovered it was his. 'Cunning as ever,' said the *Eye*, 'he set about trying to spoil his rival's scoop by telephoning the *Mail*'s easily shockable editor, Sir David Fester.' (The real name of the late editor of the *Mail* was Sir David English, but for reasons that were never quite clear to anyone, the *Eye* called the newspaper grandee Fester. Perhaps it was a tribute, of sorts.) 'I think you ought to know,' Kelvin cheerfully warned Fester, 'that your tart is actually a man.'

The horrified Fester was galvanised into action. His news editor, Ian 'Mad' Monk, so nicknamed by *Private Eye* – who years later pops up in the Rooney narrative as the soccer star's PR man, working on press releases admitting that the star had been going to see prostitutes – immediately contacted *Mail* hack Paul Henderson, who was 'minding' the delightful Nicola at a hotel in the London suburbs, and ordered him to establish her gender. (To be fair to the *Mail* editor and 'Mad' Monk, it may not have just been prurience that led them down this track. Nailing down the tale that the DPP had lost his job to a tranny could have been a bloody good story.)

'I will do almost anything for the *Daily Mail*,' replied Henderson, an amiable Cockney, 'but I won't examine a tart's fanny.'

Monk's next idea was to send for Dr Cope, the *Mail*'s company doctor. But *Private Eye* reported the good doctor was unavailable. So the magazine alleged the assignment was passed to hackette Tracey Harrison, who carried out a gynaecological survey of Nicola's pudenda and sounded the all-clear.

The editor and news editor still weren't happy. What if Nicola was a man who'd had a sex-change operation? Fortunately, it was the right time of the month: Harrison reported that she had personally witnessed evidence of nature doing its thing. Whereupon, belatedly, reported the *Eye*, it occurred to Sir David Fester that perhaps Kelvin had been pulling his leg.

The full comic majesty of this tale cannot be grasped, my friends, until later on in the life of our hero, but it is worth noting that one of the main figures in the scandal of the silly man in the public eye and the two tarts stars in a subsequent arrangement of the old, old story, more than a decade later, and that when Fleet Street is presented with a selection of tarts and claims that 'she must have been with a silly man', they sometimes make terrible mistakes and pick entirely the wrong tart. Watch this space.

Roon of the Rovers, the Boy Wonder of Crocky, was going from strength to strength. He first turned out for a proper team – as opposed to knockabouts in the street – as a substitute for the youth team of the Wezzy. Rooney came on towards the end of the game, and scored. The fixture was for Under-12s. Little Wayne was seven years old.

John McKeown sat in the Copplehouse pub in Liverpool, nursed a pint of shandy and recalled the moment he saw Rooney play football.

> This kid blew me away. I was running the Under-10 team at the pub, the Copplehouse Colts, and I got a phone call from another guy, John Reilly, who was running the Under-12s at the Wezzy. He said he'd got this kid who was too young, but was I interested? Well, my team was struggling. I got in touch with his mum, and the lad came along for a trial. I remember a warm-up. Someone put a cross in and Wayne did an overhead kick and put it into top corner. His vision stood out, he was far in advance of all the other kids. He could see something before it could happen. It was like he could envisage it.

McKeown, wholly unprompted by me, was touching on Rooney's genius. Young Wayne was not Doctor Who. He could not travel backwards or forwards in time, he could not surf along a rip in the space–time continuum. But he could look up at a ball falling towards his part of the pitch and work out where it might land and where he could kick, head or chest it at a speed so lightning fast that it would appear to less talented people that he had the gift of foresight.

McKeown continued.

> And he was a winner. A big boy, brawny, unafraid. If he hadn't been a footballer, he could have been a runner or a boxer. His dad was a big

boxer. For a boy that age, seven going on eight, he had powerful leg muscles, powerful thighs. He could kick the ball with a force that was far beyond his years.

We raced around to his mum's and signed him up, and then he started scoring goals. Our crowds got bigger and bigger. Before it had just been mums and dads. But word got round that this kid is a bit special. He was a joy to watch.

I asked him how he coped with the other kids, and they with him. 'He was very quiet, very well mannered. Never rowdy. Very shy. The other kids appreciated him. Mum and Dad never missed a game. Even when his kid brother, Graeme, played for the Under-9s, they would split up, so there would always be one parent supporting each boy.'

Did he ever see anything of Rooney's famous red mist?

He was never dirty. He didn't need to be. He was too skilful. But other kids, other managers, targeted him. They knew that if they could take out Wayne, they had a chance. He was never booked, never even spoken to by a referee. And he had great lumps kicked out of him. I've got a video of a terrible tackle when this boy took lumps out of him. And he just got up and walked away. He's only a boy. It must have been hard for him. He didn't have to train. He had natural ability. He was born to play. In one season for the Walton and Kirby League, he scored ninety-plus goals.

The legend says ninety-nine goals, and, as ever, the journalists have gone with the legend.

McKeown's partner coach at the Copplehouse Colts was Nev Davies. He told Geoff Sweet of the *News of the World* that 'Wayne was unbelievable, always playing in the team a year above'. Davies said they had Roo for eighteen months. He scored on his debut and once hit twelve in a fourteen-goal onslaught. From the off Davies thought he would be better than Michael Owen and Robbie Fowler. He always had big strong thighs and was more in the Alan Shearer mould, riding the tackles and playing with a fantastic awareness. He was so good he never practised with the team. He was a throwback to when lads learnt their craft in the streets.

It's hard to get it straight that the football star-in-the-making they were all raving about was seven years old.

But everybody has to start somewhere. For example, at roughly the same time that Little Wayne was banging in goals for his first pub club, Moscow's finest were accusing a young wheeler-dealer of stealing a train carrying fifty-five wagon tanks of diesel worth nearly four billion roubles. His name? Roman Arkadievich Abramovich – the Russian who went on to become the billionaire owner of Chelsea Football Club, which I've read is a team of some minor importance in parts of west London, and an outfit that fancied buying up Rooney the star.

Abramovich is now a big player in the pantomime of British football, so his early career, running parallel to, if 2,000 miles to the east of, young Rooney's, is worth having a look at. Did the owner of Chelsea really nick a train? Surely that can't be right.

Russia is like the Wezzy. You go there at your peril. But it's never boring. In late 2006 BBC1's *Panorama* sent me to Moscow to investigate who poisoned ex-KGB man Alexander Litvinenko in London with four billion becquerels of polonium 210. The man who ordered the hit, according to some, was none other than then President – now Prime Minister – Vladimir Putin himself. Litvinenko had written a book, *Blowing Up Russia*, accusing Putin of being behind the bombing of two apartment blocks in Moscow in 1999. Putin blamed Chechen terrorists but others – journalists, opposition MPs – wondered aloud whether the bombings had been carried out by Putin's secret police, the FSB. Litvinenko wasn't the first Russian to die mysteriously after having accused Putin of blowing up Russia, but the sixth.

In that light, the Wezzy's not so bad after all.

I was on the Litvinenko trail – as it happens, finding out about a great Russian troublemaking journalist called Yuri Shchekochikhin who had been mysteriously poisoned in 2003: his skin fell off him after a trip to Ryazan, a town where another 'Chechen' bomb had, some say, been actually planted by the FSB – when some bloke with snow on his boots, who had been a friend of Shchekochikhin's, gave me a sheaf of papers in a pub. It was a copy of what appeared to be the initial police charge sheet against Abramovich, and a case number: 79067. True or untrue, it makes for fascinating reading. The charge sheet, dated 9 June 1992, says that Moscow police suspected that Abramovich, while working as a director of a small business called AVK, based at 108 Leningradskoe Shosse, Moscow, aimed to embezzle or misappropriate state property on a particularly large scale by swindling the Ukhta Oil Refinery by means of a fictitious order issued on 28 February 1992 and other documents known to be false. The train, carrying 3,585,337 kilograms of diesel fuel, had been destined for Moscow but the fake warrants led to it ending up in the Russian micro-colony of Kaliningrad on the Baltic. The charge sheet appears to suggest that Abramovich may have been in custody at one point, and calls for more investigation to be carried out. But something happened and the whole case was kicked into touch. *Nep + S*, a local paper in Ukhta, reported in 1999 that the prosecution failed and spun a confusing tale of a last-minute intervention by a mystery benefactor.

Abramovich has denied ever nicking the alleged train. In the biography *Abramovich: The Billionaire from Nowhere*, Dominic Midgley and Chris Hutchins write that one of his senior lieutenants approached the Russian: 'I asked him about the train story. I felt bad about doing so but I felt that I had to know the truth. He simply looked at me and said, "It never happened."'

Back in Crocky, Little Wayne was playing an angel, of sorts. Jeanette Rooney's favourite photograph of her boy is young Wayne, aged nine, wearing a shiny blue suit, red bow tie and red sash for his first communion, with his hands clasped together. He looks like a little cherub, though the smile gives a slight hint that in a few years' time the cherub might be able to kick the living daylights out of you, if he was so minded. But there is a genuine niceness and innocence about the photograph: you cannot look at it and not smile. Rooney admits that he hated both the sash and the bow tie, and the moment he got home he tore both off.

Although Crocky has a love–hate relationship with its most famous son (some damn Rooney for leaving Everton and the city of Liverpool), most are proud that one of their own has made it to play for England. His old primary school, St Swithin's, still loves him. Little Wayne's former head teacher, Tony McCall, does nothing but gush about Roo in Sue Evison's book: 'Wayne was always a very respectful pupil.'

McCall says that whether Roo was on the football pitch or the stage, he always gave everything his best shot. He came alive on a pitch. He was always very, very shy but he came out of his shell when he was playing football. He was good in his lessons, always tried to give of his best, never caused any problems.

The unauthorised biographer can only read this stuff and go into the corner and have a little cry.

I tried – you hang out in Crocky for more than ten minutes doing your utmost not to look like a policeman or a social security investigator or, worst of all, a reporter – but I failed miserably to come up with any other story than this: Little Wayne Rooney was, when on the ball, a genius; when off it, a reserved but thoroughly normal kid. He wasn't the Archangel Gabriel, but no one in Liverpool 11 is. He never did anyone any great harm, never robbed anyone, never beat anyone up. The women who run the library in Crocky – they lend books behind steel shuttering you'd normally associate with a bullion reserve – remember the three Rooney boys: 'We used to get a bit worried about the behaviour of the younger two, giving us a bit of cheek, but young Wayne never gave us any trouble. He'd be with them, but at the back. If there is one word to sum him up, it would be shy.'

Throughout his boyhood young Wayne's bedroom was a shrine to Everton: blue was the colour of his wallpaper, his bedside lampshade, his posters, and he even had a car number plate in the window spelling out his club's name. Roo's great hero was Duncan 'Big Dunc' Ferguson, once described by one of the papers as 'icon, hooligan, man of principle, shameless mercenary, tender bird lover, vicious thug, generous teammate and waste of space'. Ferguson was a brilliant, erratic and tortured Rangers, then Everton, centre-forward, who was more often in trouble than not.

Big Dunc was fined for butting a policeman in 1991, fined for kicking a Hearts fan on crutches in 1993, and then later that same year put on probation for assaulting a fisherman in an Anstruther bar – one wonders whether the fight started with a crack about bloaters – but the incident that blackened his name happened in April 1994. Rangers were playing Raith Rovers and Ferguson had a nasty falling-out with the Rovers' John McStay, a disagreement which culminated with Big Dunc head-butting the rival player. It was stupid and foolish, but hardly unknown on a football pitch, where tempers can get out of hand. The Scottish football authorities got tough, and the police north of the border began a long, painstaking investigation which led, eventually, to a prosecution.

In the meantime, Big Dunc decamped south and switched to Everton, becoming young Wayne's favourite player. Big Dunc knew how to endear himself to the Blues. At a press conference on Merseyside, he was asked whether he would ever play for Liverpool and replied: 'Who?'

The striker swooped, he scored, he ran rings around the opposition and then, when he was playing very well for the Toffees, the fracas in Scotland caught up with him and his case finally came to court. Ferguson was convicted and ended up serving a 44-day jail sentence in Glasgow's Barlinnie Prison. It's not exactly the Black Cat Club in St Tropez.

Wazza says in his autobiography that he wrote to his hero in prison when he was around nine years of age. Little Wayne told him he shouldn't be in jail, and that he and his mates were desperate for him to come back and play for Everton. Ferguson wrote back, thanking Roo for his letter. There is a picture of Wayne, his two younger brothers and Big Dunc, towering over them with a silly scowl on his face.

A few years later Rooney and Big Dunc would be Everton teammates. As role models go, Big Dunc is not exactly Scott of the Antarctic – a posh bungler whose lack of concern for his shipmates led them to be soaked in pony piss as the crew was housed directly underneath the pony stalls on the ship to Antarctica; he valued ponies over huskies in extreme cold against all common sense and preferred walking to skiing on snow – or the founder of the Boy Scouts, Lord Baden-Powell, who in 1939 noted in his diary: 'Lay up all day. Read *Mein Kampf.* A wonderful book.' Of the three role models, Big Dunc seems the least ghastly.

A blurred photograph of Little Wayne tells the story of this time better than anything else: it shows the star, his face a mass of freckles and sticky-out ears, his head almost disappearing into a baseball cap, clutching two trophies, one of them the 'Copplehouse Player of the Year'. His T-shirt shows off a brace of Everton stars beneath the Gothic script 'Dogs of War'.

Merseyside had other 'dogs of war' for Everton's puppy of war to admire and emulate, if he so chose. One was Davey Ungi, another Johnny Phillips, a third Curtis 'Cocky' Warren, and they were all successful local entrepreneurs on Merseyside. But none of them was raved about in the chamber of commerce.

It's a credit to young Rooney that he did his best to avoid the city's gangsters when he was growing up. But, once he was successful, they wouldn't leave him alone. Organised crime was to prove yet another massive pressure – along with the tabloid celebrity meat grinder – with which the young footballer had to contend, and, as far as his reputation was concerned, fail. His repeated visits to prostitutes – not just on one occasion, but several times – opened up the Wayne Rooney legend to being preyed on by the underworld.

The prostitution racket is often protected and run by organised crime. Sleep with a series of prozzies, and someone pretty nasty is likely to know all about your secrets and be willing to sell them to the highest bidder. To understand how the gangsters succeeded in getting their hooks into the Wayne Rooney legend, it's important to know the background of a murderous turf war that started in his home city when he was just nine years old. It's a story that takes in race hatred, animal savagery, official incompetence, the failure of the War on Drugs – *The Onion*, the American version of *Private Eye*, says: 'The Drugs won' – and the raw power, in our society, of greed.

If you think Wayne Rooney is rough, think again.

Davey Ungi was an amateur boxer from a family of white Irish toughs, shot dead in mysterious circumstances; Johnny Phillips a psychotic black bisexual drug dealer who reportedly had the Aids virus but used to bugger his drug debtors openly on the streets of Liverpool. And Warren? He is reputedly Britain's richest career criminal.

Once upon a time, a Scouser in a shell suit with the head of a bullet on the neck of an ox turned up at the Squires Gate helipad in Blackpool and went for a flying lesson in a helicopter. He paid £750 in cash. The notes, like snow in the Christmas carol, were deep and crisp and even. The chopper flew up and away over the Irish Sea, leaving the effluent plume from the Mersey and the metal prick of the Blackpool Tower far below. The chopper flew north over the grey, scudding sea to the peninsula of Barrow-in-Furness where they turn out nuclear submarines for the Royal Navy. The Scouser pointed to a big square of grass down below, the grounds of the non-league Barrow Athletic Football Club, and said: 'I own that.' A preposterous boast – but it turns out that he had an estimated fortune of £185 million.

The scally's nickname, 'Cocky Watchman', is, some etymologists say, Scouse slang for a crooked caretaker, and he was, some say, the Cali cartel's agent for northern Europe. Her Majesty's Customs & Excise had a different name for him: Target One. Warren did a long stretch in the tough Nieuw Vosseveld prison in the Netherlands, where inmates are advised to bring their own bars of Camay. In 1997 Warren got twelve years for importing enough cocaine into Europe to keep the London advertising industry happy until the year 2050. While he was inside, a Turkish murderer called Cemal Guclu started hurling apparently unprovoked abuse at Warren in the prison yard in September 1999. Guclu tried to punch Warren, who pushed him against a wall, knocking him down. Guclu moved to retaliate but Warren kicked him in the head three or four times, killing him. Warren got four more years, was released, went to Jersey, started to make some phonecalls from a payphone that the police were interested in, got nicked again and in December 2009 got thirteen years for plotting to import drugs.

Meanwhile, British customs officers and policemen, working in tandem for a Dutch judge, are trying to unpick a fraction of Cocky's missing millions. Forget Kenneth Noye. He was just a fence, albeit for the Brinks Mat gold bullion robbers, and one with a nasty temper. Forget the Krays. They were just pathetic minnows. Law enforcement on the track of Cocky's treasure have thus far uncovered some £20 million, though they have yet to get their hands on it. They suspect that he is worth a lot more. One customs officer on his case suspects he might have £150 million buried away. Another former associate has referred to a fortune worth £185 million. Cocky, through his solicitor, says he has been fitted up by a 'whisper campaign' by Customs, that he only owns two very small properties in Liverpool and that reports of his 'multimillionaire status' are grossly exaggerated. Well, maybe.

On the other hand Cocky may well be the richest criminal in British history. Law enforcement sources say some of it was stashed in tax havens and Swiss banks, some of it placed in a beautiful flat in Liverpool's fancy Wapping Dock development, bang opposite the Customs museum, a small fraction on motors, normally a quietly unfussy Lexus, air con as standard, some of it on office blocks, some on 200 properties in the north-west, mainly let out to DHSS claimants. Not forgetting, it was reported, a mansion in the north-west, a villa in the Netherlands, a casino or two in Spain, a disco in Turkey. The interesting question is, where's all that money now?

Cocky, with his Desperate Dan pecs, his head shaved as round and smooth as a billiard ball and his thick black eyebrows marching across his face like lunch-seeking millipedes, doesn't look the part of a multimillionaire entrepreneur. But he is. Successful drug barons are smart, streetwise, yes, but subtle too and, above all, intelligent and keen to use intelligence. And Cocky was very good indeed.

I remember vividly the first time I ever heard the name Curtis Warren. Veronica Guerin, the brilliant Irish journalist, had been shot dead in Dublin in the summer of 1996, for going after the heroin barons who were making themselves rich while a generation of Irish kids were getting suckered on smack. Her mission had been simple: follow the money. *The Observer* sent me off to find out who, and why, and how. And what were the names of the British Mr Bigs.

In Dublin, I saw a young mother, who was eight and a half months pregnant, inject herself with heroin because her craving for smack was more powerful than her love for her unborn child. The unborn baby was a junkie, too, quivering inside her stomach for the heroin. When it was born, the first thing the doctors did was put it on infant methadone, to ease its pain. It was one of those things you see with your own eyes and cannot believe and never forget.

In search of the British Mr Bigs, I had gone to a pub to meet a Customs investigator, the late Bill Newall, who at that time was working for the heroin target team. Bill had hollow legs and an ear for a good story well told. Bill had 'called the knock' on many heavy-duty nasties, including a number of Turkish heroin traffickers, and on some more amusing outlaws, including a judge he had nicked for smuggling too much booze from the Continent back in his yacht.

I asked Bill about the Mr Bigs, the ones that always get away. He took a pull on his pint and said: 'Then you've got to go to Liverpool. And ask them about Curtis Warren.'

Who?

'He's nothing much to look at. The usual big Scouse tough guy in a shell suit. But this one is good. He doesn't drink, smoke or use drugs. He's got a photographic memory for telephone numbers, numbers of bank accounts and the like. We've been looking for where he keeps his stuff. On a computer? In notes? No way. He carries it all inside his head.'

Curtis Francis Warren was born at home on 31 May 1963, his father a mixed-race sailor with the Norwegian Merchant Navy, his grandfather listed as a coffee manufacturer in the Americas. His mother was Sylvia Chantre, the daughter of a shipyard boiler attendant and a mother with a Spanish name, Baptista, originally from Bird Island, South Africa. The young Warren was brought up in the Granby district of Toxteth, which wasn't then, and isn't now, the Cheam of the north-west. It looks bomb-damaged, but then you recall that the Luftwaffe haven't been this way for more than half a century. The Toxteth riots in the 1980s provided the coffin for the area's reputation. That, and the sad fact that insurance rates for the Toxteth postcodes are some of the highest in the country.

Today you can see the scrotes hanging out, on the lookout for coppers, Customs, strangers. The taxi driver who took me around offered the following advice: 'It's fine for you to walk around and chat to people. Just give me all your money first.'

But from these lowly origins, Cocky became so rich he made it on to the *Sunday Times* Rich 500 list, the highest-placed mixed-race plutocrat in the country. The odd thing about all this wealth is that he had, as they say, no visible means of income. On the contrary, the word was Cocky had made the lion's share of this fabulous sum of money importing stupendous amounts of heroin and cocaine, guns and amphetamine tablets, the drugs direct from the Colombian narco barons themselves.

He left school around the age of eleven, and was picked up every now and then for bits and pieces of crime. Tony Barnes, Richard Elias and Peter Walsh, the authors of his compelling biography *Cocky: The Rise and Fall of Curtis Warren, Britain's Biggest Drugs Baron*, had no luck whatsoever in getting Cocky's family or schoolfriends or teachers to talk about his early years. Nor did I.

Liverpool cops say Cocky started out life on the doors as a bouncer, then he moved up a level and began organising bouncers. He became friends with a fellow bouncer, Mike Ahearne, who grew up to be Warrior in the TV show *Gladiators*. Another pal was Johnny 'Sonny' Phillips, a black bouncer and a ferocious enforcer. A third was Stephen Mee, who later made a name for himself by leaving a prison van, without prior consent, in the middle of the Pennines.

While still in his teens, Cocky was selling heroin. By the late 1980s, he had moved into the wrong kind of snow, big time. He teamed up with another drugs trafficker with style, Brian Charrington, who worked the north-east of England, to Cocky's north-west. Like Cocky, Charrington was enormously wealthy, but had no obvious means of income. Charrington had a yacht. Well, doesn't everyone?

The two of them went to France on British visitor passports. Once in France, they took out their cached ten-year passports and flew to Venezuela, which is next door to Colombia and awash with cocaine. There, the two men fixed up a deal to import huge amounts of coke in steel boxes sealed inside lead ingots, which were not so easy to slice open and impossible to X-ray. Customs were suspicious of the lead ingots. They had cut into one ingot in a first shipment of lead from South America, but had found nothing and let the whole shipment through. Too late, Dutch cops tipped them off that the coke really was hidden inside steel boxes deep inside the lead ingots. They just hadn't drilled into the lead deep enough.

Customs stopped a second shipment, found the coke, and arrested Cocky and Charrington. They had them bang to rights. Oh, no, they hadn't. It turned out that Charrington had been working as a police informer.

The effect of the police championing Charrington as a valuable informer was to torpedo Customs' case. When Charrington walked, the case against Cocky at Newcastle Crown Court in 1992 fell through, too. Legend has it that Cocky went back to the ashen-faced Customs officers, gnashing their teeth at this reverse, and said: 'I'm off to spend my £87 million from the first shipment and you can't fucking touch me.'

Cocky's Liverpool lawyer has denied this boast, but the legend is the better story.

Three years on, in 1995, Warren sat, informally, at the centre of a vast industrial combine. One police officer described it like a wagon wheel, with Cocky in the middle and great spokes leading from it – and down each spoke huge amounts of cocaine and heroin would flow. But for Warren's organisation to function effectively he needed soldiers out on the streets, selling his wares and protecting his interests. They, too, made grotesque sums of money – and that attracted envy and unpleasantness from rivals. This was the background to a 'straightener', a bare-knuckle fight that March between Davey Ungi and Johnny 'Sonny' Phillips.

Phillips was Warren's top muscleman. It is hard to describe just how frightening Phillips was in his heyday. You crossed him at your peril. He pumped iron, guzzled steroids, buggered men, shot people. He had all the trimmings, a showcase wife, a snazzy car and a fine house. (Much of inner-city Liverpool boasts superb Georgian architecture. But the ships' captains and brokers have long since moved on.) One police officer who visited the Phillips home in an official capacity uncovered the reality behind the bling when he discovered 'there was dogshit in the middle of the kitchen floor'. Another detective added, 'No matter how much Chanel you spray on shit, it's still shit.'

Davey Ungi was one of the very few men in Liverpool who dared to challenge Phillips. The Ungis are originally from the Philippines and made a name for themselves in the Mersey tugboat business. They were related by marriage to the wider Fitzgibbon clan, a close-knit extended family of white Liverpool Irish whose members were in and out of the nick, and hospital. In February 1995 Colin Fitzgibbon, aged twenty-four, was walking home in the Kensington area of the city when he was shot in the back with a shotgun. Three men were charged with attempted murder, including one Mark 'Sonny Boy' Osu. The charges against him were later dropped.

The mainly black Warren organisation, centred in Toxteth, and the mainly white Ungi–Fitzgibbon families, based in Dingle (it sounds twee but it isn't), were at loggerheads over the right to control the doors of the city's nightclubs, the prize being, it is said, if you control the doors, you control the drugs. The 'straightener' fight, which took place on 20 March, was formally over the ownership of Cheers, properly described in *Cocky* as a 'dismal, flat-roofed concrete block' which, in a previous life, had been a Conservative club. Ungi won the fight, though Phillips's seconds claim that he cheated and secretly concealed a knuckleduster under flesh-coloured gloves. This is nonsense. Phillips was a huge, steroid-enhanced monster, but Ungi was an amateur boxer of quality, and he won, fair and square.

But, more fundamentally, the fight was about dominance and control of black-market Liverpool – drugs, guns and prostitutes – and whether the mainly black Warren organisation or the white Irish Ungis would be top dog. And that's why the straightener straightened nothing.

The very next day someone tried to shoot Ungi and missed. The word on the street was that the wannabe killer was Johnny Phillips, who had not taken his defeat well. On 1 May, Ungi was driving his car along Dingle's North Hill Street, not far from the city centre of Liverpool, when he slowed down for traffic lights. A black Volkswagen Golf GTI blocked the road. Inside were two black men. Ungi objected and he was shot dead with a Tokarev 9mm, an old Soviet pistol, dirt cheap and as reliable as a Russian tractor and Liverpool's then weapon of choice.

Condolence messages for Ungi filled the *Liverpool Echo*.

'Davey was an innocent man gunned down in the street by gangs for no reason whatsoever,' wrote his widow Jean. At a shrine of flowers where his brother fell, Ronnie Ungi, then thirty-two, made a public appeal for anyone who saw anything to come forward: 'All he had was a straight fight in a pub and this is how they retaliated.' Ronnie Ungi had no truck whatsoever with the suggestion that his brother had been a gangster. 'I don't know where these rumours have come from. If you check my brother's background you will see that he has no criminal record, he has never been in trouble with the police. It has got nothing to do with racketeering or drugs and that's it.'

The anger was real and uncontrollable. The race issue ratcheted up the tension. On 2 May an unknown arsonist poured petrol through the door of Cheers and lit a match. Two days later, six houses were sprayed with bullets in Halewood, a few miles south of Toxteth. Battle had commenced. Half a dozen more people were shot in the next couple of months.

To deal with the screamingly obvious suspicion, Phillips turned himself in to the cops and presented them with his gold-plated alibi for the 1 May shooting of his boxing rival. Then, perhaps to deal with his grief, he went on holiday to Jamaica.

When Phillips returned from his break in the Caribbean sun, he was arrested at Manchester airport for the attempted murder of Davey Ungi – the unsuccessful one that took place the night after the straightener on 20 March. While Liverpool was in the middle of a full-blown gang war, Warren, ever the cautious risk assessor, moved to Holland. But not Amsterdam. He went to the lowly dorp of Sassenheim, where he set up shop in a fancy but not overly pretentious villa called Bakara. He hung a boxer's punchbag from the attic ceiling and checked out the world from four slits in the roof. North, east, south and west were covered. It was a substantial house with a big garden, but most of the rooms were empty. It was almost as if he was imprisoned by his own ill-gotten wealth. To kill time, he phoned his Merseyside mates on his mobile, or 'portie', always keeping a sharp eye on the latest gossip.

He didn't know it, but someone was listening in to his phone conversations. But being Cocky, he didn't make anything easy for law enforcement.

No names, only nicknames.

So, according to *Cocky* the biography, he chatted about the Werewolf and the Vampire, Cracker, Macker and Tacker, the Bell with no Stalk, the Egg on Legs, Lunty, Badger, Boo, Twit and Twat, Big Foot, the Big Fella, the J Fella, the L Fella and many more.

Cocky's conversations were taped by the Dutch police and are known as the 'Dutch Product'. The transcripts show that he was a subtle player of the gangster game – for example, gently admonishing the brother of a bouncer who was causing trouble. They provide an insight, too, into what was going through his mind. The odd thing is that, rich as he was, Cocky couldn't stop himself from shipping in more coke. Maybe it was the buzz. That must have meant more to him than the money.

The new plan was a variation on the old coke-in-lead trick. But this time the coke was going not to Britain but to Bulgaria, where Cocky had interests in a winery. There, oxyacetylene torches would cut through the lead ingots, and the coke would be retrieved. It would then be cooked into liquid and – here's the clever bit – held in suspension inside bottles of Bulgarian red wine. The Plovdiv plonk with the kick of a Colombian mule was going to be shipped back across Europe to Liverpool, from where the coke would be taken out of suspension in Cocky's labs and sold at a 2,000 per cent mark-up to the nation's grateful coke addicts.

Neat, huh?

Meanwhile, one rumour on Merseyside had it that Warren himself had ordered the killing of Ungi, and had even had his own two hitmen, Bunji and Jackson, bumped off to cover up the loose ends. Warren's chum Tony Bray put this to the great man. Unbeknown to both, Dutch police and Her Majesty's Customs & Excise were listening in. This is the transcript of the conversation:

TONY BRAY: Tell you what, you know, the shite they think up is unbelievable. The special people [maybe this is crap code for the Special Branch?] have got the plod in Jamaica looking for the bodies of the other two.

CURTIS WARREN: Yeah?

BRAY: This what they've got down: you give the order to do the other fella [David Ungi], they done the business for you and then you got them out to Jamaica, right?

WARREN: Yeah.

BRAY: They wanted more money to keep their mouth shut. You have got connections with gangsters there, so you got them slotted. Fucking mad, isn't it?

WARREN: Yeah.

BRAY: They've got you down as fucking putting the hit out but you got them slotted because they [wanted] some more money to keep quiet. Fuck, so now they're all looking for these fucking two bodies in Jamaica.'

WARREN: Mad, aren't they?

In October 1995, Phillips's house in Aigburth and his £30,000 BMW 328i convertible were sprayed with automatic fire. He, his wife and child were lucky not to get hit. The next month David Ungi was laid to rest. A thousand mourners stood packed outside the church while 150 family and friends attended the funeral service within. The *Liverpool Echo*'s In Memoriam column ran to five whole pages, including a tribute from his mother Vera, using David Ungi as an acronym, beginning 'D for Distinguished, A for Admirable. . .' and ending with, as the writers of *Cocky* note, 'I for Incomparable'.

That year there had been forty-two shootings in Liverpool, with twenty-nine people injured or dead.

And still it went on. When writing about gangsters and the victims of gangsters it is hard not to succumb to the pornography of violence. A year and a day after the straightener, Phillips was shot four times in the stomach and chest by an unmasked gunman toting, yes, a Tokarev. Phillips only survived because he was built like a brick outhouse. He recovered, but went mad. He had been taking massive amounts of steroids to boost his strength after the shooting.

Bray told Warren, who had now moved to Holland, what the latest was – and, again, Warren was being listened in to by the Dutch police.

> BRAY: He's on the really heavy thing.
> WARREN: Charlied up?
> BRAY: No, the one worse than that.
> WARREN: Rocks?
> BRAY: Yeah. He's on that. His head's properly gone.

The violence continued. In May 1996 Stephen Cole went for a quiet drink with his wife and a couple of friends. Cole, a former reserve for Liverpool FC and a black bouncer, was, some say, trying to move in on the club-door trade, and others say the heroin and cocaine market, in Liverpool. They didn't like that. Cole and his small party were drinking in the Farmers Arms public house on Longmoor Lane in Fazakerley, a stone's throw from Aintree racecourse, when a convoy of up to a dozen vehicles arrived in what Merseyside Police called 'a very carefully planned operation'.

As Cole was returning from the bar to where his wife and another couple were sitting, a gang of about thirty men wielding machetes and knives went for him. They hacked him to pieces. As he lay dying in a pool of blood, one of the attackers sprayed CS gas into his face.

A typical post-mortem lasts ninety minutes. This one took six and a half hours because what remained of Cole was a jigsaw of slashed body parts.

On 24 August 1996, Phillips died of a massive heart attack. The Liverpool coroner is rumoured to have said that he had never seen a heart muscle so big. Davey Ungi had been avenged, and many people in Liverpool breathed a sigh of relief.

That October, a ship had docked in Rotterdam, and part of its cargo was a container load of coke-in-lead. Its rightful owner, Curtis Warren, was fast asleep in his new Low Country home when the Dutch version of the SAS moved in with stun grenades and the like and busted Cocky and his gang. The Dutch went hunting in six addresses. They found the container and got out a pneumatic drill and the long slog of drilling into the lead started, each ingot being about one metre cubed. Eventually the drill noise changed pitch, the metal filings became lighter and a fine white powder flecked the drill head. They drilled a hole big enough for an arm to reach in, and repeated the process.

Hidden in the lead was 400 kilograms of 90 per cent pure cocaine. At some of the other places the Dutch cops raided, they found 1,500 kilograms of cannabis resin, 60 kilograms of heroin, 50 kilograms of ecstasy, crates stacked with 960 CS gas canisters, a bunch of hand grenades, three guns, ammo and almost £400,000 in guilders. The coke, the heroin, the dope, the E and the rest would have netted a cool £125 million. Tax free.

The Dutch judge gave him twelve years. That's much less than he would have got for major drug trafficking in Britain. On the other hand, some law-enforcement officers were concerned that friends of Cocky might have considered a little bit of jury-rigging: a live bullet through a letter box here, a night with a stunning whore there, and then the threat of embarrassing phone calls. Dreadful, really, to suggest it, but then Customs investigators have suspicious minds.

The death of Phillips and the arrest and conviction of Curtis Warren did not bring an end to gangsterism in Liverpool. Far from it. But they did bring one change. They appeared to knock out the Warren organisation. After Warren's conviction in 1997, Ranald Macdonald, a senior Customs investigator, said: 'With the conviction of Curtis Warren an entire criminal organisation has effectively been destroyed.'

The word on the street was that the Ungi–Fitzgibbon family became top dog. Drugs, whores, guns? Well, you certainly didn't hurry to Warren's prison in the Netherlands or Phillips's grave for those. The Ungi–Fitzgibbons, the rumour machine says, decided to move their entrepreneurial skills a tad upmarket and get into two new, perhaps related, businesses: funeral directing and massage parlours.

One day, not so very far in the future, a valued customer for the second type of service would be Wayne Rooney.

4

BOY MEETS GIRL

The gangsters did not yet have England's footballing genius in their sights. He was, after all, only nine years old. Before long, word of Little Wayne's gift reached the football scouts. First to glimpse the Rooney talent was retired train driver Bob Pendleton, who came across the future England player in a fashion wholly consistent with Liverpool 11. Pendleton was asked by the treasurer of the Walton and Kirkdale junior football league to collect unpaid refereeing fees owed by Copplehouse Under-10s. Patrick Barclay, then with *The Guardian*, tracked down the debt collector's tale: 'The treasurer asked if I could go and get them,' said Pendleton. 'I walked down to where they were playing and was talking to the manager when I saw a little fellow. He was so comfortable on the ball. I said to the manager, "Who is the little fellow?" and he said, "You're joking, aren't you? That's young Wayne Rooney."'

Pendleton recalls: 'From the word go, the things he could do with the ball, the goals he could score. Even then, he was one of them players.' The Everton talent spotter immediately realised that young Wayne was a seriously gifted young man. But the moment the youth wing of a big club signed up a lad his first priority had to be with them, not the pub team, so Pendleton, according to McKeown, agreed to wait until the Copplehouse Colts had finished their season and won their cup, and then sign him up.

It was only a matter of days. But, unknown to Pendleton, Liverpool had also sniffed the air. An Anfield scout had been at the same Copplehouse game and got their offer in first, asking Roo's dad immediately after the game if young Wayne would come along to their training ground, Melwood, for a trial. As McKeown told it: 'He ripped apart the other kids, just played at a level far better than them. He scored a few goals, too. The other kids had Boss, AstroTurf-friendly shoes on, but Wayne only had a pair of normal trainers. He still managed to compose himself and play well. But Liverpool didn't welcome him. He had his Everton shirt on. They ignored him.'

Roo didn't get on well with the Liverpool coaches, and that was because of something screamingly obvious: he was wearing an Everton shirt. The problem for Roo is that, being a lifelong Blue, sporting the Toffees' colours was as natural as brushing your teeth, but you can easily see why their sworn enemies on Merseyside might not think too highly of such unwitting defiance. Roo was asked to attend a second trial for the next week, but, in the meantime, Pendleton heard about the trip to the enemy and acted. He invited the Rooneys to come to an Everton trial. Pendleton said:

> I just introduced myself to the parents and said I'd like to take the young man into Bellefield [Everton's training ground]. The look on their faces – because they were Evertonians – said it all. I was on to a winner. Later, I went over and had a little chat with Ray Hall, the training manager, and said, 'I'm bringing the little fellow in.'

The second trial for Liverpool and the first for Everton fell on the same evening. The Rooneys stood up Liverpool and went to the Everton trial. The young soccer star had come home – it was the team he adored, and he loved every single thing about the club: the stadium, the *Z Cars* entrance, the fans, the players. The Toffees signed him up that very evening, after one training session. Ray Hall said: 'I didn't even need that as proof. You get an experienced scout sitting there with his cup of tea quivering while you're talking to the lad, and you know he's a special talent.'

He was on Everton's books. Missing out on Wayne Rooney was a decision the Kop would live to regret.

Roo says in his autobiography that he was desperately excited about his news and needed to tell the most important person in the world. Going like an express train, he zoomed from the Everton training ground home to tell his mum. She wasn't there but at church, taking part in the rehearsal for his brother Graeme's first communion. In church she was sitting next to the mother of Francis Jeffers, another Everton academy star, 'and when I told her the news she burst into tears'.

Roo told his mates, who were so delighted they celebrated by having a kickaround in the street. Though if he hadn't got in, his mates would probably have commiserated with Roo by having a kickaround in the street.

Hall vividly recalls seeing Rooney's star quality shine when the Everton Under-10s played Manchester United, away. It was only a little while after the Man United training programme had processed talent like David Beckham and all the attention was on who next was going to emerge at Old Trafford. And then people began to realise that they were looking at the wrong end of the pitch. Everton Under-10s beat Manchester United Under-10s 12–2, with young Wayne scoring six of the twelve goals. Hall told Jonathan Norcroft of the *Sunday Times*: 'It was an eight-a-side game with small goals, yet Wayne executed this overhead kick that flew straight into the net. There was a big crowd, but the place went silent. Someone, Wayne's dad, I think, started clapping. Suddenly everyone, the United parents included, was applauding.'

Tim O'Keefe, coach of the Liverpool Schools Under-11 side, is yet another coach who was gobsmacked by the precocity of Little Wayne, who broke the team's scoring record of seventy-two goals.

> We could never really coach Wayne because he had such ability and was just ahead and did his thing. He was once running through the middle with only the centre-half to beat and teammates wide on either side. Me and one of the other coaches were telling him to give it wide and his dad was telling him to take the defender on. Instead,

he ignored us all and just looked up and hit it in from thirty-five yards. Then he looked over at us and shrugged his shoulders before giving that big smile of his.

This description tallies with dozens of other Rooney genius goals. They all sound like the same goal, over and over again. They are not – but all carry the hallmark signature of Wayne's space-traveller's goal-scoring trick. He is many intergalactic light years from the goalmouth, sees his opportunity and uses his enormous firepower to knock one in before defence and goalie realise that he could be a threat. Arsenal were to find out what it was like to be on the wrong end of the Rooney kick-from-outer-space trick a few years on.

When Little Wayne was ten, he was chosen as Everton's mascot for the derby game with Liverpool – there could be no higher honour for a schoolboy Toffee. The huge bonus of being picked as the mascot was that you were allowed to have a couple of shots at your own goalie in the warm-up. You can guess what happened next. Normally the tiny player would be massively awed by the great occasion and just tap the ball gently into the goalie's gloves. But the little so-and-so had been honing his skills all week and Everton goalkeeper Neville Southall was taken totally by surprise. The first ball young Roo lobbed over his head into the back of the net; the second clipped the crossbar. Southall, the portly Wales goalkeeper, didn't see the funny side. Wayne thought Southall called him a 'flash bastard'.

If he hadn't been a footballer, Wayne sometimes suggests he could have made it in showbiz. Or that's the laughably absurd boast that follows from his first performance in the public eye, when he and his mates for a youth-club competition put on the musical *Grease*. Little Wayne played Danny, the part played in the movie by John Travolta.

The way Rooney tells the story in his autobiography gives you a feeling of what it must be like to be brought up in Crocky, when there was never quite enough money to go around. All the boys in the *Grease* spoof had been given black leather jackets for Christmas, so that they looked like mini-Travoltas. After they had done the song, they twirled their jackets above their heads and launched them into the audience, at which point their mums raced to get hold of the right jacket. Otherwise they would've lost their Christmas presents. You can't imagine that happening just like that in Tunbridge Wells.

Grease has been a theme in Rooney's life. He first realised that he had a chance with Coleen when she offered to lend him her video of the musical – it was as good as her saying, 'I'm hopelessly devoted to you . . .'

Little Wayne's other sport was boxing which, as we know, ran in the Rooney blood. So it's possible he could have ended up king of the ring. But it never quite worked out like that. He did go to a boxing club at Croxteth Sports Centre, run by Uncle Ritchie, his dad's brother. Wayne messed around, skipping and sparring, but he never actually stepped in the ring. He says in his book that he had a strong punch – and no one is going to contradict him.

But football was his great love. He was so bent on winning that some of the coaches found him 'goal greedy'. It took a while before they were able to make the boy play for the team, and not just for himself – but that's a common problem for every football coach that's ever breathed.

Neil Dewsnip was a coach at Everton's academy and nurtured young Wayne for much of his teenage years. He was 'not tall, but he was always powerful' as a child. At every level, he played with school kids much older than him. At Under-12 level, he played for the Under-13s; at Under-15 he played for the Under-17s and even the Under-19s. By sixteen, of course, he was playing with the big boys.

But at one stage, they had to bring the precociously skilful player back into his own age group – fourteen – 'to stop him getting beaten up and allow him to regain his confidence'.

It was at fourteen that Little Wayne suffered from two separate problems that, for the very first time, stood in the way of success. The first was physical: he began to get terrible pains in his knees, and then his back too. He tried to hide the pain from the Everton coaches and physio, lest they drop him for good. The downside to all 'football academies' for kids who are young and gifted is that your star quality can vanish with puberty, and Little Wayne was streetwise enough to observe that at least some of his fellows at the Everton Academy were not being invited back for another year. The thought of that happening to him was terrifying, and yet sometimes his knees were so full of fluid they had to be drained, and the pain would last an hour and a half. He told the Everton physio about the problem and Osgood-Schlatter disease was diagnosed directly. It's a fancy term for growing pains, when youngsters who shoot up in adolescence suffer short-lived aches in their joints, particularly their knees. Little Wayne recovered from the growing pains, and got his natural athleticism back.

His second problem was psychological: he felt uneasy with one of his coaches at Everton, that he wasn't getting along with him. He admits that he gave him some stick, which, of course, made everything worse. Big Wayne came to the rescue and played honest broker. Roo's father knew how he felt, but he also realised what the coach was trying to achieve. He gave Roo a telling-off, said the coach knew what he was doing and told him to get on with it and cut out the cheek. Rooney says in his autobiography that he buckled down and got on with it.

That conclusion comes a little too breezily. The fact is that Wayne Rooney had a troubling and prickly relationship with authority figures: sometimes they can be a club team manager, like David Moyes, sometimes a captain of England, like David Beckham, sometimes referees, of English or any other nationality you care to think of. His disciplinary record, since he hit the big time, is not wonderful. The one thing that Roo did not learn at Everton was how to control his temper, how to accept an adverse decision gracefully and how to conduct himself maturely on the football pitch. That's not for want of Everton FC trying. Maybe, by the time the club got their hands on him, it was too late. You can take the boy out of Crocky, but you can't take Crocky out of the boy.

Pendleton, the Everton scout who first spotted Rooney's talent, was asked by Barclay if he ever hoped to pull off his talent-spotting success a second time. 'No, Jesus,' he said. 'A good friend said to me, "You only find one of them in your lifetime, so sit back and enjoy the ride Wayne is going to give you" – and I am enjoying it.'

There was no doubting the boy's precocious talent. The sharks were beginning to circle. If Wayne kept on developing, without a career-killing injury, the coaches in the north-west were starting to sense a footballing great might be on their hands. And you could make a lot of money out of that – millions of pounds' worth. The key to the money was control of 'the asset'. The stakes were not small. So long as Rooney can stay playing he has the potential to earn £100 million or even more from football and sponsorships over the next ten years or so. A smart agent could earn a good percentage of that – a prize worth perhaps as much as £10 million, maybe more, and one you don't give up without cursing your luck.

But for the time being, Wayne was safe and secure under the Everton umbrella, knocking in as many goals as he could, still enjoying street footie with his mates. It's this image of Wazza and his pals knocking a football around the back streets of a council estate that the advertisers and the brand-makers were to drool over when Rooney's career hit the stratosphere. Many people in the game have mourned the passing of street football, killed off by modern life and the fear that there's a paedo on every street corner. Some of the game's greatest talents, including Pelé and Maradona, grew up playing urban footie. But that was a generation ago. Rooney says he played endlessly in the streets with his friends without a problem. That is true, but it may be because Crocky's deprivation means that it is socio-economically a throwback to the 1960s.

Even today, not that many people in Liverpool 11 have their own cars. The streets, certainly around Roo's first home, on Armill Road, are curiously empty of vehicles. Also, Rooney's tight-knit extended family, with loads of cousins all living nearby, were the perfect form of 'child security' – but that, too, is increasingly uncommon for many people in Britain, who have moved away from their old extended families. His childhood was out of sync with much of modern Britain – and maybe modern Britain is the loser.

Little Wayne's schoolwork at De La Salle wasn't much to write home about. His Year 8 report, for July 1999, when he was thirteen, shows that he got nought in geography – he hadn't turned up for the exams – and nought in Spanish. His other marks show an absence of academic genius: 40 per cent in maths, 49 per cent in science and, curiously, 60 per cent in religious education. He boasts in his autobiography that his report shows that he could do it, when he could be bothered.

One line in that school report prefigures some tabloid headlines later on: 'General targets: Get to class without any distractions, i.e. gambling.' Roo explains in the autobiography that gambling meant 'Jingle', a playground game where he and his mates would chuck 10p or 50p bits at a wall: the one who lobbed his coin nearest to the wall scooped the lot. The teachers hated it, Rooney says, but it doesn't exactly sound like high-rolling in Monaco.

Once he got into trouble for taking his favourite football into the science lab, where it was promptly confiscated. In a red mist, Rooney kicked a hole in the wall, denied doing it, but then had to confess when a teacher playing Sherlock Holmes discovered the remains of half the wall embedded in the front of his shoe. He got two days' suspension for that. If, say, Prince Harry had been brought up in Crocky – an unlikely thought, worth savouring – one wonders just how much better he would have done at school than the young Rooney.

But perhaps the most impressive 'school report' is the one his schoolmates haven't made. The absence of evidence on Friends Reunited or in the tabloids that Little Wayne was a thug, a bully, a love-cheat, a serial killer, a sociopathic psycho is worth noting – because had there been anyone claiming that he was a bit that way, then it would have come out. What you see is what you get: a bit of a lad, brilliant at soccer, not obviously the next Lucasian Professor of Physics at Cambridge University, but not someone his much less successful, much poorer schoolmates want to slag off in any serious way. They must have liked him.

To be a winner at football, to make it at Everton, Little Wayne knew that he had to keep his nose clean. The distractions were ever present in Crocky: drink, drugs, crime. In the autobiography he comments on realising that some of his mates were sniffing glue and smoking weed. He confesses that he tried to smoke an ordinary cigarette once, but never liked it. Later, he saw that some of the people he knew on his Crocky council estate were getting into drugs, big time. They have since become addicts and, he says, look terrible.

It does happen. A football coach who first spotted young Rooney's genius mentioned that one of his – the coach's – relatives was Craig Charles. The Liverpudlian TV star was born in Bootle, which is a milder, posher, slightly less homicidally scary version of Crocky. Charles started out as a player for Tranmere Rovers, then became 'Susan Williams', a trans-gender punk poet with attitude, then got the part of Lister, the Scouse smeghead but signed-up member of the human race in the cult mock-sci-fi classic *Red Dwarf*, before moving on to *Coronation Street*. Later, Charles popped up on the front page of the *Daily Mirror*, snatched in video stills whiling away a four-hour taxi journey between London and Manchester, snorting crack cocaine from an old drinks can. He copped a caution and is back broadcasting.

Thankfully, Rooney never snorted his talent up his nose.

However, one suspects that Little Wayne wasn't quite the angel depicted in the First Communion photograph all the time he was growing up in Crocky. He admits that he had a mini-motorbike, a Yamaha PW80, which had three gears, no clutch and no licence. He rode it around his council estate in Crocky when no policemen were at hand. The sight of Little Wayne coming at you on a mini-Yamaha at 30mph wouldn't be to everyone's taste. And the model of alcoholic sobriety doesn't quite ring true: ambitious sportsmen have to keep off the bottle, true, but the odd binge never stopped Sir Beefy Botham from knocking a cricket ball out of the ground.

Rooney does pass on one story about him being surprised in a pub, but the angle is that he was an innocent – a man falsely accused. One day a busybody member of the public noticed that young Wayne was sitting in his dad's other local, the Dog and Gun (before it shut up shop), and telephoned Ray Hall, the head of the Everton academy, to complain about the errant young star wasting his time in a pub. Hall sent a scout round to check out the allegation of Little Wayne's under-age drinking, only to find that he was just watching the football on telly.

What kind of a drinking story is that?

Just like what happened on his cousin James's eighteenth birthday: everybody else may have been knocking back the booze, but Wayne goody-two-shoes Rooney nobly declined the demon drink. The way Rooney tells it, the dominant colour in his life is a very light pastel beige.

As a schoolboy player on Everton's books, Little Wayne fell naturally into the lap of the first smart agent who saw him play, and one with good connections to the Blues and even the Rooney family. His name was Peter McIntosh. He saw Rooney do his stuff, was astounded and signed him up on 12 December 2000. McIntosh and his Proform outfit ran a modest stable of home-grown Everton talent, with a bit of grit from Tranmere Rovers – Birkenhead's bonny boys on the other side of the Mersey, locked, it seems forever, for pernicious and unnecessary reasons, down in the basement of the Football League. McIntosh ran not very well-known names like Leon Osman and Tony Hibbert, and Jason Koumas, who moved from Tranmere to West Brom for £2.25 million. McIntosh already had a Rooney on the books, Little Wayne's older cousin, Thomas Rooney, who was then playing for Tranmere, the son of Uncle Ritchie, who ran the boxing club in Crocky.

McIntosh comes across as an affable man, a natural gentleman, with no side to him. He has, though, a chronic addiction to blazers. Roo's mother Jeanette is, by common consent, someone you would not want to cross swords with. McIntosh gave an interview to Sue Evison in which he sidestepped the issue as well as he could. He said that Jeanette is what you might call a strong character. He added that she knew her stuff, wasn't one of these women who don't know anything about football. She knew about the offside rule, she knew when a player was playing well or badly. And her belief in Wayne was total.

Big Wayne and Peter McIntosh pale in comparison with the dinner lady from Crocky as the big influence in his life. But McIntosh did his best: making sure that Little Wayne didn't make any obvious mistakes, or sign his life away to the football equivalent of the Foreign Legion.

Meanwhile, the buzz around young Wayne grew louder. As time sped by, McIntosh's problem was that Rooney's genius was no longer a secret. Down the East Lancs Road, the great beast of Manchester United was beginning to stir. Other teams were also intrigued when they heard reports of the new Boy Wonder. The honours and accolades continued to pour in. In an outing for the England youth team against Scotland, Rooney scored the opening goal, and two months later he got another against Canada. He was a fixture in Everton's FA Youth Cup side, his favourite season 2001–2, when it seemed he couldn't help but score goals. He got two against West Bromwich Albion, then two more against Manchester City, a goal against Nottingham Forest and two more against Spurs in the semi-final. Tottenham manager Glenn Hoddle waxed lyrical about him, as did Liverpool, but the message from Everton was very clear: Rooney was theirs, and strictly not for sale or any other entreaty.

The semi-fiction employed by the Football Association is that players under seventeen shouldn't earn any serious money and are free to go anywhere, lest they be unfairly swayed by the first big team that comes their way. It's a noble attempt at giving young players a bit of leverage against the Big Money that rules English soccer, and it doesn't always work. Clubs, desperate to hang on to talent, use all the obvious tricks to keep potential stars on their books until they sign properly on their seventeenth birthday. But Everton had no problems with Little Wayne: he and his family were Blue, through and through. The side has a real family atmosphere, full of malarkey and messing about, and the Rooneys loved it.

When he was sixteen Roo signed a kind of football version of a prenuptial agreement, committing him to the Blues. It kept the other clubs at bay, at least for the time being. That season, coming to a close in the spring of 2002, Everton had more than their fair share of injuries. In April Little Wayne travelled to Southampton with the team proper as a substitute. Roo records in the autobiography that the fans were shouting for him to come on, but it never happened. Had he been called from the subs' bench, he would have beaten Joe Royle's record as the youngest-ever Everton first-team player.

Wayne aches with pain whenever he is forced to sit on the substitutes' bench. If there is one thing that winds him up, it's watching others playing football when he isn't. Little Wayne was due to come on for Everton in the next game, but the fixture clashed with an England Under-17 game for which he had been picked, and national call-ups take precedence over league games, so Joe's old record stood.

England did well in the Under-17 World Cup, before they were defeated by Switzerland. But there was one final game in that season, the FA Youth Cup Final, in May, against Aston Villa, over two legs. Word had reached the Toffees that their new hero was on great form, and an astonishing 15,000 Everton fans turned up for what was only ever going to be a youth game. Roo scored the first goal and pulled up his shirt to reveal a T-shirt underneath with the slogan 'Once a Blue, Always a Blue'.

The T-shirt had been the idea of Roo's cousin Toni, also, obviously, an Everton fanatic. The Toffees lost the game 4–1, and a couple of years later they lost Rooney, so soon the slogan on the T-shirt would no longer be a proud boast but a curse that would haunt the star.

Meanwhile, Rooney's mind turned to romance. If you are thinking that Coleen was his first childhood sweetheart, then you would be wrong.

To be fair to Coleen, nowhere has she ever claimed that she was Roo's first childhood sweetheart. That label may have been stuck on her by hacks, oozing saccharine from every pore, putting Coleen in the grotesquely difficult position of having to deny what was first an implication, which then morphed into an assumption, and then became a fact without her ever uttering it.

Hunteroo's take on his pre-Coleen love life is so dull it's more fun reading the instructions on a bag of cement. He writes that he had his first so-called girlfriend when he was about thirteen, whom he went out with for about two months. That ended and when he was fifteen he had another girlfriend for about seven months. But there's one thing everyone agrees on: young Wayne fancied Coleen something rotten from the word go. In *Grease* terms, she was the one that he wanted.

Wayne has had a rough press, because he looks like a Scouse wide boy with far too much money. Coleen has had a rough ride too, for no particular good reason. She was, by common consent, one of the brightest, prettiest girls at St John Bosco, and was always going to make something of her life. She has also got herself out of Crocky, which means that when she sees a chance, she takes it.

Her family are Liverpool supporters, her father a devout Catholic. Transparently good people, they adopted a young girl, Rosie, who turned out to be suffering from a disease called Rett's syndrome, which eats away at the sufferer's nerve system, causing a terrible progressive paralysis. None of that has prevented Coleen from getting the bucket-of-shit treatment. *Private Eye* has an excellent satirical column called 'Glenda Slagg', in which the wilder excesses of Fleet Street's women-for-women's journalism is ridiculed. But even Glenda at her bitchiest would be hard put to match Australian acid queen Amanda Platell, who wrote in the *Daily Mail*:

> No number of designer makeovers can disguise the fact that underneath she is Vicky Pollard with money, just as no amount of crash diets can really change that sweet, tubby little figure. She is flogging her chavdom for all it is worth while she can, as even Col knows she has the shelf life of a pork pie.

This is vitriolic even by La Platell's standards and has been belied by later events. Stand-up comic Jenny Eclair gave it to Coleen with both barrels when she was crowned the face of Asda, a supermarket chain so prolier-than-thou that its technique of imprinting its advertising brand is for its adverts' customers to spank themselves on their arched buttocks. The comedienne wrote: 'You cannot be a style icon and the face of Asda, as Coleen is. That – literally – would be having your frozen chocolate gateau and eating it. Coleen is as exotic as a catering-size bag of chips, but possibly slightly duller. She is the Chav Princess' – spankety-spank.

Ah, but Coleen is now worth an estimated £8 million. How galling must that be? The backwash of bitching and sniping Coleen has attracted is oceanic. Coleen's life – thus far – shouldn't provoke this concentration of sulphur. And yet it does. There is something about Coleen that brings the claws of Fleet Street's minxes out and there seems to be nothing that she can do about it. By falling in love with the brightest footballing talent of his generation when she was still a schoolgirl, Coleen has somehow hit a double jackpot: she has her youth and she has loads of money. There is also a whiff of revolting old-fashioned snobbery: that a young woman from somewhere vulgar with bus stops should never make it on to the

front cover of *Vogue*. It shouldn't be allowed... her kind are not suited...
blether, blether, blether.

However, there are times when Coleen functions as her own worst
enemy. Coleen told her very own life story in 2007 – at that stage,
all twenty-one years of it – in her very own autobiography, called,
imaginatively, *Welcome to My World*. The book is a tribute to the
colour pink. Pink jacket, pink glitter title, pink inside cover page, pink
handwritten bits, pink prose. Some of that, at least, was tap-tapped out by
a chap called Harvey Marcus, who appears in the book credits as 'Edited
by...'. Harvey pops up once in Neon, an electronic newspaper archive, as
'celebrity editor' of *Marie Claire* magazine, drooling at the chops about
Angelina Jolie, so he is clearly a journalist of some stature. These celebrity
chaps like lists. On page 210, Coleen–Harvey treat us to a list of Coleen's
top ten favourite bags:

1. Fendi Spy
2. Fendi B
3. Chloé Paddington
4. Thomas Wilde, with skulls on the front
5. Chloé Betty
6. YSL Muse
7. Chanel classic padded
8. Fendi Baguette
9. Chloé Silverado
10. Balenciaga classic

Welcome to my World reads like a savage dystopian satire on the
mindlessness of Western consumerism, though that does not seem to
have been the original objective. Nevertheless, there are some funny bits
in it and Coleen has an honest turn of phrase that occasionally punches
through the self-regarding photographs, the listing of bling and the fancy
parties and places 'me and Wayne' have been to.

They've been yachting on the south of France, they've swum in the
Caribbean and they've been partying at Beckingham Palace but they

first hooked up in front of the chippy thanks to a dodgy bike chain in Crocky. Coleen tells the story in her book. She was riding on the back of her friend Claire's bike when the chain broke just in front of the fish and chip shop where Wayne and his mates were hanging about. The damsels in their distress called for help and Wayne Rooney played the gallant Sir Galahad. She says, slightly acidly, that she has since learnt that Roo is not a handyman, but that night he managed to fix the bike and a date was booked to thank him for his courtesy.

Having bagged that prize, they got chatting and Wayne established that Coleen had been to amateur drama classes. He chipped in with his *Grease* story, she mentioned that she had the video, he asked Coleen whether he could borrow it that very night, he tailed her home, got the video and they went round the back of the Queen of Martyrs church and true love was sealed with a snog.

It's not exactly Elizabeth and Mr Darcy in *Pride and Prejudice* but this is Croxteth, Liverpool 11, after all. He's got loads of money, she's beautiful, ping and pong; he can appear thick, she's bright, yin and yang. They were hooked on each other.

The first photograph of Coleen appeared in the *Sunday Mirror* in February 2003, and it says something about her cosmic self-confidence today that she allowed it into her autobiography. She is wearing a black puffa jacket with the hood up, blue skirt and blue socks as she walks to school. It looks as though it is raining in Crocky. The image is not wholly flattering. In her book she says that the moment she appeared in the newspaper loads of her relatives rang to congratulate Crocky's latest celebrity. She's often said that she finds the media intrusion into her life pretty ghastly, but she has the honesty to confess that she loved her first brush with fame: 'You laugh at yourself being in this national newspaper, and it's strange, and funny. That day I must have looked at that same picture at least fifty times.' As photographs go, it wasn't that bad – she could have been opening the door to receive flowers, like the wife of one of our former Prime Ministers.

There is an honesty about Coleen's reflection on her first moment of fame which is quietly impressive.

The first big press interview she gave wasn't with Saccharine Sue of *The Sun*, but with the *Sunday Mirror*'s Zoe Nauman in 2003. The *Mirror* photographed Col in a silver spangly number. She looked like she was done up in foil, oven-ready, at gas mark 5. In the clearly staged photographs she seems unhappy, not herself, with a tense stuck-on smile as though she was having second thoughts about appearing as Miss BacoFoil 2003. But Coleen comes across as she is – no Bette Davis or Dorothy Parker, at least not yet – but a lively, thoughtful, decent teenager, and one who is already a little wary of the press. Nauman reports Coleen's views on Roo: 'He tells me he loves me all the time. We are like best friends. When I am with him I feel really relaxed. He is really caring. You wouldn't think so on the pitch but there is a soft side to him.'

Coleen told Nauman how the couple slowly fell in love:

> At first we were just mates, but then we began to spend more time together. Then we became best friends and soon realised we liked each other more than that. When I first started seeing Wayne I was a bit nervous, but as I got to know more about what he was like, I realised how understanding he is.

But the first great test of their love raised the question not of just how understanding Wayne Rooney was of Coleen, but of how understanding she would be of him.

And his dark side.

5

'NO TIP OR NOTHING. THE CHEEK OF THEM, THESE MILLIONAIRES'

It would be hard to imagine a more squalid place in which to perform the act of love. Diva's is the name, but the brothel's address gives a truer sense of the scene: Aigburth Road, Dingle, Liverpool. Diva's is round the back from a tatty row of shops that runs along the A561, the old arterial road from north Cheshire into Liverpool, parallel with the Mersey. The area is full of red-brick Coronation Street-style terraces, run down, grim, the only splashes of colour lime-green cardboard octahedron ads promising punters discount prices for pies in a bakery. Dingle is where the former Tory MP and wannabe Mayor of London Steve 'Shagger' Norris – he of the five mistresses – comes from. Perhaps there's something funny in the water.

Diva's is tucked behind the main drag, down an alley blocked off by a high metal fence, and accessed only by a barred metal gate. The brothel runs along the first floor, its windows protected from the odd brick by steel mesh, the whole effect unwelcoming.

Two paint-bespattered concrete steps lead the punter through the heavy metal framework to a corrugated security door, up a flight of stairs to the top where he is greeted by a barred cage. Smile, you're on *Candid Camera* – with sound to boot. But never mind, discretion is assured. Unless someone flashes around £200,000, when it's negotiable. So that's how the world got to see video footage, fuzzy, but unmistakably the real thing, showing Wayne Rooney's tendresse for prostitutes, some youngish, some, allegedly, not so young. . .

It's impossible to imagine that anyone would be interested in the global sexual humiliation of a Scouser in a trackie unless he happened to play for England, so one has to conclude that fame on the football pitch brought with it shame in the bedroom, as night follows day.

Everything went right for Wayne Rooney in 2002, and also everything went very wrong – although it would take two more years before his foolishness would come to light. But the precise history of that shaming – and the likelihood that gangsters made a lot of money out of it – is a story that does little credit to the participants.

For Rooney, the footballing highlight of 2002 was the moment when he came on as a substitute and did his trademark shot from outer space and smashed the ball into the back of the net – but this time the other side wasn't a pub or youth team, but Arsenal.

When Everton played Arsenal on 19 October 2002, Rooney had yet to stamp his talent on his own team, still less the national game. David Moyes, the Everton manager, was still umming and aahing about playing his new talent from the off. Finally, towards the end of the match, Moyes pulled off Tomasz Radziński and on Rooney ran. Roo had watched Arsenal's Frenchmen run Everton ragged for most of the game. His first mark in English football was typically explosive. Receiving a mis-hit pass from Danish midfielder Thomas Gravesen, he looked up at the Arsenal goal, and from the far side of the galaxy he launched a photon torpedo at the Gunners' goal. Keeper David Seaman, fresh from being cheekily lobbed by Ronaldinho in the summer's World Cup, was not just beaten but dazed, and would wake up to headlines screaming 'SEAMAN BEATEN BY SIXTEEN-YEAR-OLD FROM THIRTY YARDS'.

Arsenal manager Arsène Wenger had lost his run of thirty-one unbeaten games. But he was honourable in defeat:

> To lose our record is a big disappointment, but at least we lost to a
> special goal from a special talent. Seaman had no chance with their

winner. There is no goalkeeper in the world who would have stopped that goal. He's the biggest English talent I've seen since I took over at Highbury. He is supposed to be sixteen, but I didn't know that sixteen-year-olds could do things like that. He has everything you could dream of – intelligence, quick reactions, strong running with the ball. He has huge potential. He's more than just a goal scorer. He is not the guy who just stands in the box and waits to score. You can put him on the wing, you can put him in the centre, you can put him behind the striker. He can play people in and dribble – I like strikers who can do that – and he's a clever, natural footballer. He's special all right. The guy can play.

His own manager, David Moyes, paid homage: 'It was a wonderful goal, a wonderful finish. There are special players who have graced the game down the years and Wayne can go on to become another.'
But then Moyes went on to lower the temperature:

I won't let him get carried away – he hasn't scored all week in training. Sometimes we have a bit of a go at him for trying unrealistic shots from that range but this time I felt with the space in front of him that he had a serious chance to score and he did it pretty well.

One can perhaps sense something – even when Rooney is still sixteen – of a tension between Moyes and his star player. Moyes is an excellent manager, shepherding a team with a historic lack of cash to punch well above its weight, every season. He clearly felt that it was in the best interests of the team and young Rooney to keep him grounded – at exactly the moment when the hyper-ambitious boy from Crocky wanted it all.
The Everton fans, however, had a new god, and worshipped him with an intensity that might have been on the wrong side of idolatry. 'Phil the Blue' gave his memory of the day on the Toffees' website:

At the Everton–Arsenal game. Rooney scores that memorable wonder goal. We went to the Winslow after the match for a pint. When everyone was reading the *Pink Echo* and it was dead quiet, I stood on a table and looked at a picture of Rooney on the telly and shouted: 'Rooney, I'd walk a hundred miles over burning hot coals just to stick pins in your shit.' And sparked off the biggest chorus of 'Rooney, Rooney, Rooney' with about 200 *Pink Echo*s being waved in the air.

Such hero worship is hard to deal with at the best of times, for the most well-centred of people. It's no great surprise that his success went to Roo's head. A few days after his seventeenth birthday, Rooney started to visit Diva's on Aigburth Road, and surrendered his reputation to some not very nice people. Worse, he became a bit of a regular and his visits began to be noticed by the cops, taxi drivers and soccer fans. The only thing Rooney didn't do was put an announcement about his trips to the brothel in the personal ads of the *Liverpool Echo*.

It was only a matter of time before word spilled to a reporter. First off the mark was Graham Johnson, then of the *Sunday Mirror*, and one of the most feared tabloid 'operators' on the face of the planet.

Johnson sold his granny into slavery in 2004 and then bought her back on expenses. (Oh, all right, I made that bit up.) His record of journalistic scoops tells its own story. Before he worked on the *Sunday Mirror*, he reported for the *News of the World*. There his scoops included 'VIRGIN'S FORSAKEN ORGAN FOR A DUET WITH HUNK IN JAIL', 'JARVIS LOOKED LIKE A TRAINSPOTTER BUT HIS LOVING DROVE ME LOCO – KISS AND TELL EXCLUSIVE', 'NAOMI STOLE MY BOOBS! SUPERMODEL HAD BODY-DOUBLE – EXCLUSIVE' and 'VAMPIRE SEX CULT PREYS ON VIRGINS'.

One has to drop the snooty tone for a moment and reflect that that last one sounds like a bloody good story, if true. Johnson has knocked out some proper stories, mainly at the *Sunday Mirror* – nailing racists, crooks, gun dealers – and he's reported well from places like Kosovo. His photograph is on Google Images, if you look hard enough. I recognised him from the wars of former Yugoslavia and remember his presence: wary, tough, guarded, with a Scouse accent so thick you could spread it. Anyone who covered that episode of man's inhumanity to man, while the rest of Europe sat on its hands for too long letting Slobodan Milošević get away with mass murder, is not all bad.

He's written up his investigations in a book, *Football and Gangsters: How Organised Crime Controls the Beautiful Game.* Johnson says that the first lead about Rooney's visits to a brothel had come up about eighteen months before the story appeared, in the winter of 2002. A taxi-driver contact had called Johnson to say that he knew a fellow cabbie who had witnessed Roo being turned away from Diva's. At the time of this first lead, Roo was only seventeen and had just popped up on to the national stage after his goal from twenty-five yards out against Arsenal.

The editor of the *Sunday Mirror* turned the story down for the time being, and Johnson parked the tip. Two years on, in 2004, Johnson heard gossip from the same taxi-driver source that the brothel had managed to capture Rooney on its CCTV camera and record his voice too.

The greatest story ever told on the Aigburth Road was splashed all over the front page of the *Sunday Mirror* as a World Exclusive on 22 August 2004, though the hard evidence for it was all taped back in November 2002. Johnson's copy kicked off the story in the standard tabloid way: foam-flecked hysteria, barely suppressed. It hit virtually every single tabloid gong – seedy, gong! Sensational pictures, gong! Football wonderkid, gong! Back-street brothel, gong! Wayne, gong! Vice den, gong! Sex, gong! Rooney, gong! Sex with prostitutes, gong! Sex with Cowgirl prostitute who was a mother-of-six, gong! Sex with a kinky boots prostitute, gong! Sex with a PVC-clad prostitute, gong! Sex with a PVC-clad prostitute who was in fact a grandmother. Gong! Gong! Gong!

Back in the *Sunday Mirror* office, orgasms all around.

The paper screamed:

ROO IN A VICE DEN:

- HE VISITS 8 TIMES AND HAS SEX WITH A GRAN IN A PVC SUIT
- HE CONFESSES: I DID USE PROSTITUTES. I'VE BEEN STUPID
- SENSATIONAL STORY, PICTURES AND ADMISSION: PAGES 2, 3, 4, 5, 6 AND 7

Any celebrity knows that if their story commands more than a couple of pages in the tabloids they are in the doo-doo ever so deep. Rooney bagged the paper from the front page to page seven. That's not good. The snaps were grainy but pretty damning. The photograph on the front page was a still from the brothel's CCTV video, showing Rooney's unmistakable angry potato face, with a caption shouting: 'SHAME ROONEY: WAYNE IS CAUGHT ON CCTV INSIDE THE SEEDY BROTHEL'.

On page two, three still photographs tell their own story. The first one is captioned 'I'M COMING: Rooney heads for sex room carrying his shoes'; the second, 'I'M RUNNING: Cowgirl runs from the room as police arrive', showing a topless cowgirl on the hoof; and the third, 'WE'RE OFF: Rooney (background) and his Liverpool star friend in brothel.'

The proof that Rooney had visited Diva's was the CCTV footage of him, and, the cherry on the cake, audio on the tape too.

The paper ran a minute-by-minute account of one trip to the brothel when Rooney and an unnamed friend who plays for Liverpool are caught on camera. Rooney's pal goes into bat – as it were – first, while Rooney has a snooze on the sofa. That's not too surprising because it's past two o'clock in the morning.

A few minutes before half-past two the police buzz on the brothel intercom. Cowgirl shoots out of the room where she'd been entertaining Rooney's friend, wearing just her knickers and boots and carrying her black cowboy hat. She's panicking that it's a police raid and that she will end up in the papers because of who her clients are. But it's just a routine patrol and the police move on. She goes back to her job of work, then it's Rooney's turn, then both men leave.

Everyone says: 'Ta-ra!'

The *Sunday Mirror* breathlessly quotes Friends of Cowgirl who quote her as saying: 'I'm quite a panicky person. All I was thinking was that I didn't want to get caught with Wayne Rooney and a Liverpool player – it would be all over the papers.'

She was right about that. Sticking to the cowgirl theme for a bit, one week later *The People* stepped in and joined the fun.

They'd bought up Cowgirl. Or at least that was their claim. The story was illustrated with a snap of Cowgirl sporting a cowgirl hat, a shoulder holster for her gun, a rootin'-tootin' neckerchief and a low-cut frilly waistcoat as worn by all the best cowgirls. Her face was blodged out, but the caption ran: 'Romps: Cowgirl wore skin-tight Wild West outfit during sex sessions with football stars.'

The People's Chris Tate reported that Cowgirl's only meeting with Rooney was in November 2002.

Cowgirl, originally from Birmingham, claimed that they did the business, she gave him a kiss on the cheek and he was off.

The *Sunday Mirror*'s Cowgirl and *The People*'s Cowgirl don't quite add up. If it's the same cowgirl, it's odd *The People*'s cowgirl doesn't refer to the arrival of the coppers in mid-bonk with Roo's mate, while the star sleeps, which is the comedy highlight of the *Sunday Mirror*'s cowgirl story. Also *The People's* cowgirl is a mother of two, the *Sunday Mirror*'s a mother of six. Perhaps she is the same cowgirl, but forgot her four extra kids.

And there is always the ugly possibility that there may not be one but two cowgirl slappers in Merseyside. Of the two girls, the *Sunday Mirror* had the CCTV tapes, so they had the right cowgirl. The other cowgirl, perfectly cowgirly in every other respect, may have been milking *The People's* teat.

Funnily enough, cowgirls do pop up in Rooney's own book. But not in the way you might expect. He tells the story of when he was a wet-behind-the-ears thirteen-year-old and went on a team trip to America, and stayed in Dallas. He didn't think much of the waffles for breakfast, but he did appreciate being a spectator at the rodeo shows, where, he notes, 'Some of the girls were dressed as cowgirls.'

Johnson's somewhat different type of cowgirl story went on and on. Pages four and five are devoted to the kiss 'n' tell story of Gina McCarrick, she of the kinky boots. She describes Rooney not wholly affectionately as having a face 'like a smacked arse'. When they got down to the fast bowling, as it were, she said, 'There were a few little grunts'. She thought not of England – is patriotism on its last legs? – but of which Pot Noodles she would enjoy when this particular maiden was over: the chicken and mushroom or the beef one? The *Sunday Mirror* helpfully ran a photograph of said chicken and mushroom Pot Noodles as a useful guide to readers.

Not-very-turned-on Kinky Boots Gina had hoped for a big tip, but she claims that Rooney even waited for his £5 change – her fee was £35. She concluded: 'No tip or nothing. The cheek of them, these millionaires.'

It is fair to point out, again, that the very worst the ladies of the night at Diva's have to say about Wayne Rooney is that he is sleepy and not a good tipper – but I would be astonished if anyone from Croxteth would be. It is also fair to add that if there was good evidence of Rooney behaving nastily to any of the sex workers the *Sunday Mirror* would have told us all about it. But Rooney appears to have treated the prostitutes decently.

There is a second video/audio tape, of a second trip to Diva's.

Graham Johnson and the *Sunday Mirror* got the perfect tabloid hit because they managed to extract a full confession from the Rooney camp. It came from Rooney's public relations man, Ian Monk, an old Fleet Street creature with an interesting, indeed a bit of an embarrassing, past himself, of which more anon. Rooney's confession statement read:

> Foolish as it now seems I did on occasions visit massage parlours and prostitutes. It was at a time when I was very young and immature and before I had settled down with Coleen. I now regret it deeply and hope people may understand that it was the sort of mistake you make when you are young and stupid.

Rooney was denounced from the tabloid pulpits for his whoremongery, but, idiot that he was, one cannot help but feel a pang of pity for him. The celebrity industry loves its victims to have sex with the wrong people, and Rooney duly obliged, more than once, with a moronic lack of discretion. And yet one should bear in mind the humane reflection of Anatole France: 'Of all sexual perversions, chastity is the most peculiar.'

Diva's was squalid, but, more to the point, it was smack bang in the middle of Ungi–Fitzgibbon gangland, whose grip on the dark side of Liverpool life was strong. As we know, their biggest rival, the Warren organisation, was in serious trouble, with the leader, Curtis Warren, in jail in the Netherlands and the gang's most ferocious enforcer, Johnny 'Sonny' Phillips, pushing up the daisies.

Young Wayne Rooney would have heard of people like Warren – his

arrest and conviction had been front-page news in the *Liverpool Echo* –
and would have picked up whispers about the Ungis. But neither he nor
any of his drunken mates would have realised that when they popped
into Diva's for a bit of slap and tickle, they could be handing over their
good names to people who know people who kill people.

In his book Johnson explains that he was warned by an underworld
contact that Diva's was under the protection of a mob boss from a
notorious crime family, known as The Pizzaman because of his ability to
deliver contract killings to your door.

The Pizzaman is connected to the Ungi gang.

Rooney's visits to Diva's were worse than foolish. He was potentially
risking placing his reputation in the hands of gangsters, albeit unwittingly.
And they could profit from that mistake, twice. Once because they could
end up getting some of the prostitutes' pay – because that's how the
game works. And twice because the brothel's CCTV had caught Rooney's
face on camera, and some people would pay big money for that, and the
gangsters would get a cut of that, too – because that's how they work. But
to imagine that the Ungi–Fitzgibbon gang were the only gangsters who
were interested in exploiting the young soccer star in late 2002 would be
very wrong.

In fact, there were so many people who lived on the edge of the
profession of violence who fancied profiting from the Wayne Rooney cult,
one could be forgiven for forgetting that he was becoming a very fine
footballer indeed.

6

THE HAIRDRYER, THE DODGY AGENT, THE GANGSTER, HIS FRIEND WHO KEPT HIS .45 MAGNUM UNDERNEATH HIS MOTHER'S FLOWERPOT, AND THE LEFT LEG IN THE LAY-BY

On 22 March 2009, a foot attached to a left leg was found in a green holdall dumped in bushes behind a lay-by on the A507 near the village of Cottered in Hertfordshire. The leg had been severed at the hip. One week later a left forearm popped up on a grass verge on Nomansland Common, near Wheathampstead. The arm had been dismembered at the elbow and wrist.

Two days after that, in a cattle pen in Asfordby, near Melton Mowbray, Leicestershire, a farm worker chanced upon a head, partly decomposed, minus two upper front teeth. The eyes, ears and tongue had been cut away. On 7 April a right leg surfaced in a lay-by on the A10 near Puckeridge, Hertfordshire. A headless, handless torso turned up in a ditch in Gore Lane, Standon, Herts four days later. The torso was found in an olive-green Gullivers suitcase, the same make and design as the holdall containing the left leg. This case involved not only missing body parts but matching luggage. The police put two and two together, as it were, and discovered that four of the parts – left leg, head, right leg, and torso complete with right arm and stump of left arm – belonged to the same unfortunate person. He was dubbed 'Jigsaw Man'. (That leaves a left forearm out there somewhere.)

No hands, no fingerprints, see. But the killer was, as well as being completely psycho, a bit thick. In the modern age, DNA technology means that the police can trace corpses in a way they could never do two decades ago. For the moment, they knew he was white or Asian, between 5ft 6in and 5ft 10in, his shoe size between seven and nine, aged between his mid-40s and early 60s, heavy – between 16 and 17 stone – suffered from eczema, had thick, discoloured little toenails and had broken his lower left leg when he'd been a teenager. He had no tattoos or scars from surgery. And – almost certainly the cause of death – he'd been stabbed in the back.

Literally.

So what's the gruesome consequence of a psychopathic killer's handiwork littered across the Home Counties in matching luggage got to do with Wayne's world?

Wait and see.

A few weeks after his seventeenth birthday in December 2002, Young Rooney won a *Blue Peter* badge. You don't generally give *Blue Peter* badges to grown-ups. In that regard, he was still a child. At exactly the same time, he was also an adult goldmine, an investment target that the Big Money in Football could not resist.

The previous summer one man in particular had eyed up Everton's great talent, and wanted a slice of the Roo action. British football's super-agent, Paul Stretford, has dark hair turned shock white, is a bit podgy, boasts a friendly smile and a good manner with people.

In the spring of 2002 he was interviewed by Alex Hayes of the *Independent on Sunday*, and set his stall out on the moral high ground. The man who started business as a football agent from a cellar in his family home in 1987 took time out with Hayes to moan about some of his fellow agents:

> While I think we are sometimes an easy target, I do also believe that some agents leave themselves open to attack and criticism. True, there are going to be times when it is a little difficult because you're on a different side of the table to the managers, but I believe there is always a middle ground. I've managed to be successful because I've made sure all parties are satisfied.

Stretford banged the drum for better standards: 'I'm really worried about the lack of professionalism and I am frankly appalled at the behaviour of some of the so-called agents that certain players have signed with.'

The über-agent argued that sloppy standards resulted from the attempt to clean up agents in the wake of the Rune Hauge bungs affair. Hauge, a Norwegian wheeler-dealer, represented John Jensen and Pål Lydersen during their transfers to Arsenal in the early 1990s. Allegations were made that the then Arsenal manager George Graham had been paid a £425,000 'bung' to sign the players. Graham was later found guilty by the Football Association after admitting receiving an unsolicited gift and was suspended for a year. Hauge was banned for life from operating as an agent by FIFA (the international governing body of football) in 1995, but this was cut back to two years' suspension.

This mess required the authorities to tighten up – and that's what provoked Stretford's scorn.

> These rules and regulations are a nonsense. FIFA overreacted to something they thought was prevalent, although it was in fact anything but. What they have done is create an industry. And what that has done is create problems. As a result, any Tom, Dick or Harry can now easily become an agent. To stop this onslaught, I would like to see our organisation, IAFA [the International Association of Football Agents], totally restructured. That's why I have signed a

petition calling for a specific charter of conduct within our business. Travel agents have it, so why shouldn't we?

If Stretford's reforms were put in place, he said, 'the game would be a lot cleaner'.

It's worth remembering Stretford's pieties about purifying the game as the Rooney drama unfolds.

As time went by, a second man came to covet Everton's youthful star – Sir Alex Ferguson, the brilliantly competitive, bleakly aggressive and comically bad-tempered manager of Manchester United. Ferguson's habit of swearing his head off at players, at anyone in earshot and, some say, at passing aircraft has earned him the nickname 'The Hairdryer'.

The flinty Scot may well be the most successful manager in British footballing history, but he was once sacked by St Mirren for 'unpardonable swearing at a lady on club premises'. For his part, Ferguson believes that he was unfairly treated by the Paisley club. The definitive work on the great man is *The Boss: The Many Sides of Alex Ferguson* by Michael Crick, who makes the point that 'Ferguson swears all the time, by the way, at most people'.

He is a ferocious disciplinarian of the swaggering stars on the pitch and there is no doubt, given his astonishing record of success at Old Trafford, that somewhere inside Ferguson's brain chemistry is a deep, intuitive understanding of how to get eleven men to kick a ball in the right direction more often than not.

Stretford and Ferguson live in roughly the same posh bits of Cheshire's suburban sprawl, just to the south of Manchester, which, some say, ooze 'nouveau riche' vulgarity, all fur coat and no knickers.

To understand a little more about how Stretford hoovers up football's talent we must call on 'The Most Hated Man In England' (for a few days): Stan Collymore, former striker for Nottingham Forest and Liverpool, sex beast, dogger and the man who infamously beat up his then girlfriend, TV weathergirl Ulrika Jonsson.

In the early 1990s Collymore was a rising twenty-year-old star at

Southend with a golden future when Stretford came knocking at the door. Collymore, in his book *Stan*, describes the approach. Could this have been a pointer to Team Stretford's recruitment methods deployed for Wayne at the beginning of the next decade?

Collymore recalls:

> Stretford's pitch was based around the ethos that he would be totally devoted to me. He didn't have many clients so that allowed him to work like a slave for his chosen few. His attitude was very much that it didn't matter what time of the day or night it was, he would always be available if I had a problem and I needed to call him. If I allowed him to represent me, he said, all I would have to worry about was my football. He would take care of the rest. He was hungry and ambitious and I liked that. So I went for it. I signed with him. He came to watch me regularly that season. He was always there for me.

And then, as time went by, the passion cooled and there were times when, much to Collymore's frustration, Stretford wouldn't return his calls immediately, and he wasn't always there for Stan.

Collymore complains, in particular, of the time when he was bored with Nottingham Forest in the mid-1990s. His goal-scoring record was so good that he was a contender for the top flight, and he harboured a dream of playing for Manchester United. He claims in his autobiography that there was some interest from Ferguson, so he was 'gutted' – footballers are never disappointed – when he learnt that Andy Cole was in the process of being snapped up by Man United instead of him. Cole was another client of Stretford's.

Doing a fair impression of a Moaning Minnie, Collymore says in his book:

> I tried four or five times to phone Stretford on his mobile and he was very curt with me. He kept telling me that he couldn't talk. That went on for four or five days although it seemed like an eternity . . . The fact was that Stretford had shoehorned his other client into Manchester

United at my expense. There was nothing I could do about Fergie's opinion, but the fact that my own agent didn't even have the bollocks to call me was infuriating. Eventually, he returned one of my calls. He was embarrassed.

Stretford, according to Collymore, smoothed him down with the possibility of going to Liverpool.

Some time later, when Rooney left Everton and signed for Manchester United, Paul Stretford's then agency, Proactive, got from the Reds deal £½ million up front, £½ million guaranteed over a relatively short period and £½ million if Wayne stayed with Manchester United for a given time – a prospective £1½ million in all if everything worked out. Some time after that, in 2004, three men were tried for blackmailing Stretford – demanding money with menaces. At the blackmail trial defence barrister Lord Carlile raised the possibility of a conflict of interest for the agent and suggested that Stretford's aim was 'to milk the cow from both ends' – a charge Stretford pooh-poohs. Still, everyone knew that being Rooney's agent was a bit like having a key to a goldmine.

In late June 2002 Wayne Rooney Senior wrote a strangely worded letter to the star's first agent, Peter McIntosh – nicknamed 'Peter Mac'. It began 'Dear Sir/Madam', which was odd because Wayne Senior knows that Peter Mac is a man, not a lady. Two years on at the blackmail trial Carlile correctly deduced that the letter had been written by someone at Proactive, the agency which Stretford then ran. It was a kiss-off letter so brutal they couldn't be bothered to establish the gender of the addressee. The letter spelt out that when Rooney's contract with Peter Mac ended in December that year, he would be moving on. Paul Stretford had snapped him up.

Was this a simple business switch? No.

To understand how the beautiful game really works, you have to know something of the background to one of the principal characters in the dark side of Roo's story.

The Spitfire, the Dyson vacuum cleaner and the two-on-a-bike hit are all great British inventions. But whereas the Second World War fighter is defunct, the Germans now our gallant European allies and great hosts for World Cup 2006, and the eponymous cleaner manufactured in the Far East, the two-on-a-bike assassination is a still-active 'Made in Britain' success story. The motorbike roars up, engine racing, the hitman on the pillion unloads his weapon into the head and torso of the hapless victim, and then the driver flicks his wrist and they're gone. And the only ID is of two men in helmets in a blur.

Rule Britannia, etc.

The firm credited with the invention of the two-on-a-bike wetjob is the Adams family, specifically a gang of three brothers from north London, not to be confused with the much less scary Addams Family. Uncle Fester, Morticia and Itt don't kill real people. The Adams family gang are cold-blooded psychos, er, correction, highly respected London 'faces' who have made a fortune rumoured to be as high as £100 million from protection rackets, drugs and prostitution, enforced by up to twenty assassinations, or poppings or toppings in the argot. (All journalists go over the top. Gangsters don't, in the ordinary way, employ PR men or lobbyists to set the record straight. Gangsters don't sue for libel. So it's wholly possible that the two numbers about the Adams gang, £100 million fortune and twenty murders, are absurd exaggerations. But it is fair and accurate to report that the Adams gang have a bob or two, they are tough and they frighten the living daylights out of people who don't, as I do, go behind the couch the moment the Cybermen pop up out of the drains in *Doctor Who*.)

Until very recently, the gang was led by three brothers, Patrick, Terry and Tommy, who has the stylish good looks and understated charm of a well-made axe handle. The Adams gang were and are not stupid. Not for them gala displays of over-the-top ostentation. Tommy owns a £500,000 three-storey town house in King's Cross, not far from his mum and dad's place. Older brother Pat spends most of his year in his villa in Fuengirola on Spain's 'Costa del Crime', living the quiet life. Terry has lately been a guest at Her Majesty's Pleasure in Belmarsh prison, having done a deal with the Crown Prosecution Service, copping a guilty plea in return for one specimen charge of money-laundering a million pounds. He's due out in June 2010.

Back in the 1980s, word of the family's easy relationship with violence hit the streets. People who crossed them ended up looking good in funeral parlours. The Adams gang were so feared that, according to one copper, they got the credit for hits that were nothing to do with them. A series of bit players – accountants, minor runners, a Hatton Garden jeweller – whispered to have got involved with the gang and then been tempted to turn Queen's evidence turned up very dead.

In the early 1990s *The Observer* asked me to do a story about the mounting pile of victims of hitmen. The corpses included the Great Train Robber Charlie 'the Silent Man' Wilson, gunned down by a pale-faced assassin on a yellow mountain bike in April 1990 at his mock-Moroccan home in Malaga, Spain. The hitman shot Wilson's dog, too. Wilson was, some say, running drugs.

Six months later another alleged drug trafficker, Roy Adkins, was shot five times in the head as he sat in a hotel bar in Amsterdam. Although both killings took place outside British jurisdiction, police suspected British fingers pulling the triggers. Brendan Carey was killed in the Prince of Wales pub on the Caledonian Road, London, also in 1990. The next year saw the end of Billy Fisher, a known associate of the Great Train Robber and cocaine trafficker Tommy Wisbey. In April 1991, David Norris was shot dead in Bexleyheath. In February 1992, 'Mad' Frankie Fraser was wounded outside Turnmills wine bar in Clerkenwell Road. In March, Roger 'the Growler' Wilson, a south London off-licence owner, and David Wilson, a Lancashire accountant, were killed in two separate incidents. In May, Graeme Woodhatch was killed inside the Royal Free Hospital, Hampstead. In January 1993, multimillionaire Donald Urquhart was killed. On 2 June, Jimmy Moodie, on the run since a breakout from prison thirteen years before, was killed while he was standing drinking in the Royal Hotel pub in Lauriston Road, Hackney. A few days later, cocaine junkie and drug rip-off merchant Tommy Roche was gunned down as he was working on a bus stop lay-by opposite a McDonald's near Heathrow.

And then people would just disappear. One was an enforcer for the Adams gang known as Gilbert Wynter. He vanished in 1998 after there'd been gossip that he might have been double-crossing them by skimming off drug profits. His bits and bobs are thought to be buried underneath the Millennium Dome – now the O2 arena. Another vanisher was a hoodlum known only as Manchester John.

Time and again, I would go for a pint with a copper – most often a detective sergeant – and ask him who was behind this slaughter. The copper would look left and right, mock nervously, but with a hint of trepidation, and say: 'The word on the street is that he' – fill in name of stiff – 'crossed the family.'

What family? I would ask.

'The Adams family,' the copper would say, meaning brothers Pat, Tommy and Terry, and ask for another pint.

It is wholly possible that these policemen were just getting free beer for spreading old gossip. What could be more fun than winding up some lah-di-dah nancy boy from a posh paper by telling him a load of rubbish. But was all of it tosh?

London has its fair share of gangsters. The Krays are simply the best known, and the easiest to write about because they went to prison for a long time and are dead. The Arifs are a gang of south London toughs it does not pay to cross. North London is full of Turkish-Kurdish heroin gangs. The Albanians and the Russian mafia are doing very nicely. But the one London family everyone seems to agree you really don't want to mess with is the Adams gang.

To repeat, there is no compelling evidence proving a connection between the Adams gang and any of the killings listed above. Some of the killers have been charged, some convicted, and the courts heard not a sausage about any involvement from any member of the Adams gang. But – how can I put it succinctly? – the Adams gang don't inhabit the same moral universe as, say, the lady behind the till in the Oxfam shop.

The family was targeted by a secretive police unit, part of the National Crime Squad, set up in a semi-rural police station in Hertfordshire. That's odd, you might think, because the family were based in the Barnsbury council estate in Islington. Why didn't the Met go after them? The gossip was that the Adams gang had bought some policemen in the Met, which, as they don't say on *Crimewatch*, is considered by some critics a little bit bent. What happened was that, time and again, good Met officers were poised to strike when the family suddenly appeared to be tipped off and were somewhere else on the day. The Adams gang appeared to be untouchable. They were also rumoured to have their hooks into a Tory MP, although that was probably just showing off.

The coppers in the National Crime Squad unit who went against the Adams gang were hand picked; the whisper was that the whole team had been checked out by MI5. The joke was that they all chewed bits of straw, drove tractors and had funny rural accents – like the Wurzels – and came from places like Devizes, Knitting Sodbury and Middle Wallop-on-the-Poke, because policemen in the sticks are less bent than their colleagues from the metropolis.

In the mid-1990s the Wurzels managed to pick up a lead on the Adams gang which was, for once, not blown by a bent copper. They were moving huge amounts of cannabis, not quite enough to keep north London stoned off its head for the rest of time, but tons and tons of it. Tommy had a simple wheeze to keep everything secure. He ran his business from the back of London black taxis, using two former school chums from Islington, Michael Papamichael and Ed Wilkinson, as his runners. It was all done by word of mouth with people he had known since England last won the World Cup. An impregnable set-up. Or so it seemed.

The straw-chewing Wurzels went one better. In the middle of the night, they nicked the target taxis, pushing them by hand from where they were parked so that their engines didn't start, and swapped them with replacement lookalike taxis, fitted with the same registration numbers, while they drilled micro-bugs into the back of Tommy's vehicles, and then switched back the now-doctored originals. The take was spectacular. The Adams gang were moving shipments of high-powered cannabis, of up to three tons at a time. They were also into cocaine in a big way. And, the cherry on the Bakewell tart, Ed Wilkinson let slip that he hid his Magnum .45 in his mother's flowerpot.

Doesn't everyone?

The police arrested the gang and the case came to court in 1998.

The cops were expecting a trial lasting months but suddenly all three defendants coughed. Tommy Adams got seven and a half years and was ordered to pay £1 million in a confiscation order. Wilkinson got nine years, Papamichael six.

As Tommy was led downstairs to do his time, he burst into laughter.

The word on the street – as they say – is that the Adams gang have gone into respectable retirement. Maybe. Maybe not. In 2000, evidence emerged of an astonishingly cunning fishing expedition. Organised criminals had sought out those who might betray them, the grasses on the payroll of the cops. Somehow Mark Herbert fell into their lap. A not-quite-as-boring-as-he-looked civil servant, he worked as a clerk in the Crown Prosecution Service and had access to pure gold, the real names of thirty-three underworld informers. For a mere thousand quid, he flogged the files to the organised crime group, and that meant he risked making thirty-three dead men walking. The cops were on to it, and Herbert got banged up for six years for selling top-secret police intelligence. And the name of the organised criminals that corrupted Herbert? The whisper is the not-so-very retired Adams gang. Whatever they're up to, it's not exactly Saga Holidays.

So what's all this London gangster stuff got to do with Roo? Well, on 13 November 2002, a strange meeting took place in the bleak soullessness of Heathrow's Le Meridien Hotel. Among those present were John Hyland, Dave Lockwood of X8, which had transmogrified into something called IMRA Consultants Ltd., Peter McIntosh of Proform, former Everton player John Ebbrell, Liverpool legend Kenny Dalglish – who had two million shares in Proactive – Rooney's new agent Stretford, chief executive of Proactive, and one Tommy Adams, newly released from prison.

He'd got time off for good behaviour.

And Jigsaw Man? What's he got to do with Wayne Rooney's circle?

Oh, it turned out the dismembered corpse known as Jigsaw Man was one Jeffrey Howe, a blameless kitchen salesman. He'd been murdered and butchered in his ensuite bathroom and his body parts dumped around various counties by his lodger, psychopath Stephen Marshall, thirty-eight, with the assistance of his lover, prostitute Sarah Bush. Marshall had told police that he had chopped up Howe but he hadn't murdered him, and was sent to trial.

But Bush had told another hooker, Sophie Franklin, that Marshall 'killed Jeff. He stabbed him in the back.' Sophie said that Bush had 'rambled about the bathroom being covered in blood, how they poured bleach over him and drained his blood down the plughole. She talked about a dismembered foot, wrapping body parts in plastic and Marshall going for a drive in the country.'

Halfway through the murder case, Marshall confessed to murdering Howe and was sentenced to thirty-six years. But after the trial ended it emerged that Marshall is now the prime suspect and/or the prime witness for four more gangland mystery murders, including those of Gilbert Wynter and 'Manchester John', which date back for more than a decade from his time as an enforcer for the Adams gang. Body-builder par excellence, Marshall, who boasts a 52-inch chest, had become handy with a meat cleaver, knives and, when occasion demanded, a chainsaw. Based at Belugas nightclub in North London, Marshall would chop up bodies and then others would ensure the body parts would vanish. Marshall's mistake was to use his old meat cleaver technique on poor old Jigsaw Man but to forget to do the smart thing with the back end of the operation. You can't just dump body parts in lay-bys.

In the good old days, before Paul Stretford had run into Tommy Adams, Psycho Marshall had called Adams 'Uncle Tommy' – exactly the kind of man you'd want your sports agent to hang out with.

Not.

7

'HE COULDN'T WRITE PROPERLY AND DIDN'T SEEM ALL THAT BRIGHT' – CALL GIRL ON ROONEY

None of the pressures ratcheting up inside Wayne's World – the baby-oil sessions in the gangster-protected brothel on the Aigburth Road; the most feared criminal family in Britain taking an unhealthy interest in his affairs; the growing tabloid monster interest – appeared to trouble his game. That went from strength to strength.

But, first, a word in passing in defence of estate agents. As a breed, estate agents are overmuch maligned. Too often, they are portrayed in the media as cliché-riddled scumbags out for a fast buck who don't give a monkey's what they sell to whomsoever, so long as they get their percentage. Their detractors claim, wholly unfairly, that your average estate agent might inspect a fungoidally damp shack of two rooms and a void in the earth for a toilet with a garden contaminated with 2,3,7,8-tetrachloro, paradoxide with diethyl phthalate and polyhexo built on the slopes of an active volcano, and write it up as a 'bijou medieval-effect residence with enhanced garden nutrients, convenient for thermal springs'.

Spare a thought, then, for the hard-working professionals of posh estate agents Kinleigh, Folkard and Hayward of the King's Road, Chelsea. The good people of KFH were naturally alarmed when two scallies out 'on the rob' marched in one midwinter weekday and began to case the joint. An informant told the tale: 'One of the agents simply refused to give the pair any details of their properties. The two scallies were asked to leave the premises or police would be called. The agent thought they were burglars who had come to London to "case" some big houses before robbing them.'

The duo weren't robbers at all, but, reportedly, Mr Wayne Rooney and defender Alan Stubbs, who were having a quick look at house prices in Chelsea before the match in December 2002. The Everton football source who told the story to the papers alleged that 'all the lads were crying with laughter when they found out. The estate agent had mistaken them for a couple of scallies on the rob.'

A spokesman for Kinleigh, Folkard and Hayward, whose Chelsea offices are near the Stamford Bridge ground, told one paper: 'I have heard about this incident. I am not allowed to comment on it, but we wouldn't normally judge people in this way.'

In his autobiography, Rooney describes the story as 'total rubbish'. Of the two groups of people – professional footballers from Merseyside and London estate agents – I'm with the former.

Dog must eat dog. That is rule number one of the pirate code of Fleet Street, and it would be quite unsporting to give any other journalist the benefit of the doubt when it came to their word against that of the Croxteth Cyclone. However, there are times when the papers pick up on something and get it half or, more often, a quarter right. Take Nick Henegan, football writer of the *Daily Mirror*, who wrote in his paper about a tattoo on Rooney where his lower back meets his upper buttock: 'The italic mark at the base of his back, just above his shorts, looks like the letters IREN. Or it could spell "gran" as a tribute to his grandmother Patricia Morrey, 78.'

Nearly there: the tattoo on the Rooney (upper) arse spells 'THEN'. It's a gag carried out with one of his old Crocky mates. The pair of them went round Liverpool, always saying to each other, 'OK, then?' His mate got 'OK' tattooed on his bottom and Rooney 'THEN'.

His first tattoo bears the legend 'Coleen' and is placed on the top of his right arm, where it joins his shoulder. He got that tattoo from a shop in the Quiggins centre in the heart of Liverpool.

'Coleen' and 'THEN' are a far cry from David Beckham's more spiritual body etching. One of Beckham's nine tattoos spells out the name of his beloved Victoria but it is penned in Hindi rather than English because Beckham thought it would be 'tacky' to have it tattooed in Shakespeare's tongue. Tragically, the tattooist got his Hindi wrong, so the tattoo actually reads 'Vhictoria' rather than 'Victoria'. A second Beckham tattoo is in Hebrew, from the saucy Song of Songs, and reads: 'I am my beloved's, and my beloved is mine, that shepherds among the lilies.' This is a hymn to fidelity which, given the former England captain's alleged record between the sheets, makes one wonder whether Roo's 'THEN' was the smarter choice.

Some people look down their noses at body art, but Beckham, despite all his tattoos, remains a style icon. Rooney himself admits that his make him look 'like a cartoon version of a burglar'. Perhaps he should have got 'Choleen' and 'THHEN' in Babylonian-Cuneiform. That would've impressed the lads down the Wezzy.

Right from the start of his career on the national stage, the image of a street yob stuck to him like chewing gum to a shoe. His game has always had the raw aggression of street football, and playing in the Premier League changed nothing. Rooney and, perhaps more importantly, his family and advisers did nothing to sidestep the stereotyping when England manager Sven-Göran Eriksson handed him the award for BBC Young Sports Personality of the Year in December 2002. He picked up the award with his tie knotted a couple of inches above his waist and furiously chewing gum. Who gives a damn?

Well, at least some of the punters. One J. Wooster, of High Wycombe, Buckinghamshire, wrote to the *Express* to complain: 'The young football genius, Wayne Rooney, was let down by his gum-chewing, slovenly appearance.' Callers to Nicky Campbell's BBC Five Live phone-in the next morning moaned on and on about Rooney's appearance.

Everton's chief spin doctor, Ian Ross, hit back:

The whole thing is preposterous and has been blown out of all proportion. In a world riven with problems, I could not believe a major radio station was wasting its airtime on such an inconsequential matter. It is evidently easy to forget Wayne Rooney was still sixteen until a few weeks ago. If people didn't like the way he dressed, maybe they are short of something to worry about. A lot has happened to this boy in a very short time. He's a shy lad who happens to be a footballer. Appearing on live television would scare the living daylights out of many a seasoned performer, let alone a teenager from Croxteth. At least Wayne Rooney chose to wear a suit and tie, which is more than could be said for Sir Steven Redgrave or Sam Torrance. I haven't heard questions being asked of their sartorial elegance.

You can't rig phone-ins. I've been on the Campbell show, as it then was, to talk about the horrors of the Russian occupation in Chechnya: wholesale destruction, terrifying use of torture, savage killing by vacuum bombs – they suck people's lungs inside out – and hardly a person called in. A young soccer star like Rooney chews gum and the world calls up to complain.

In a sense the hope that the young Wayne could be a model ambassador for his sport and his country was wholly unrealistic. He was brought up in one of the roughest parts of one of the roughest cities in Britain. He behaved exactly like you'd expect a boy from Crocky to behave, and all this episode represents is a failure of comfortable people to imagine what it must be like to be born into a society where money is scarce and half your neighbours are on the social.

Having said that, Roo does make the point in his autobiography that his mother was not best pleased, and the wrath of a Crocky dinner lady is to be avoided at your peril. This was the first big occasion where the papers went gunning for him. Until this point nobody had really come down hard on him before. He found the episode troubling – it didn't square with all the praise of him being a breath of fresh air, a brilliant player. Now he was just a yobbish young thug. It didn't occur to him that both views might have an element of truth.

Off the pitch yet another pressure emerged: jealousy. In early November

2002, *The Sun* screamed: 'THUGS FORCE WONDERBOY WAYNE OUT OF HIS HOME'. The paper reported that vandals used nails to puncture the tyres of Rooney Senior's Ford Galaxy in two separate attacks, forcing the Rooneys to move home. Neighbours in Crocky said that Big Wayne had had to shell out £140 on new tyres after the attacks. Doreen Driscoll, seventy-one, a neighbour, told the paper that it was horrible. Doreen said that Roo was a lovely young fellow and everyone around here loved him, especially the kids. It was probably people from outside doing this.

On the pitch, Rooney wasn't doing an awful lot to build up the impression of a gentleman player. In the first four months playing for Everton at the top level, he had been booked four times. The pressures on the young star were immense – and perhaps the hardest to deal with was the expectation that, as a footballer, he could do no wrong. For example, when Everton played Charlton in November 2002, thousands of T-shirts emblazoned with the slogan 'Saint Rooney – youth is temporary, class is forever' were on sale outside Goodison Park. During the warm-up, Rooney's classic 'outer space' shot into the net from thirty yards off brought a huge cheer, a racket only matched by the tannoy news of Liverpool's defeat at Middlesbrough – announced twice for Everton's 'hard of hearing'.

But manager David Moyes, ever cautious, kept Rooney on the touchline for seventy-three minutes. Instead of rocketing in the goals when he finally came on, Roo created a loud and stupid bang with a reckless challenge against Charlton's Chris Powell – and was promptly booked by the referee.

The Everton fans didn't seem to mind. One of the club blogs records a fan's reaction to the foul against Powell: 'When Rooney nearly snapped the defender's legs in half. The ref booked him and Rooney started pointing in his book as if to say: "wot did I do?" Sum fella behind stood up and said: "Fuck him off Wayne. Don't give the bastard your autograph."'

Another Everton blogger recorded: 'The ref was booking Rooney when a shout goes up, "hey! Yer bastard! Leave him alone! He's only 16!"' (He had just turned seventeen, but you get the drift.)

Moyes had a difficult time reconciling the fans' adoration of Everton's

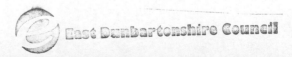

outstanding star with the practical problems of running a team – some of whom, at least, could be forgiven for being just a little bit envious of the teenage idol – and keeping Rooney grounded. Burnout was a serious worry. Some say that Michael Owen's prodigious talent was squandered because he was played too often, too young, causing too many injuries at the peak of his career.

In mid-December 2002 Everton defeated Blackburn Rovers 2–1, the match winner knocked in by Rooney. Moyes gave an interview, reported in the *Daily Mail*, which contained a subtle blend of admiration for his number-one star and wariness of what too much indulgence might bring. At the start Moyes reflected on Rooney's innate genius: 'I've never come across anyone like him in my life. Being on a football pitch is completely natural to him. He does things without even thinking.'

Then came the buts. Moyes warned: 'There are outside influences that could have a detrimental effect on him, and you have to be wary of that.' Was this a discreet reference to the gangsters who lay in the shadows? Moyes continued:

> The years between 17 and 20 are difficult for any lad, especially one in the spotlight. Let's face it, we're probably trying to take away his adolescence. We're effectively stopping him doing the things most teenagers do, and people have to understand the importance of that. We can't keep an eye on him all the time and it's vital we get support from everyone to make sure his development continues uninhibited. I'm convinced he has what it takes to handle all that. There's no big ego with Wayne. He's a down-to-earth lad who'd ideally like to be left alone to get on with playing football. The good thing is he isn't the sort to get carried away. I'd be the first to slap him round the ears if he did. Mind you, he'd probably hit me back!

Indeed, Roo might.

Moyes's conclusion was fair: 'He puts the fear of death into opponents at times and gets spectators out of seats. But there's plenty of scope for improvement.'

In self-discipline, for one. On Boxing Day 2002, when Everton played Birmingham City – a team, you may recall, that scored no goals at all during the entire reign of Pope John Paul I – the red mist flared again. Once more Moyes had kept his star off the pitch for the majority of the game. He bounded on, like a tiger late for his lunch of tethered goat, and ran for what he judged to be a fifty-fifty ball. Instead, he slammed both sets of studs into the other side's Steve Vickers, leaving him with a gaping hole requiring eight stitches. The referee produced a straight red card. Moyes asked the referee to look at a video replay of the incident in the hope that the decision might be rescinded. It was not.

After the game, Moyes defended the boy from Crocky:

> I'll be reviewing the situation carefully. If you look at Everton's recent record in terms of discipline, it may seem referees are not very keen on us at the moment. I will not be asking Wayne to change in any respect. You people [the media] are saying he is a bit rough and tough, but his enthusiasm is part of his game. I'm not going to stop him challenging for the ball.

The sending-off made Rooney the youngest player in a Premiership game ever to be sent off. Nevertheless, the golden reviews of his football continued. And he was having fun. Rooney loved Everton and Everton loved Rooney. He was adored by the fans but, perhaps most important of all, most of his fellow players grew to like and respect the boy from Crocky – and they signalled that in the classic Liverpool way by giving him an affectionate but dismissive nickname: the Dog. Rooney told Sue Evison that they called him the Dog at the club – he'd been called that since he was thirteen. They used to call him Wayne but then it suddenly changed and he still did not understand why he was the Dog.

Defender Alan Stubbs – the Everton teammate Rooney was allegedly with when the two men were allegedly suspected of being scallies by a posh firm of estate agents – came round to Rooney's new house in upmarket Formby and was standing at the bottom of the stairs, shouting: 'Dog, Dog, are you there, Dog?' Rooney explained to Evison that there were workmen in the house and the door was open so he had just wandered straight in. Coleen and Rooney were still asleep. It took Alan a bit of explaining to the workmen. He wasn't after their real dog, Fizz, but the best young player in England.

On 28 December 2002, Everton played Bolton at Goodison Park. The game provided a meeting of two stars: former Real Madrid defender Ivan Campo, playing for the Wanderers, and the seventeen-year-old Crocky boy. The first challenge went all the young man's way. Campo was left dozing in the mud while Rooney was a blur of blue. The Gwladys Street end (where Everton diehards hang out) erupted: 'Rooney's gonna get ya.' The result was 0–0, but Rooney made all the running, was declared Man of the Match and was unlucky not to have scored.

He allegedly made good that deficiency later that same night when he made love to a call girl in a derelict flat and gave her a billet-doux for her to remember the romantic encounter:

'To Charlotte, I shagged u on 28 Dec. Loads of Love, Wayne Rooney.'

And remember it she did, two years on, with a little help from Fleet Street's finest, under the headline 'ROONEY'S SEX WITH VICE GIRL'.

There's thick. There's thick as two short planks. And then there's unimaginably, gob-stoppingly, stupidly thick. And, finally, there is Wayne Rooney leaving an 'I shagged u' note for a prostitute. As the man said, you couldn't make it up.

The tragi-comic sexual indignities of Rooney and Charlotte were not paraded in front of the nation's bacon and eggs until July 2004, but, again, one has to remember that 2002 was Rooney's *annus mirabilis*, his first great brush with fame – and he had yet to seriously encounter the dark side of the celebrity coin. The daft boy had only just been given a *Blue Peter* badge, after all.

The king of sleaze-sleuthing on Merseyside, Graham Johnson, got the story again for the *Sunday Mirror*. This, then, is the snapshot of Rooney's life as a seventeen-year-old as observed by the call girl.

Rooney and his pals had had to go to an escort agency because, by late December 2002, the star had got the red card from Diva's. Making money from prostitution is still a crime in Britain, but the police tolerate brothels to prevent a greater social evil – young women selling their bodies on the streets with no 'protection' at all – from flourishing. But if you push it too far and take the piss, the vice squad has the power to close down a brothel with a snap of its fingers. Rooney was too young, at seventeen, and, far, far worse, he was too famous. The word in Liverpool was that when he turned up at Diva's, Everton fans would get to hear about it, and small but noisy crowds of lads would start chanting 'Rooney, Rooney, Rooney' at two o'clock in the morning.

OK – maybe not the world's greatest entertainment – but it was cheap and funny. However, you could imagine that might annoy some of the more respectable neighbours trying to get a decent night's sleep, and it was hardly discreet or low profile. Diva's closed its doors to the Everton star. So Rooney and his pals turned their attention to escort agencies, and one they found in the phone book was called La Femme. (The agency has since dropped Charlotte and her sister for talking out of turn.)

Charlotte told Johnson that that night the agency had got a call for three girls to go to a flat in Crocky. Charlotte, her twin sister Katie and a third escort girl who was never named found a dilapidated flat, set amid Crocky's usual charms of graffiti-strewn, abandoned dens that look like they've seen better days. The door was opened by a man who called himself Mark. She said she recognized him from the Jolly Miller pub where she worked some of the time pulling pints. Inside the flat were three men, one bald, one fair haired and Wayne Rooney.

Cunningly, he was wearing a brilliant disguise – a Father Christmas hat was sitting on top of his head. As disguises go, it might be seen as less successful than a fake plastic moustache and a pair of thick glasses. It's not going to fool three streetwise girls from Merseyside and it didn't. It seems perhaps a little odd that Rooney didn't try harder to disguise himself, if indeed that was what he really wanted. Or perhaps the lads had only decided on an escort late on, when access to convincing disguises was limited. And/or drink had been taken in the course of the evening. The trio from the escort agency hadn't arrived until nearly 2 a.m., which suggests Rooney and pals might have been partying a little beforehand.

Not to beat about the bush, Charlotte popped the 'Are you Wayne Rooney?' question. He was in a bit of a tricky situation.

Quick as a flash, Rooney said: 'No, I'm a boxer.'

Brilliant.

Charlotte knew who he was. She had clocked his mug in the local paper the previous day. Worse, Charlotte considered the man pretending to be a boxer to be 'dead ugly'. Her inner feelings chimed with many of her gender: in 2007 a research firm, Onepoll, sampled 4,000 female sports fans, who plumped for Roo as the ugliest sports star of all time.

Perhaps it also isn't a coincidence that one of Rooney's buddies is Ricky Hatton (Rooney carried out Ricky Hatton's prestigious *Ring* magazine belt in his knockout victory over José Castillo in June 2007), another sports star whose looks are, ahem, less than flattering.

Charlotte, Katie and the other girl were billing £140 a pop. Charlotte told Johnson that they wanted the cash 'up front', which was pretty fair, seeing as how they'd arrived at a grim flat in the middle of Crocky. In the event – and again suggesting that calling out the escorts was more a spur-of-the-moment decision than pre-planned – the lads didn't have enough bread on them and Rooney handed over his bank card to another lad to draw out some readies. Yes, they do have cash machines in Croxteth, Liverpool 11, and they apparently work, because friend of Roo returned with the money and Charlotte said that 'I saw his name on his bank card,' confirming Rooney's identity, as if his face hadn't already given the game away.

The girls paired off with different guys – Katie with Mark, the third girl with the aforementioned baldy, Charlotte with Rooney. Given that Charlotte reported that four men greeted them at the flat, the fourth man appears to have opted out of paying cash for sex. Or maybe he was broke. Charlotte and Rooney ended up in the scruffy bathroom and she provides the readers of the *Sunday Mirror* with perhaps the most detailed home-décor appraisal of a bad-sex venue ever.

The bathroom, she notes, was not properly decorated and the peach paint was peeling off the walls. It needed a good clean, and the bin was tipped over and rubbish had spilt out. The tiles on the bathroom had paint splashed on them. Charlotte proceeded to strip, and Rooney likewise. According to Charlotte, she was laughing all the time because she couldn't believe she was having sex with Wayne Rooney.

They went back to the bedroom, rejoined Katie and Mark, and lay down on the bed. It was at this point, in this atmosphere of post-coital merriment, that Charlotte asked Rooney to sign something to prove it to all her mates, like an autograph. Roo promptly ripped the corner off a small piece of paper and wrote his billet-doux. Charlotte explained to Johnson: 'He was pissed.'

Silly boy.

Charlotte added, bitingly: 'He couldn't write properly and didn't seem all that bright.'

If you were looking for a ten-word summary of Wayne Rooney off the pitch back in the day, Charlotte's assessment is the one to beat.

But that wasn't the end of her encounters with Wayne Rooney. On New Year's Day 2003, Everton played Manchester City, two mid-level teams playing out a draw that was considerably duller than the 2–2 scoreline suggests. Rooney was booked for the fifth time that season. He'd played well-ish and, yet again, manager Moyes took his young star's side in the disciplinary matter – but Roo's red mist was beginning to become a major problem, a weakness that other teams would identify and try to capitalise on. Our hero had an Achilles heel. The media stylised him off pitch as a yob and that fuelled the association in the minds of football officials between Roo and violent play.

The elephant trap was blindingly obvious: cunning rival players would start diving the moment robust street footballer Rooney went for a ball within yards of them, but Roo, being a bit of a pachyderm, sometimes couldn't think of a way out of the trap. Every now and then he still can't, and the haunting fear is the brilliance of his natural game is only a whisker away from a red card. That's what makes watching him so fascinating – he can win or lose a match in a tenth of a second.

That New Year's Day night, Charlotte was in the Jolly Miller, the pub where she pulled part-time shifts and had first encountered Mark. On this particular night, Mark happened to be there and invited her to a party at his place later that evening. Charlotte told Johnson that after a while Rooney arrived with his mates, having taken drink, sporting denim trainers, a grey T-shirt and blue trackies – the pure Crocky look – but clutching a bottle of Cristal champagne.

Cristal is the filthy rich chav's bubbly of choice. The brand, produced by Louis Roederer, flogs at £200 a pop and enjoyed, until recently, gangsta rap chic. Cristal is so called because of its clear crystal bottle, created, so the story goes, for the paranoid Russian tsar Alexander II, who feared 'being bumped off'. They made the glass see-through because the tsar was afraid of assassins concealing weapons inside an ordinary dark green champagne bottle. (Just because the tsar was paranoid didn't mean he was wrong. Russian revolutionaries got him in 1881.)

In the nineties Cristal was adopted as the ultimate status symbol by black American rappers, who refer to it as 'Cris' or 'Crissy'. Hiphop mogul and music industry King Midas Jay-Z in his number one hit 'Hard Knock Life' toasted the bubbly thus: 'Let's sip the Cris and get pissy-pissy.' But times change. In 2006, *The Economist* asked new managing director Frédéric Rouzaud whether the gangsta rap association might harm the marque. He replied: 'That's a good question, but what can we do? We can't forbid people from buying it. I'm sure Dom Pérignon or Krug would be delighted to have their business.'

Some of the rappers thought this reply a bit snooty and a simple 'thank you' would have been more gracious. Cris is now boycotted by the gangsta rappers. Both P. Diddy and Jay-Z have said, on their more recent albums: 'Fuck Cris'.

I've never drunk Cristal, and even though Wayne Rooney drinks it, I'd stick to park bench cider. It has the same effect.

This time Charlotte and Rooney did not hit it off and soon Charlotte and Katie left the party.

January was two-faced for the young star. In the middle of the month he was formally presented to the football experts in the press to mark the occasion of a fresh sweetheart deal with Everton. His pay had gone from £80 a week as a sixteen-year-old, then £90 a week when he hit seventeen in October, to around £14,000 a week. It was the first big deal brokered by his new agent, Paul Stretford, and made Rooney one of the highest paid teenagers on the planet.

Manager Moyes had forbidden Rooney to speak in public thus far, so the press conference was the first occasion for the world to judge the star as an orator. In reply to a question about the deal, he replied in a whisper that you needed a hearing trumpet to pick up: 'I'm very delighted.' It quickly became clear that, genius though he may be on the pitch, the boy from Crocky, as a public speaker lacked that killer kick. It wasn't the words he spoke so much – they made sense – but the timidity and hushed voice with which he spoke them. Away from the television cameras and the mass of the writing press, he gave a pooled interview to the *Liverpool Echo* that was distributed to the rest of the media. He told his local paper that his ambitions were to play for Everton and keep doing what he was already doing. He said there had never been any doubt in his mind that he would sign for Everton. This was something he'd always dreamed of.

But he reflected, a little, on the flipside of fame, too, admitting that sometimes it was really hard having to deal with all the attention, especially when people were outside your house. That was the downside and he just wished it would go away.

That kind of attention came at the end of the month, when *The Sun* reported on a Rooney failure that must have been supremely irritating for the young star: 'IF ONLY HE COULD PASS A DRIVING TEST LIKE HE CAN PASS A FOOTBALL'. The story hit every footballing cliché in the first sentence: 'Footie wonderkid Wayne Rooney was as sick as a parrot last night – after failing his driving test.' The paper reported that he had flunked the easy written theory exam, and now had to apply to take it again. One of the star's friends spoke anonymously to the tabloid, in a way that might make you wonder whether he was indeed a friend. When he got the results, said the friend, he was gutted, adding that Wayne was an amazing footballer, but he was not that bright academically. The paper went on to give readers a flavour of the intellectual rigours of the theory exam: 'Objects hanging from your interior mirror may a) restrict your view; b) help you concentrate; c) provide entertainment; d) improve your driving.'

The Sun gave a handy hint: 'Here's a clue, Wayne – the answer is not b, c, or d.'

In February 2003 David Moyes called Rooney over at the start of a training session and told him: 'You've been called up for England.'

Roo leapt to the assumption that meant the Under-21s, and asked, according to his autobiography: 'Is Hibbo in?' meaning his Everton teammate Tony Hibbert.

Moyes replied: 'No, Tony's in the Under-21s. You're in the full England squad.'

Roo was going to play his first game for the England big boys. The game was a friendly against Australia, at West Ham, but part of the run-up to the vital qualifiers for Euro 2004. In *My Story So Far* Rooney (or his ghost Hunter Davies) sets out perhaps the most thrilling moment in any footballer's career, the time when they first enter the squad as part of the national team. Roo's Uncle Eugene gave him a lift down to the Sopwell House Hotel in St Albans, close to Arsenal's training ground, where the England team were going to hone their skills. Rooney had lunch with the other players, then retired to his room for a quick kip before a strategy meeting at three o'clock led by Sven-Göran Eriksson. Roo fell fast asleep, dead to the world. The hotel had to find a spare key and shake Rooney awake before he caught up with the briefing, which was, as you might expect, not worth missing a snooze for.

This was the very first occasion for Rooney to meet David Beckham and the other England stars. Clearly it wasn't that inspiring or he would have managed to stay awake.

Amongst the names you would kind of expect – Frank Lampard, Stevie Gerrard, Sol Campbell – there was his old mate from Crocky, Frannie Jeffers. It's an indication of the snakes-and-ladders nature of modern football where those two boys from Crocky have ended up – one is at the top of the ladder right now, a multimillionaire and a fixture in the England squad, and Jeffers is struggling to find a top-flight football team to take him on.

Goalkeeper David James was the joker in the pack, hyperactive, cracking jokes, always the comedian. Rooney himself isn't a natural wit – at least, not in public – but there's something about him that makes people laugh and he's not mean spirited or miserable about being the butt of a joke. That he doesn't mind being laughed at is one of his best qualities. Pretty soon the England team were enjoying some of the Rooney family pantomime. The story goes that the England players were forewarned about Roo's mum, Jeanette. Word of her strength of character had reached the England dressing room. When someone asked what time kick-off was, England and Liverpool striker Steven Gerrard said: 'When Wayne's mum gets here.'

The match against Australia was the usual England disaster, with England losing 3–1 to the Socceroos. But Rooney came on in the second half, aged just seventeen years and 111 days, and so, at that time, England's youngest full international player.

Rooney's second England game was on 9 March, against Europe's minnows, Liechtenstein. The score was 2–0 before Rooney came on, but he was fast becoming an England fixture.

Later that same month Paul Stretford held yet another vexed meeting about who should run Rooney's career. The venue was the Novotel in Euston, just opposite the station and among those present were Stretford, the rival wannabe agent John Hyland, and convicted drug smuggler and feared gangster Tommy Adams.

It was that month, too, when Charlotte the call girl was on her own in the city of Liverpool queuing for a sandwich at lunchtime and saw Rooney and his mates in front of her. She told the *Sunday Mirror* that Rooney kept turning around at her, pointing and laughing at her. As she tells the story, she is stuck in a slow-moving queue waiting for a salmon sandwich, damned if she is going to run away from them. Up ahead of her – and, she felt, laughing at her – was the city's most promising footballer and his mates. She said that she thought he was bragging that she was the girl he'd shagged over the bath, and telling everyone that she was a prostitute. That's how shame and embarrassment can suddenly strike you: when you're doing something else entirely and a mistake comes and hits you in a completely unexpected way. She didn't speak to him, she said, concluding: 'I hate him.'

The idea of revenge – a dish best served ice cold – didn't come into it. Not then.

8

'YOU SCHEMING LITTLE PRICK'

You can learn a lot about a man by finding out what makes him laugh. Wayne Rooney's favourite comedian is Roy 'Chubby' Brown, a roly-poly act who is so deeply unpolitically correct that he is pretty much banned from terrestrial television. Brown sports Biggles-style flying goggles and silly multicoloured coats, and his patter with the audience features the Anglo-Saxon word 'cunt' rather a lot. His routine is a very deep shade of blue. He invites his audiences to call him 'Fat Bastard' to which refrain he replies: 'Fuck off.'

It's not exactly Ibsen.

Brown smashes taboos. Middlesbrough born, he shocked a Catholic social club in his home town by pointing to a crucifix and saying: 'I see you got the bastard who nicked the video.' Brown disputes one claim made against him, that he is for ever banned from Bradford after the appalling fire at Bradford City Football Club in 1985 in which fifty-five people lost their lives. Brown denies that he opened an act complaining: 'Why wasn't I invited to the barbecue?'

The first intelligence that Roo loved Roy Chubby Brown and had committed to memory his entire 'Jingle Bollocks' act appeared in a piece in the *News of the World*, in April 2003, headlined 'WAYNE'S WORLD'. As media maulings go, it was mild to the point of insignificance: 'BIG NIGHT OUT IS TABLE TENNIS AT YOUTH CLUB; LOVES J-LO AND IMITATES

ROY CHUBBY BROWN; STILL RIDES A BMX AND PLAYS FOOTIE IN THE STREET.'

The *News of the Screws* was miles away from the hot stuff: the serial visits to Diva's, the session in the peach-painted bathroom with bright-as-a-button Charlotte, the two different sets of gangsters – the Ungi–Fitzgibbon gang and the Adams gang – hovering in the wings. But even so, many people would feel it intrusive to find the titbits of their lives and photographs of happy times littered across perhaps the beastliest paper of them all. The paper sourced its exclusive to 'the pal who knows him best', Cousin Thomas Rooney, who was earning £80 a week as a Tranmere Rovers trainee at the time. Cousin Thomas told the paper: 'He's still our Wayne. He does normal things, he will just ring us and ask where we are, then come and just sit around talking. That's what he did after playing for England against Turkey.'

Cousin Thomas continued: 'The only difference was we all wanted to know about the players. We were like, "What's Beckham like?" "What about Gerrard?" Wayne was just: "Yeah, they're OK." It's amazing Wayne meets these people now. We both still have their posters on our walls.'

England had won the match against Turkey 2–0. Rooney didn't score but he was made Man of the Match. The most fun to be had was prompted by England skipper David Beckham wearing an Alice band to keep his blond locks at bay. He took exception to the Turks' 'questioning my sexuality'. Once the Three Lions had gone two goals up, Beckham, by way of retaliation, started blowing kisses at the Turks.

Bitch.

The free market in football talent – globalisation – is one of the great boons of the modern world. Panics about terrorists – real and imagined – aside, it is worth reflecting that both my grandfathers fought in the First World War, and my father fought, as a ship's engineer, in the very Western Approaches celebrated by the Wezzy, in the Second. The curse of fighting wars in Europe has been lifted for my generation, and the prospect of my kids – or, say, Wayne Rooney – ever being compelled to go to war for their country is laughable. The globalisation of the beautiful game has something to do with that. Not a cause, maybe, but a correlation that has happened alongside the weakening of national barriers, national boundaries and nationhoods. It is harder to nourish hatred of the foreign, the different, if you know and admire players from, say, Congo, China and Germany. When a foreign player steps out for your team, the question is not 'Where's Didier Drogba from, then?' (Abidjan in the Ivory Coast) but 'Is Drogba any good?'

There are, as ever, downsides to globalisation. Big Money gets interested in big teams. Little teams generate little financial interest. So in the last ten years seriously rich merchant capitalists from Russia (for example, Roman Abramovich buying Chelsea) and the United States (for example, Malcolm Glazer buying Manchester United) and the Middle East (for example, Sheikh Mansour bin Zayed Al Nahyan and his pals buying Manchester City) have bought into Britain's national game. Big Money from countries like Thailand and China are forever thinking of committing to British teams. This influx of Big Money from abroad has boosted the fortunes of the already favoured.

Lesser teams, like Everton, Sheffield Wednesday or Stoke City, seem doomed never to be graced with the Midas touch. The distortion of wealth in British football, with a small number of teams having too much and the general run having too little, is a consequence of the globalised market.

Despite the global financial crash, the immense and continuing wealth of Great Britain is a magnet for foreign talent; the market is unfettered; football requires no great expertise in language, social graces or cultural sensibility – or it would be back to Crocky with you, Rooney. Britain is also a tolerant society, its big cities especially so, compared to, some say, France or Russia. That means a large number of the world's best players come to Britain to play. The specific downside for some local British players is that they lose places and fall down the league table because they are not as good as the world's best. But it's not worth the bother of importing foreign talent for lower down the football league, so the less sexy sides have markedly fewer exotic, foreign-sounding names than, say, Manchester United or Chelsea.

Take Tranmere Rovers, for example. (Tranmere means, in Old Norse, 'sandbank of the crane birds', if anyone's interested. I am because I support them, although no one I've ever met does.)

Of the twenty-three players in the current Tranmere squad, seventeen are English, one Welsh, one Irish, one Australian (if Hot England really is a foreign country), one Jamaican, one from Grenada and one from the Ivory Coast. By comparison, of the forty players in the Manchester United first team squad, only thirteen are English, with four coming from Northern Ireland, two from Scotland, one from Wales, two from Ireland, three from Brazil, two from France, one each from Netherlands, Bulgaria, South Korea, Serbia, Portugal, Ecuador, Italy, Poland, Belgium, Senegal and Germany, and two from Norway.

The point is that home-grown top-level footballing talent is now more than ever at a premium: when it comes to picking an England team and more importantly, as far as Big Money is concerned, picking English talent to peddle your wares – Coca-Cola, the Ford Motor Company, blah blah blah – the pressure is on a small number of English or British players in the big teams. Race adds another factor. There are many brilliant black or mixed-race English players, but the businessmen who decide sponsorship deals appear to think that white English players are the best commercial bets on which to shower their goodies.

But there is no such thing as a free lunch or a free massive sponsorship deal. The corporate majors much prefer good corporate behaviour: no drunken orgies, no visits to massage parlours, no brushes with gangsters, no atrocious behaviour on the pitch. And no sexual gratification with prozzies, thank you very much.

Wayne Rooney seemed almost the perfect ambassador for England. He was white, English-English and hugely talented at the beautiful game. The men in the boardrooms in London, New York and wherever looked up Rooney, ran their fingers over the projected profits and smacked their chops. The corporates fell in love with Wayne Rooney.

Little did they know.

The good news – or so it seemed for the corporates planning to bet big money on their new fatted calf – was that Rooney had found a good woman. Fuzzy, out of focus, shot from what looks like half a mile away, but the *News of the World* was proud to boast: 'PICTURE EXCLUSIVE: WAYNE AND COLLEEN PHOTOGRAPHED TOGETHER FOR THE FIRST TIME'.

It's Coleen, not Colleen, but the sequence of long-lens paparazzi shots showed that 'ROONEY AND HIS STRIKER' were, by early April 2003, definitely an item. Misspelling aside, the two teenagers got the full treatment. They were spied upon by a total stranger, photographer Nigel Bennett. He used his zoom lens to take a series of pictures of the couple, she dressed in a powder-blue top and white jeans, he sporting a T-shirt, trendy combat trousers and Becks-style designer shades.

Rooney still hadn't passed his driving test – he admits, rather winningly, in his autobiography that he failed the easy-peasy theory test twice – but for a private chat they went out and sat in the McLoughlin family car, a Renault Clio. The *News of the World* captions to their smudgy snaps are the best the hacks can do, a hint of the Monty Python 'nudge, nudge' sketch: 'SLOW BUILD-UP: THEY GET INTO PARKED CLIO FOR A CHAT; HALF-TIME: THEY EMERGE BEFORE GOING FOR A CHINESE MEAL; TOUGH OPPOSITION: WAYNE'S TEAM-MATES ARE FERRIED IN LIMOS.'

The accompanying copy was no better. Under an 'Exclusive' headline, Jane Atkinson and Matthew Acton reported that the couple later went to the Kung Fu Chinese restaurant in St Helens, where they feasted on vegetable spring rolls, main courses of mixed veg chow mein and sweet and sour chicken with fried rice, all washed down with a glass of Coca-Cola each. The bill came to £40.

This is the kind of rubbish that gives journalism such a bad name. It's not only mindlessly, pointlessly intrusive – in what universe is a couple going for a £40 Chinese in St Helens a story? – it is, far, far worse, extremely boring. There's another point worth making: even though Rooney was now established as a top-flight Premiership player, with two England caps to his credit, his family and friends, the fans who'd seen him inside and outside Diva's, the call girls, madams and bouncers who had all witnessed him behaving badly, had, thus far, all kept mum. He could be forgiven for thinking that he might be invincible.

Throughout 2003 Rooney worked hard at making his place in the England team a permanent fixture. In May, after the close of the football season, Sven took the England team out to La Manga training ground. The inevitable shots of the players and their totties lounging around the pool created a riot of headlines back home in grey old England:

'THE WAYNE IN SPAIN . . . AND HIS GIRL IS FAR FROM PLAIN!' – *The Sun*

'A GOLDEN BEACH, A BEAUTIFUL GIRL, A SUNNY SIESTA AND THE DAILY MIRROR: WELCOME TO WAYNE'S WORLD' – *Daily Mirror*

'ROONEY'S GIRL GETS A TASTE OF SUN, SEA AND SOAP' – *Daily Mail*

The soap angle was the freshest news story, that Coleen had landed a bit part in Channel 4's *Hollyoaks*, a dreary soap opera about a dodgy community college in the north-west featuring teenagers few of whom are ever hideously obese or acne riddled. The nightspots and bars in the show get burnt down every now and then, to keep the plot moving on. Coleen did do her bit part on *Hollyoaks*, but the acting career hasn't yet taken off. The calls from Hollywood have yet to stack up but it is fair to report that the Money behind *Hollyoaks* at the time was Phil Redmond, a professional Scouser who has a reputation in showbiz for being very prudent – some would say tight – with his cash. The point is: Coleen may not have succeeded with the Phil Redmond organisation, but that doesn't mean she can't act.

(A million years ago I worked on a TV pilot show for the Redmond organisation about what naughty tricks the nasty newspapers get up to, to be presented by Jeremy Paxman. The show was pants, the expenses absurdly restricted, but in a gap between filming, Paxo and I went to see the film *Robocop*, and spent the weekend obeying the titanium-clad robot's four prime directives:

1. Serve the public trust.
2. Protect the innocent.
3. Uphold the law.
4. Classified.)

Back in La Manga *The Sun*'s copy contained one clue that all in the garden was not rosy: that the couple kissed before fans started coming up for Wayne's autograph. The *Mail* spelt it out: that the couple had to retreat to the sanctuary of the team hotel when England fans among the guests started coming up and asking for autographs.

It's great to be paid to sit in the sun, but it's not wonderful if the public are around you 24/7, hassling you for your signature. The bad news for the couple, who were still both aged seventeen, was that they didn't have a home of their own and that, back in England, Wayne's repeated failure at the driving theory test meant that they couldn't go out on their own, even for a drive. One can only imagine how those frustrations would add to the sense of pressure from the media, which was now apparently happy to run any old rubbish about the young star and his girlfriend.

On the pitch, Roo wasn't all that dazzling. Against Serbia and Montenegro in early June, he put in a workmanlike performance. Against Slovakia, a week later, he bombed so badly he was substituted in the second half. The papers were universal in giving the Crocky boy the thumbs-down. *The Guardian* reported:

> For the first time in an England shirt, Rooney was showing his age. The ball was bouncing off him, and he was failing to reach crosses aimed at his head. There were one or two nice pieces of continuity play near the halfway line, but in the danger areas nothing was happening for him. A 25-yard shot lifted wildly over the bar did little to help as England pressed for an equaliser, and when Owen fed him 10 yards from goal in first-half injury time, his gauche attempt to turn and play the ball back spoke of a loss of the confidence that had won him so many compliments after his first starting appearance against Turkey two months ago.

The Guardian was terse in summarising how Rooney rated: 'Burn-out? Big-headedness? Butterflies? These questions will be submitted to the inquest. Maybe we were all guilty of high expectations because, however indefatigable, Rooney's performance was engulfed in anticlimax. 6/10.'

The Star was equally unimpressed: 'This was the night the boy wonder discovered the harsh realities of football at this level. Rarely involved. Withdrawal was a merciful release.'

So was the *Daily Mail*: 'Anonymous in first half. Out of sorts and too much out of the box. Subbed. 5/10.'

The Sun summed up: 'Wayne Rooney: Minutes on pitch: 58. Pass completion: 3%. Tackles won: 1. Tackles lost: 9. Clearances: 0. Rooney was taken off just before the hour mark, after a night he will want to forget.'

So what might have been eating at Wayne? Why might he have been off his game? To find out, we have to follow the white rabbit down the bunny hole. Or whatever.

> 'Twas brillig, and the slithy toves
> Did gyre and gimble in the wabe,
> All mimsy were the borogoves,
> And the mome raths outgrabe.
> Beware the Jabberwock, my son!
> The jaws that bite, the claws that catch!

The unique selling point of the four-star Lord Daresbury Hotel near Warrington is its *Alice in Wonderland* theme: the book's author, the Reverend Lewis Carroll, was born in nearby Daresbury Village. The hotel is, as a result, a shrine to heritage Britain and so cluttered with bits of *Alice* verse and *Alice*-themed knick-knackery in honour of the polymath, mathematician and all-England weirdo fantasist. To Victorian nonsense verse the hotel has now added a second claim to fame: that it was the place where some daylight shone briefly on what really goes on inside British football.

On 4 June 2003, inside the Kingsley suite – named after Carroll's friend Charles, author of *The Water Babies* – two men are chatting. One is Dave Lockwood, who is a business associate of a Scouse hard man called John Hyland, who has taken over the interests of Roo's first agent, Peter McIntosh. The second man is Stretford, six months in the Rooney saddle, black eyebrowed, white haired, rumple suited and podgy.

First comes the comi-tragedy of low-level football. Lockwood gives us a clue why Hyland and Co. were so pitifully eager to get some share of the Roo action. Representing soccer stars past their best is like selling plastic bags of cold sick to Claridge's. You're flogging wounded egos for ever-diminishing amounts of money to people who would rather buy something else. The Crissy champagne has gone flat, and instead they're offered Lambrini.

Lockwood, who is clearly a good storyteller, starts talking about Irish international and gently sinking star Jason McAteer, who, in June 2003, has ended up with Sunderland FC. The team, Lockwood moans, appeared to be so broke that they would not pay the garage bill when McAteer banged his Aston Martin against the gate at the training ground. Or perhaps Sunderland FC aren't daft and don't choose to throw their money around.

'How can you possibly drive a ninety-grand motor into a post?' Lockwood wails to Stretford. The two men are joined in mutual despair at the antics of the players they have to represent. But, comedy over, Lockwood and Stretford are locked in a seemingly irreconcilable dispute. Lockwood wants Stretford to sign something, which Stretford doesn't want to do.

Suddenly, three men burst into the room. The trio are led by Scouse huckster Hyland, a boxing promoter who works on the fringes of soccer, and two strangers, unknown to Stretford, who are clearly on Hyland's side of the argument.

Hyland is bald, with black-frame glasses and a blacker mood. He looks like the Hood, the baddie in TV's *Thunderbirds*, after a night out on the tiles and without the bits of string that hold up the puppet – same egg-shaped dome, same furled brow, same narrow eyes. Hyland had taken over McIntosh's interest in Rooney in the last months of the old contract, and he wanted some of the Roomania franchise. Hyland demands that Stretford sign the agent-pays-agent contract – his reasoning being that Stretford had poached 'the asset' and that wasn't straight. To make the point, he has brought along two softly spoken lawyers, er, correction, two bruisers. They make a living in the cage-fighting business, which is not exactly providing tea and jam for the Women's Institute.

Chris and Tony Bacon are Aussie musclemen who have swapped the
golden sands of Bondi Beach for the muddy soup of the Manchester Ship
Canal. Chris used to be in the Australian SAS, the didgeridoo version of
those funny Action Men who wander round with black bars over their
eyes in photographs in badly written paperback books boring everyone
rigid with stories about how tough they are.

The Bacons are now pioneering Britain's stab at cage fighting, in
which contenders who have had their brains surgically excised enter a
seven-foot-high metal cage and thump the living daylights out of each
other. (The bit about having their brain removed I made up.) Biting, head
butting and eye gouging are out, everything else is in. Chris Bacon boasts
on his website: 'As long as combatants fight within these boundaries, and
some additional prohibitions such as kicks to the groin and strikes to the
throat, "anything goes".'

Let's apply the rules of cage fighting to writing about the men behind
cage fighting. Shaven-headed Chris looks like quarry aggregate in suit
and tie with a generous Neanderthal forehead and two eyes the colour
of smoking bleach exhibiting all the intelligence of a Bernard Matthews
turkey.

Anything goes, eh? His brother Tony looks milder, but you wouldn't
want to sit next to him on the bus. Lest he break the springs.

'I'm the muscle,' Chris Bacon announces to Stretford in one of the all-
time-great entrance lines, while Hyland slams his fist down on the table,
which is a shame, because the table hasn't done anyone any harm.

Hyland, shouting to Stretford: 'You scheming little prick.'

Chris Bacon: 'If you want to play the gangster bit, bring any man you
want into it. Doesn't mind me, it's one of those. . . honestly, that's my
game. Do you understand that?'

Stretford, cowed, frightened: 'Yeah.'

Hyland is roiling with anger, seemingly a few moments from bursting
into physical violence. The Bacon brothers don't look ever so very nice,
either.

Hyland was putting pressure on Stretford to sign a very unusual
contract. The terms weren't great, from Stretford's point of view. They

wanted Stretford to sign a new agent-pays-agent contract, effectively handing over half of Proactive's take of Rooney's millions for the next ten years. Hyland's interest was somehow connected with Lockwood's X8 outfit, also known as IMRA Consultants Ltd. The draft contract was an agreement between IMRA and Stretford's Proactive, which would last ten years. Payments due from Proactive were to be indemnified personally by Stretford himself. IMRA had the right to audit Proactive's accounts and the right to control any decisions taken over Wayne Rooney's career. The IMRA contract didn't ask for Stretford's testicles in a kebab, lightly cooked and served in a white-wine sauce with heart-shaped croutons, but that must have been an oversight.

Weeks before, Stretford had told Hyland where to put the IMRA contract – 'to stick it up his fucking arse' – over the phone, but it wasn't so easy face to face. Hyland shouts at Stretford and repeatedly bangs his fist on the table. Tony Bacon stands to one side, silent, intimidating, but Chris Bacon leans over and adds to the general atmosphere of threat. Stretford looks as though he would very much like to be somewhere else.

Two minutes after they stormed in, the three left the room.

Lockwood, appearing to affect astonishment, asks Stretford: 'Got a fucking candid camera?'

'No,' says Stretford.

The word he was looking for was 'yes'.

What Hyland and the Bacon brothers don't know is that Stretford may look dim but he isn't stupid. Uncannily expecting something like this performance, Stretford had gone to the trouble of hiring a very kosher security outfit. Enter Tom Lockhart, Queen's Gallantry Medal and Queen's Commendation for Valuable Service and a former special forces surveillance and technical surveillance expert. Lockhart used to be Her Majesty's Bugger, but not in the homosexualist sense. After leaving special forces, Lockhart had worked for Tim Spicer's Trident outfit in Sri Lanka on counterterrorism.

Kitting out Stretford in a Jabberwocky-themed hotel in Cheshire with a secret camera and audio microphone was, for Lockhart, child's play.

He gave Stretford a sports bag with a hidden camera in it and told him to plonk it so that the pinhole camera could spy on the action.

So when Hyland and his heavies charge in to monster Stretford they don't know they are doing so live, on candid camera. They're stinging him by coming mob handed. He's stinging their sting by getting it all down on videotape, courtesy of Lockhart, QGM, QCVS, and they don't begin to suspect it.

Immediately after the meeting broke up, Stretford phoned Lockhart, and then he burst into tears, terrified at the pressure. Then he called his solicitor and not long after that the next people watching the performance of Hyland and the Bacon brothers were the Cheshire Constabulary. They nicked them for demanding money with menaces: blackmail.

You underestimate Paul Stretford at your peril.

But the pressure had made Stretford a very, very scared man. He had reacted badly to a disturbing incident a couple of months earlier when some idiot had fired a gun into the house belonging to Stretford's next-door neighbour. Later, it was said this shooting was not related to Stretford.

The threats by Hyland and the Bacon brothers seemed serious and menacing, and rattled him. Right or wrong, Stretford thought he was being pursued for a cut of the Rooney action, and he was being blackmailed to pay up. The whole saga would end in a criminal trial in 2004. Exactly when Stretford or anyone else at Proactive for that matter 'fessed up' to the Rooney family, reliable history does not record, but Rooney would have been forgiven for having his mind on something other than football by the time he went walkabout in the England–Slovakia game.

But the pressure – all of it, taken together, from jealous Crocky hooligans, nosy fans, warring agents, heavies and gangsters and the like – did have a major effect on Roo's life.

In the spring mindless chumps had thrown bright green paint at the family home in Crocky. This attack, taken with the slashing of the family's Ford Galaxy earlier in the year, forced them out of Crocky. His mum and dad had moved into a posh(ish) £500,000 house in the Sandfield Park area of Liverpool's suburb of West Derby – the latter apparently means 'place of the wild beasts' in Old Norse, but that's not important right now. Sandfield Park is highly respectable, but it's still Liverpool and you would never imagine, say, Margo Leadbetter from *The Good Life* settling in.

Roo moved in with his mum and dad, too. That summer, security was tightened at the new Rooney home: CCTV around the grounds, with two cameras clearly visible in a tree, and a steel plate attached to the cast-iron gates to the property and a panic alarm to the local police station, which went off with irritating frequency for no good reason.

If you were one of the Rooneys, you could be forgiven for thinking that fame wasn't all it was cracked up to be – sometimes, something more like a prison.

To get away from it all, in early July, the Rooney and McLoughlin families went to the resort of Cancún in Mexico: Little Wayne and Coleen, Big Wayne and comic-ferocious dinner lady Jeanette, and Coleen's dad, Anthony, a council bricklayer, and her mum, Colette, who had been, before she had kids, a nursery nurse. The whole party was flown out first class at Roo's expense to a private villa. One of the papers estimated the cost was £30,000 but the downside was the weather was poor, hurricane season, and the sextet had to spend too much of the time holed up in the villa because of choppy seas and tropical rain.

If you were to play a word disassociation game and someone threw at you the word 'Rooney' you'd win if you replied 'Butler'. The two don't go together. But the holiday in Mexico showed just how much money the young player was now commanding. Not only was he able to fly out himself, Coleen and their mums and dads, but they had a butler thrown in, too.

Butlers are thin on the ground in Liverpool 11, but imagine the consternation of the Crocky party when they suddenly realised that the butler had died on them. It was just their luck.

At least, that's what it looked like when Coleen's dad discovered the prone figure of the villa's butler lying on the ground, as if the victim in an Agatha Christie murder mystery.

Was it a case of a Roodunnit? Thankfully, as Rooney reports in his autobiography, the poor Mexican had only slipped on some rainwater that had come into the villa during a tropical storm, and he'd knocked himself out. He soon recovered, to smiles of relief all around. Imagine the headlines if the butler had been a goner.

There was almost another stiff on their hands when Coleen went for a swim and got into terrible difficulties. She waved to the beach and everybody else on the beach waved back, not realising that she wasn't waving but drowning. The hero of the hour? Wayne Rooney, who dived in and saved his love's bacon. Everybody go 'Aahhh. . .'

But even here, on the other side of the Atlantic in the Gulf of Mexico, the papers were on Rooney's case. A snapper from Splash News, which claims to be America's leading entertainment photo agency, caught the three Rooneys gambolling down the beach. The *Daily Mail* reported: 'THE ROONEY WALK: HOW YOUNG WAYNE AND HIS PARENTS WERE MEXICO'S MATCH OF THE DAY'.

The main picture was a wholly unflattering portrait of what the paper alleged was the Rooney family gait: 'Clad in near-identical shorts, Wayne Rooney and his parents exited the Pacific Ocean surf and trudged comically up the beach in a stiff-armed, head-bowed line. Father and son even patted their stomachs in perfect unison.'

The coverage was snotty, and geographically incorrect: Cancún lies on the east coast of Mexico, facing the Atlantic. The Pacific lies on the west coast. Running underneath this article and a string of others was a grand *snobbisme*, that people like the Rooneys and McLoughlins do not merit or deserve these riches, and they patently don't know how to behave once given them.

On 6 July the undercurrents raging around Rooney's agent became national news. The *News of the World* splashed with a very curious exclusive: 'ROONEY MURDER PLOT: GANGSTERS THREATEN TO CRIPPLE STAR AND KILL AGENT'. Written by the paper's chief reporter, Neville Thurlbeck, the article claimed that Rooney was at the centre of a terrifying murder threat in which two gun gangs had warned they could cripple the star and kill his controversial agent Paul Stretford. The agent told the paper: 'This is a very dangerous situation.' The paper reported that the gangs wanted a cut of the fortune Stretford was making by managing Rooney. The *News of the World* said Stretford refused to pay – and feared for his life after three shots were fired into his next-door neighbour's front door.

The *News of the World* article was a mangled conflation of Stretford's panic, the threats and the unrelated shooting incident involving his neighbour. The story didn't appear to come from Stretford. In the body of the copy it quotes a terse comment from the agent: 'This is a very dangerous situation and I'm now going to have to consult with a lot of people. It's dangerous for me and my family. I'm not prepared to say another word on this issue.'

Thurlbeck reported that the threats came from two notorious crime families in London and Liverpool: they made their first demands in December 2002, and in March 2003 there was the shooting incident next door. The source of the *News of the World* story, someone close to Stretford, is quoted at length in the piece, saying that Stretford was absolutely terrified about the threat to him and his family. He took the problem to several heavy-duty close-protection agencies, seeking their advice and round-the-clock protection. All professional agencies will want to know all the details about what kind of job and people they are taking on. It was clear that those at the centre of this were very frightened and that they felt genuine fear for their safety. They understood there was a death threat to Stretford and if he did not do what was wanted, Rooney would also be drawn in; he could be targeted too. It was mentioned that his legs could be broken. That could knock a footballer off his game – even against Slovakia.

The *News of the World*'s source continues, claiming that when the protection agencies heard the names of the gangsters involved and checked into their background they decided that they did not want to be involved at all, and they backed straight off. They just did not want to know; it was too hot to handle.

The Adams gang could frighten off anyone, but boxing entrepreneur John Hyland and the Bacon brothers? They may be chancers who threatened violence once but they are not gangsters – still, to be fair to Stretford, he didn't know that for certain. The *News of the World*'s source got that bit wrong.

The *Daily Star* followed up the story with a tip from an Everton-supporting gangster: 'LAY FINGER ON ROONEY AND YOU'RE DEAD MEAT'. The anonymous heavy was reported as claiming that nobody was going to harm Rooney while he was around. The heavy said he was an Everton nut, which explained his stance. He added, rather ominously, 'Even though he didn't [*sic*] know it, Wayne has got a lot of friends who'll stick up for him.'

The Cheshire police began to investigate what was really going on, but in the meantime Wayne finally passed his driving test theoretical, and was ready to do the practical. He passed it first go and his reward was a smooch from Coleen, a swanky blue SportKa from the Ford Motor Company and a £1.5 million sweetener for endorsing Ford. He was pictured with Coleen driving off into the sunset or, more likely, the Dock Road.

The downside of the Roomobile was that the insurance for driving it would be around £8,500 a year – but that was only half a week's wages for the star. The big sponsorship money was now piling in: a £2 million deal from Nike, a £500,000 deal from Coke – the soft drink, not the coking coal – and other bits and bobs. Wayne Rooney was now seriously rich. For someone from his background it must have been unimaginable, but he makes little of it in *My Story So Far*, saying that he didn't think about it very much and that he'd never really been bothered about money and never yearned when he was a kid for material things, apart from sweets. That has the Rooney ring of truth about it.

Roo went on to say that the first car he bought wasn't for him but for his cousin Toni, who had helped him write 'Always a Blue', proclaiming his undying love for Everton shortly before it died. The car for his cousin was a brand-new Mini and it cost £12,500. He said that he got a real buzz seeing the surprise and pleasure in her eyes.

His sixth England cap was against Macedonia in September 2003, in Skopje. The game had been going badly for the Three Lions. At half-time the Macedonians were 1–0 up, with a fervently patriotic home crowd cheering on the underdogs against the allegedly mighty but in reality flailing England. Eriksson called Rooney over and announced a dramatic change of formation. He would play at the base of a diamond, feeding balls to the two strikers, Michael Owen and Emile Heskey. The change of tactics worked. Rooney scored in the fifty-third minute, taking a ball from Heskey on the half volley and blasting it in the back of the net. After the game Rooney got the whole team to sign the ball. Michael Owen wrote: 'That's another of my records you've broken.' Stevie Gerrard, his closest friend in the England camp, scribbled: 'Well done, Ugly Arse.' The goal made Rooney England's youngest-ever goal scorer, but the match winner came from the boot of David Beckham, who scored in the sixty-third minute from a penalty.

Beckham and Rooney are two of the football world's richest men, geniuses both, of a kind. The journalists were beginning to establish a nice sideline in 'football genius' pieces: in 2003 *The Times* ran a story claiming that 'Scientists now believe that sportsmen such as teenage prodigy Wayne Rooney have an intelligence that matches the traditional academic kind'.

The Sun ran a piece that summer headlined 'IT'S BRAIN ROONEY', comparing Roo to chess grandmaster Garry Kasparov:

> Russian Garry, 40, speaks 15 languages. Scouser Wayne is almost fluent in English. Kasparov likes: politics and computers. Roo likes: BMX, ping-pong and collecting Jennifer Lopez pics. Kasparov most likely to say: 'The Morra gambit [used against the Sicilian Defence, in which White sacrifices a pawn to develop quickly and create attacking chances; in exchange for the gambit pawn, White has a piece developed and a pawn in the centre, while Black has nothing but an empty space on c7] in the Sicilian Defence is fundamentally unsound.' Rooney most likely to say: 'I'm over the moon.'

But there was some intellectual firepower backing up this stuff. It wasn't all tosh. A 2002 press release from the University of Sheffield headlined 'BEND IT LIKE BECKHAM' is a prime example. It quoted Dr Matt Carré of the University of Sheffield Sports Engineering Research Group, who explained that they had developed a wind tunnel technique which had enabled them to analyse in detail, for example, David Beckham's sensational goal against Greece in the 2002 World Cup qualifiers. Dr Carré said:

> We know that the shot left Beckham's foot at 80mph from 27 metres out, moved laterally over two metres during its flight due to the amount of spin applied and during the last half of its flight suddenly slowed to 42mph, dipping into the top corner of the goal. The sudden deceleration happens at the moment when the airflow pattern around the ball changes (from turbulent to laminar mode), increasing drag by more than a hundred per cent. This crucial airflow transition is affected both by the velocity and spinning rate of the ball and by its surface seam pattern. So, working from instinct and practice, Beckham was instinctively applying some very sophisticated physics calculations in scoring that great goal.

The Times ran the press release, and more. It quoted Howard Gardner, a professor of cognition and education at Harvard University, who argued that the body is a conduit of the mind and that kinaesthetic intelligence – highly developed coordination, dexterity and expertise in using the body to relate thoughts and feelings – is muscle memory acquired through experience. Gardner said: 'There are all kinds of excellences and geniuses. It is up to society to determine which are going to be honoured at a particular historical moment.'

Stretford was even quoted, in thoughtful mode, on the subject of Rooney's genius:

> I wouldn't presume to know as much as a football coach but I imagine that if we had the technology to look into his head we'd see that he sees everything at a slowed-down pace. While everyone sees the football being played at 100 miles an hour, it's all slow motion in his mind.

But even geniuses – or maybe especially geniuses – have trouble to face. On the same day that *The Sun* told the world that Rooney had passed his test, it added: 'Meanwhile, a man appeared in court yesterday charged with blackmailing Rooney's agent Paul Stretford. Boxing promoter John Hyland, 41, was remanded on bail by JPs in Runcorn, Cheshire.'

9

'YOU'VE RUINED MY DAUGHTER'S NIGHT'

Rooney and Coleen have been cast, maybe unfairly, as the King and Queen of Chavdom. It all depends on what being a chav means to each critic, and some can't hack it. They do get the palm, however, for the most romantic engagement on a BP petrol station forecourt, ever. Coleen tells the story in *Welcome to My World* of the couple's engagement on Monday 1 October 2003. She conceded that it was 'not exactly romantic in the traditional sense'. The night was meant to encompass a meal at a Chinese restaurant, although Coleen claims that she changed her mind on the way there. (That meant that Rooney had a red-hot ring in his pocket. He needed to ask her pretty damn quick, or else that special, private moment would be gone.)

On the way back home, Roo pulled into the local BP garage, parked up and reached inside his pocket and brought out a beautiful emerald-cut diamond engagement ring the size of an asteroid.

She said yes.

Coleen phoned her mum and they went home to an engagement banquet of her mum's corned beef hash, sausage and beans, washed down with champagne. It's that kind of detail that makes reading her book so corrosively addictive. Where in the literature of our time can you read of such road-smash sensibility, of the same woman having an emerald-cut diamond worth thousands of pounds being proffered on the forecourt by the fuel pumps and eating corned beef hash, sausage and beans for her engagement party?

Eh?

OK! magazine claimed a 'World Exclusive' when it ran the following story in October 2003: 'THE FOOTBALL ACE CELEBRATES HIS ENGAGEMENT TO BEAUTIFUL COLEEN'. What's fascinating about these celebrity rag buy-ups is that you know, without having the precise details to hand, that the airbrushed pictures and well-groomed facts don't tell the whole story, that you are being fed some spoonfuls of truth and some spoonfuls of PR bullshit. The *OK!* team asked Roo: 'How did you propose?' He replied:

> We went out for dinner in Liverpool. We'd spoken about it before so I think she knew. I was okay but Coleen was a bit emotional! It was a nerve-wracking moment. I don't know where or when the wedding will be – we've never discussed it. We just knew we wanted to make a commitment to each other.

That's not the whole truth, of course. *OK!* missed the critical fact of the great engagement, that it took place while the couple were parked up at a BP garage, but then critical facts and *OK!* are unnatural bedfellows. The magazine is owned by *Daily Express* proprietor Richard Desmond, whose one-time porno-empire managing director's testicles, as we shall hear, were zapped by an electric cattle gun after a disagreement with Richard 'Ricci from the Bronx' Martino, a soldier in New York's Gambino crime family – which is the kind of story you don't often read in *OK!* More's the pity.

The full monty on the petrol station forecourt engagement came out nine months later, in the summer of 2004, when Rooney spoke exclusively to the *News of the World*. He explained how he picked up the ring from the jeweller and told her they were going out for a Chinese meal, but they stopped at a BP garage because Coleen had to get the money to pay for the meal. When she was getting it, he got the box out of his pocket and had it open. She got back into the car and he asked, 'Will you marry me?' and she said, 'Yes,' and they kissed and had a bit of a hug. Roo said that asking Coleen to marry him was far worse than walking out for England. They rang Coleen's mum and told her to get the dinner on and went back to watch *EastEnders*. Coleen couldn't wait to get back and show everybody her ring. She loves it, said Roo. When they got there, her mum had put candles on the table: it was really special.

That did happen over time but the effect was not felt immediately. Far from it.

Settling down with Coleen should have calmed young Rooney. Just a few days before a vital England game against Turkey in October 2003, he blotted his copybook with referee Dermot Gallagher as Everton were losing to Spurs at White Hart Lane. The red mist came down and clouded his judgement. Every newspaper that covered the match blew a raspberry. *The Times* reported:

> Age is no longer the issue with Wayne Rooney. Neither is ability. Temperament rather than talent will be top of the agenda in Turkey and, some time in the next six days, Sven-Göran Eriksson must answer the question that will torment him: dare he put his trust in the teenager?

It took Rooney just half an hour on the turf to gob his way into the fourteenth caution of an Everton career. Manager David Moyes had kept him on the bench for the lion's share of the game, never a great way of soothing the boy from Croxteth. He came on too late, when Everton had all but lost the game, 3–0 down, tense, wound up, and started lashing out at any ball that came within half a mile of him. He rocketed into a tackle on Rohan Ricketts, the young Spurs winger, chopped up the air wildly and was given a free kick against him. Worse, Rooney started snarling.

The photograph of the confrontation between the referee and Rooney is damning. The ref is firm, implacable, his right hand outstretched, warding Rooney away from him as he prepares to reach for his yellow card. Roo's face is a study in animal hatred: his eyes like slits, his nose drawn back, his mouth a thin cut and his jaw prognathous. He looks like a wolf that's just been asked to leave Red Riding Hood alone.

Wholly unsurprisingly, Rooney got a yellow card for dissent. 'He must learn to count to ten,' said David Pleat, the Tottenham Hotspur caretaker manager, smugly. To rub his nose in it, *The Times* listed all his fourteen bookings to date. For someone who was still not eighteen, it made for bleak reading. By way of contrast, Gary Lineker, who also played for Everton (and other teams) and England, was never booked or sent off in his entire career.

But what if Rooney's animality is wholly natural, integral to his game? What then? How can an instinctive attacker discriminate between the urge to power a ball into the back of the net and the urge to get the ball in the first place? Is it possible that what makes him such a great player – his instant instinct for a kill, for a goal – is exactly the same drive that makes him see red? That the moment when Rooney learns to 'count to ten' is the moment when he starts to choke his own genius?

One week after the debacle against Spurs, Roo donned his Three Lions shirt and went into battle against Turkey at Istanbul. The pressure was intense at Fenerbahçe's heaving stadium, but Roo withstood it, and turned in a mature performance. The problem for Roo-bashers was that he was not – and never is – reliably unreliable. He can lose his temper and behave stupidly, but he can also go for long periods when he plays great football and doesn't give anyone cause to demand that he undergo a frontal lobotomy. When England left Istanbul after the 0–0 draw, but no stain attached to Rooney's reputation, you could almost hear the football writers reluctantly putting their Roobituaries back on the shelf. They wanted to write him off, but he somehow reached back to civilised behaviour and saved himself.

On 24 October the grand old man celebrated his eighteenth birthday. The day before, he had gone to Alder Hey and met some of the young patients in the children's hospital's wards, and chatted to nurses and parents. A few days later he had a massive bash for his family and mates at Aintree racecourse. He explained in *My Story So Far* that he had hoped to go to a pub, in the usual family way. But Stretford pointed out all the many problems, fairly and sensibly. If they had had a bash in a local pub, with no organisation, no one on the doors, the paparazzi would have had a field day and there might even have been a riot. Roo plumped for Aintree and invited 'everyone' from Everton Football Club – with the exception of manager David Moyes and his assistant, Alan Irvine.

Traditionally, Roo claims in his autobiography, the manager does not come to a player's party: 'It's just not done.' On reflection, he admits in his own book that this decision may have created some of the problems that he had later on.

Worse, Rooney had cut a deal with *OK!* magazine, selling exclusive rights to the party in return for a fat cheque. The *Mirror* reported that Rooney would donate the £100,000 to Alder Hey Children's Hospital. Nearly right. In his autobiography, Roo explained what actually happened. He stressed that neither he nor Paul Stretford made a penny from the party, but that all the *profits* (my emphasis) went to Alder Hey. What we do definitely know is that the hospital ended up with a cheque for £46,000, so Rooney can fairly claim, as he does in his book, that he did some good for kids less fortunate than himself. But, if the two sets of reported figures are correct in the paper and the autobiography, that would mean that the deserving children got £46,000 and £54,000 was spent on entertainment, food and booze.

It looks as though everybody wins. The sick children get charity, the celebrity gets a free bash. Hurrah! But there is no such thing as a free birthday party. You can almost miss the downside – but it does exist. The celebrity has sold his soul, or, at least, press coverage of his birthday party, to the highest bidder.

Wayne in his autobiography boasted that the food was brilliant. *OK!* gushed that the party room carried an 'incredibly imaginative' New York street theme – though what that great city has to do with Roo went unexplained. A subway train was covered in graffiti slogans such as 'Roonaldo', 'Roondog' and 'Wayne 4 Coleen'. How many subway trains are there in Croxteth? None.

Above an archway were the letters and numbers 'WR 24.10.85' –

Wayne's initials and birthdate. The magazine reported that a musical interlude was provided by Wayne's grandfather, William Morrey, who got up on stage to sing 'Happy Birthday'. The priggish prose is belied by a genuinely funny snap of pork-pie-hatted and barrel-bellied grandad Billy serenading his clearly bashful grandson. The celebrities at the bash included Andy McNair from *Hollyoaks,* Michelle Ryan and James Alexandrou from *EastEnders,* James Bourne and Matt Jay of boy band Busted, and Andrew Kinlochan, Chris Park, Mikey Green, Nikk Mager and Peter Smith from Phixx, none of whom, I have to confess, I have ever heard of.

I asked someone half my age about these people: McNair, Ryan, Alexandrou, Bourne, Jay, Kinlochan, Park, Green, Mager and Smith? She'd heard of some of them – Ryan and the boys from Busted – but said, cattily, that they were not so much B-list as Z-list. The others were, she said, sub-alphabet. I gave her a saucer of milk to thank her for her contribution.

David Moyes was, of course, missing from the party invite list. The Scot had told the *Sunday Mirror* that he disagreed with Paul Stretford about where the star's career was going. Concerning the plans for the beano, Moyes made clear his displeasure. He told the paper that he didn't think Rooney needed it, adding that he disagreed with 'his people'. He feared it smelt too much of publicity. Moyes added that he wouldn't mind if it was just family and friends, but the thing that came to his mind was trying to remember David Beckham's eighteenth-birthday party or Ryan Giggs's.

'Can you?' asked the manager, before answering his own question: 'No. Exactly.'

He could hardly have put it more pithily.

The problem for Stretford's game plan was that Rooney was, for him, never just a footballer. He was also a celebrity in his own right and, to appeal to the Big Money that wanted to pay Rooney (with his agent getting a rightful and proper percentage of the take, of course) to endorse their products, he had to have a celebrity profile to match. It was no good the Ford Motor Company, Nike, Coca-Cola or Asda throwing cash at the eighteen-year-old if he lived the life of my hero, Diogenes the Cynic, who

told the then ruler of the known world, Alexander the Great, who popped
in for a bit of a chat, 'Get out of my light.' Roo needed to throw high-
profile parties, to be seen with the in-crowd, to be in the papers for off-
the-pitch stories – the very thing that Moyes was warning Rooney not to
get involved in.

The divorce between the Everton manager and his great star had not
yet happened, but you can see it coming down the track the moment
he turned eighteen. When it came to advice, by late 2003 Rooney and
his family were minded to listen more to Paul Stretford than to his own
manager. It was an ominous sign for Everton Football Club.

The wolves were beginning, not to circle, but to gyrate around Wayne
Rooney. The talk that autumn was that Roman Abramovich – the
entrepreneur with snow on his boots who didn't steal a train back in the
bad days of Russia's Wild East – fancied him for the team he'd bought in
west London, Chelsea.

Harry Harris, the soccer writer who knows the game better than all,
called it right in the *Express on Sunday*:

> The first name pencilled in to lead Chelsea's Roman empire was Wayne
> Rooney . . . Roman Abramovich's Russian revolution at Stamford
> Bridge began with the signing of the 18-year-old Glen Johnson from
> West Ham, but Rooney has always been on the radar screen. But as
> my new book on the life of the Everton prodigy [*Rooney – Boy Wonder*]
> reveals, the powerbrokers at Goodison Park had no intention of
> selling.

Or not, as the case may be.

But all the soccer druids that autumn were saying that Abramovich
wanted to tap the Crocky gusher, in the same way that he had plugged
into the Siberian oilfield. The gossip was consistent: Chelsea wanted to
buy Rooney for £35 million – unimaginable treasure for the Toffees.

Ian 'Mad' Monk, the former Fleet Street hack with an interesting
past, and in 2003 a PR spokesman for Proactive, was quoted in one
paper, saying: 'As far as Wayne's agents and Proactive are concerned it's

Home sweet Crocky, before the football gold. I-spy the Everton car number plate in Wayne's window. (PA)

Jeanette, Roo and Big Wayne a-beachcombing down Mexico way.
(Splash News)

Young Wayne got flak for chewing gum when he picked up the Young Player of the Year gong. (AP Photo/ Kirsty Wigglesworth/ PA)

Rooney's autobiography boasts interesting insights on his favourite footwear: slippers. (Getty Images)

Right A heartfelt plea from a young United fan while Rooney was at Everton; *below* the reaction from Goodison Park once he'd gone down the East Lancs Road to Old Trafford. (Manchester United via Getty Images; PA)

That old red mist rises when the ref fails to award Roo a penalty against
Portsmouth in 2007. (Manchester United via Getty Images)

2006 World Cup quarter-final: *above* Rooney dances the cha-cha-cha on
Ricardo Carvalho's testicles and sees red; *below* an unwinking
Cristiano Ronaldo looks on as Rooney leaves the pitch,
a picture of sweet innocence. (Getty Images; AFP/Getty Images)

Roo and Paul Stretford, the dodgy agent, at a football beano. (PA)

The Liverpool boxing promoter and hard man John 'The Hood' Hyland, found not guilty of blackmail after the prosecution could no longer rely on Stretford's word. (PA)

Above The star's first car, the SportKa that Ford presented to him when he passed his driving test in 2003; *below* four years later he had progressed to a Lamborghini Gallardo. (PA)

Fancy handbag, Coleen, fancy pooch. (PA)

Wayne and Coleen in natty schmutter to promote Coca-Cola.

complete speculation. There has been no contact between anyone from Proactive and Chelsea concerning Wayne Rooney. Wayne is happy at Everton, he's under contract for the next three years.'

So that was that. The Mad Monk had spoken. The rumours that Rooney was increasingly unhappy with the Everton manager David Moyes were all wrong. Or were they? Ian Monk enjoys a splendid reputation with some journalists on Fleet Street. Graham Johnson says in his book on football sleaze that Rooney's PR guru is among the best in the world.

Others might disagree. I would be one of those others. My path crossed with the Mad Monk when, for BBC Radio Five's *Five Live Report* in 2001, I started investigating extraordinary claims about his other famous client, not the Boy Rooney, but the porno-cum-newspaper baron Richard 'Dirty Des' Desmond. The allegations were that Dirty Des had brushed against the Gambino crime family of New York.

Rooney in his autobiography complains most bitterly about journalists intruding on his privacy. Fair enough: some reporters can be horrible bastards. But not all of them. Some of us like to tell the truth, when we can stand up sober and the bosses let us. What about the people who own the reporters, who order the news priorities, who select the news agenda? Eh?

To consider Roo's grievance fairly, it might be useful to know something of the nature of the kind of people who own the newspapers. Richard Desmond is one of those newspaper proprietors who make me proud to be British. He was a big supporter of New Labour, gave them money, and then switched to the Conservative Party, and gave them support too.

Back in 1991 Desmond had made a fortune and made our country a better place. His prize assets included *Asian Babes*, *Big Ones*, *Amateur Video*, *Fifty Plus*, *Eros*, *Forum*, *Readers' Wives*, *Big and Black*, *Contact Girls*, *Double Sex A*, *Electric Blue*, *Horny Housewives*, *New Talent*, *Nude Readers' Wives*, *Only 18*, *Private Lust*, *Red-hot Pack*, *X-treme*, not forgetting *Mothers-in-Law*. The entrepreneur has since sold the mags, but is believed to have retained an interest in titty TV.

Desmond was generous on the charity circuit. He got two royals on two separate occasions, the Duke of Edinburgh and the Princess Royal (Anne), to open bits and pieces of his tits-and-bum empire, Northern and Shell. By the early 1990s, Desmond was intent on going international. He made deals in America and Europe, including one with American businessman Norman Chanes. The latter had been nailed by then US Attorney Rudolph Giuliani in 1985 for federal mail fraud. Chanes had some funny business company: one of his clients was a company run by Richard 'Ricci from the Bronx' Martino, who had already been convicted of attempted robbery and assault.

The Gambino crime family is considered one of the largest and most powerful syndicates in the Cosa Nostra, or the Mafia, and according to the FBI Richard Martino was a known soldier back then. Its former boss, the late John Joseph Gotti (1940–2002), also known as the Dapper Don and the Teflon Don, said of Martino: 'I like Ricci the kid.' According to law-enforcement officials in New York, Martino reported to Gambino captain Salvatore 'Tory' Locascio, whose father was convicted of racketeering with Gotti in 1992. Investigators say Martino's cronies include Gregory and Craig DePalma, a father-and-son team of alleged Gambino soldiers. Greg DePalma's smiling face was among those immortalised in the 1976 photo of Frank Sinatra with mobster friends.

Desmond met Chanes in 1991 over a pornography deal. Desmond has also made serious money from his Fantasy Channel and phone sex lines. In 1991 Desmond and Chanes cut a deal in which Chanes bought ads in Desmond's porn mags for Martino's sex lines. At first things went well, but the Americans began to complain they were badly out of pocket on the deal. To smooth things over, Desmond invited Chanes over to London for a charity event attended by His Royal Highness the Duke of Edinburgh in Greenwich. But the Americans were still not happy. They wanted a million pounds back, and a million on top – for the insult. In late 1992 Desmond's then managing director, Philip Bailey, went to New York. Andrew Cameron, former managing director of Express Newspapers, recounts how Bailey told him what happened next.

> He told me that he was staying at a hotel in New York and he got a
> telephone call in his room to say that somebody wanted to talk to

him about magazine distribution, so he went down. He said there were two guys who said: 'Let's go and talk about it.' So they took a stroll outside. They took him into the back of a car, a stretch limo perhaps, a vehicle of some sort, stripped him, applied a cattle prod to his testicles, put a gun to his head, drove him down along that road near the Hudson, said to him: 'You go back and tell your boss it's a short hop across the pond,' and threw him out on the sidewalk.

According to Cameron, Bailey had been cattle prodded, pistol whipped and knife slashed. Terrified, he rushed to JFK airport, where British Airways staff advised him to go to the airport medical centre, where he was given a tetanus injection for the knife wound to his face. Bailey was then taken to the Beth Israel clinic where he had a chest X-ray and a head scan.

Officer Thomas Ramos of the NYPD's 19th Precinct wrote up an extremely detailed report on the case on 24 October 1992. The NYPD was not able to complete the investigation because Bailey returned to England. There is no evidence to link Chanes or Martino to the alleged attack.

Jerry Capeci is an expert on organised crime and the Gambino family at the City University of New York. He said:

If you mess with them once, generally they'll threaten you and try to get whatever they think you owe them. If you mess with them again, they might beat you up. If you mess with them a third time and they figure they're not going to get what they came for they might whack [kill] you.

Desmond said he didn't believe Bailey was beaten up but he made a complaint to Golders Green police station and hired six British toughs to protect himself, including two men with serious criminal convictions.

One of them was James Brown, who, on 2 December 1987, had been sentenced by an Old Bailey judge to seven years for perverting the course of justice. Brown had shoved a sawn-off shotgun against the head of a man who was a potential witness in a court case, telling him that nothing would happen to him if he didn't give evidence but if he did, 'I'll blow your fucking head off.'

Desmond appointed Brown to be company secretary of a string of his porn companies while Brown was still serving his sentence. Brown, now estranged from Desmond, lives in the West Country.

A source close to Brown said that the threat to Desmond's life was real and that it came from the Gambino family. 'It was £2 million in cash or Desmond's life.' For three days Desmond agonised, and then, according to our source, he came up with the full amount. Brown delivered the two million in five Nike bags, to the back room of a London restaurant.

Wasn't Brown tempted to do a runner with the two million?

'No,' said the source. 'After it left Desmond's hands, it was the Gambinos' and you don't fuck with them.'

A spokesman for Richard Desmond said in 2001 he 'has never, directly or indirectly, knowingly engaged in any business activity with people associated with organised crime' anywhere. He 'has never, directly or indirectly, arranged or authorised any money, let alone £2 million, to be paid to any criminal syndicate' anywhere.

A year later in 2002 I took the 'Desmond's porno MD had his testicles zapped by the Gambinos' story to BBC Television, specifically BBC2's *The Money Programme*. Our TV documentary, soberly entitled 'Porn Star', delved into Dirty Des's background. Desmond's people continued to deny that there was any truth whatsoever in the story of the brush with the Gambinos. Shortly before transmission of 'Porn Star' we received a letter from solicitor Nigel Tait at the law firm Peter Carter-Ruck (which *Private Eye*, somewhat childishly, like to call Peter Carter-Fuck), asking for an advance tape of our programme. We wrote back, saying that this wasn't a normal part of the BBC's service. Tait passed on my email to Ian 'Mad' Monk, who then emailed a chum, grumbling that this would be 'a lawyer's bonanza in which RCD [Desmond] will get charged about £500 per hour for their crap letter-writing services!'

Woe and alas! Monk hit the wrong key on his computer, and his complaint about the expense and uselessness of Carter-Ruck was emailed instead to me. I wrote back to the Mad Monk, pointing out his mistake, and helpfully copied in Nigel Tait at Carter-Ruck, highlighting Monk's point about his firm's 'crap letter-writing services'. *Private Eye* somehow got hold of this story, and commented: 'Will Desmond's solicitor now be suing Desmond's PR man for libel? We can but hope.'

He didn't.

One amusing postscript to the testicles-zapping saga is that in 2005 the *Daily Mail* reported that Richard 'Ricci from the Bronx' Martino had copped a plea bargain with the FBI, the Mafia man admitting to turning the heat on Desmond's people, a story that Desmond and Co. had laughed off as a fantasy all along.

The *Daily Mail* reported:

> A Mafia mobster who made millions from internet porn sites and phone sex lines has been linked in a court case to Richard Desmond, the owner of Express Newspapers. A New York court was told that when one of Desmond's employees went to the U.S. he was abducted and tortured by thugs who told him: 'We want our money back. If your boss sets foot here, he's a dead man.' Richard Martino, 45, a member of the infamous Gambino crime family and a favoured foot soldier of the late 'Dapper Don' John Gotti, admitted personally extorting money from Desmond by threatening force in a London hotel in September 1992.

The *Mail* added that a deal between New York porn advertising mogul Norman Chanes and Desmond had been arranged. The *Mail* went on:

> But it turned sour and eventually Martino and Chanes met Desmond in London to demand their money back. According to an affidavit to the court from FBI agent Beth Ambinder, Chanes told her that at the meeting, Desmond allegedly called Martino 'stupid' and 'a commoner', saying he did not need their business. Martino warned him not to try to move his business into the US, adding: 'This is not over.' A few weeks later Desmond aide Philip Bailey, former managing director

of Northern and Shell, went to New York to identify new business opportunities for the company. According to the FBI affidavit, the night before ending his trip he was lured into a car outside his hotel by men who pistol-whipped him, slashed his face and tortured him by applying a cattle-prod type of device to his testicles.

'We're here because of your ******* boss,' they told him, according to Agent Ambinder's affidavit.

'We want our money back. If your boss sets foot here, he's a dead man. A ******* dead man.'

The *Daily Mail* concluded its report with a spokesman for Northern and Shell saying: 'Northern and Shell has not had any business dealings with any unscrupulous sections of society. We believe that the comments made by Philip Bailey are a fantasy and we never knowingly had anything other than legitimate dealings with businesses in our dealings as a publisher.'

The comedy value here – for those of us who think that press barons can run, but they can't hide – is that Dirty Des, through his lawyer from Carter-Ruck and his PR man, Ian 'Mad' Monk, denied a story that the Mafia soldier Richard Martino conspired to extract money from him, which the Mafia soldier later admitted to the FBI. To paraphrase Paul Burrell on Her Majesty the Queen, the Mafia came through for me. (Martino is now enjoying the comforts of a state penitentiary in Kansas.)

Rooney continued to play brilliantly much of the time, and atrociously not very often but too much of the time. When Everton met Manchester United on Boxing Day 2003, Rooney seemed to take the date literally. He lunged at the true star of the match, Cristiano 'Ronnie' Ronaldo, and was lucky only to collect his seventh yellow card of the season so far. It was the first reported clash between the two – but it would not be the last. (Ronnie's full name is Cristiano Ronaldo dos Santos Aveiro, but he was given his second name in the Portuguese fashion, in tribute, because his father admired Ronald Reagan – not because of his politics but because of his career as a Hollywood screen actor. Has Ronaldo lived up to the play-actor origin of his second given name? Some England fans might say that.)

A few months later Roo and Coleen felt they had good cause to curse every journalist who wrote about her eighteenth-birthday party. But most reporters don't knock out a story unless there is something in it. And, with the greatest of respect, there was.

'ROONEY BIRTHDAY BASH' was how the *Evening Standard* told the story of Coleen's eighteenth-birthday celebrations in late March 2004, just a few days before her actual birthday.

The 'bash' word turned out to be all too accurate as, according to the newspapers, the celebrations descended into a drunken brawl. The headline writers had a field day: 'PUNCH-UP AT ROONEY GIRL'S PARTY' was the *Mirror*'s effort, 'LET'S HAVE YERS ALL ON THE DANCEFLOOR FOR THE FIGHTIN'. . .' the *Daily Star*'s. 'ROONEY'S FAMILY PARTY ENDS IN DRUNKEN PUNCH-UP: DOMESTIC HANGOVER FOR ENGLAND STAR AFTER PARENTS, UNCLES AND COUSINS FIGHT AT GIRLFRIEND'S 18TH BIRTHDAY CELEBRATIONS' was the *Daily Telegraph*'s somewhat long-winded version. Pithier examples included 'WAYNE'S WILD WORLD' (*Daily Express*) and 'WAR OF THE ROONEYS' (*Daily Mail*).

The problem with all these headlines is that the hacks can't write them unless there is a smidgin of truth in them.

'ROO RIOT' was the screamer in *The Sun*. It was their exclusive, after all. The paper's Philip Cardy wrote the story with the paper's traditional understated reserve: 'MASS DRUNKEN BRAWL WRECKS HIS GIRL'S BASH. . . BLOOD FLOWS. . . POLICE END CHAOS: Cops yesterday raced to a lavish 18th birthday party thrown by Wayne Rooney for his girlfriend – as it ended in a mass PUNCH-UP.'

Britain's favourite red-top gushed that fiancée Coleen McLoughlin was in tears after her birthday party ended in a Wild West-style brawl at 3.30 a.m. Police were called after Rooney battled in vain to calm things down at a Liverpool hotel. A source told *The Sun*: 'It just kicked off like nothing you have ever seen. It seemed like everyone in the room dived into a massive scrap. There were fists everywhere – and blood, bumps and scratches.'

In *My Story So Far*, Rooney and Hunter Davies give a toned-down account of the night's events. Rooney says there was no fight or even any arguments between their families – nothing at all. He concedes there was a bit of a set-to and some people 'might call it a fight', but the punch-up was between Rooney's family and the bouncers who had been trying to clear the floor. Rooney goes on to admit that yes, punches were thrown.

Coleen's mum and dad, Colette and Tony, had reportedly booked the hotel's biggest suite, the Botanic Function Room, for their daughter's eighteenth for something like £450, but Wayne – at this stage on £14,000 a week at Everton – had chipped in something like £10,000 behind the bar.

Nitroglycerine.

There is a kind of desperate inevitability that the evening would end in a thumping contest. It started with guests arriving from Croxteth, as early as 6.30 p.m. The Botanic Room had been decorated with pictures of his fiancée, and decked out with balloons in Everton's blue and white. Coleen's family support Liverpool.

The do proper kicked off with Wayne presenting Coleen with a diamond bracelet and ring worth £4,000, then Coleen made a speech and handed out presents to her guests. Coleen cut the birthday cake, decorated not wholly modestly with a marzipan model of, er, Coleen. Not every member of the Rooney family got a present from Coleen – why should they? – this is the kind of thing that can unfairly lead to huffs being taken.

And then the disco beat began. Wayne boomed out Travis's 'Why Does It Always Rain On Me?' on the karaoke. Later, his dad, who may have sipped one half of shandy too many, got up and started singing.

By 2.30 a.m., the mass drinking had taken its toll. It looked like Culloden without the kilts. Not long after, at around 3 a.m., Wayne's Uncle Eugene took umbrage at being told the bar was finally, totally, absolutely closed. This was the trigger for the Wild West punch-up between the Rooney family and the hotel bouncers. Three big men pinned Wayne Senior to the floor as around twelve relatives went into the fray, some fists flying like threshing machines, some trying to calm it down. Uncle Eugene was by now covered in blood, his face looking like that of a victim's in some slasher thriller where they have overdone the tomato ketchup. Eugene's girlfriend Louise had someone else's blood spattering her face. Wayne's dad was still being held down by three men. Coleen's younger brother, Anthony – according to Coleen in her autobiography, the man who most makes her laugh: 'He's great at taking people off, like family and friends, and then he'll just do stupid things that really crack me up' – came close to suffering collateral damage. A family friend had blood spewing from his eye. The hotel security staff took quite a few punches.

Coleen's mum Colette was heard allegedly yelling: 'You've ruined my daughter's night.' One of the tabloids alleges that Colette swore but a friend of the family says that's just not like her – 'They're working class, all right, but gold.'

The police arrived in three patrols cars and a van.

Other than that, it was a quiet night.

10

'HE WAS A KNOBHEAD'

Friendly matches are badly named. Often they turn out nasty. Even if the game goes sportingly, friendlies are bad for generating unfortunate injuries. In August 2003 in a friendly against Glasgow Rangers, Rooney fell awkwardly, twisting his ankle and damaging his ligaments. Because he could no longer put any weight on the injured ankle, Moyes suggested that he himself take Rooney's place on the team coach while the physio drove Rooney back from Scotland to Liverpool in Moyes's own Mercedes. This was, Rooney concedes, a generous gesture by the manager, but as luck would have it, Rooney put his Barry White album into the CD player in the Mercedes, and Crocky's own managed to crock it. Rooney goes on to plead his innocence so pitifully that you have to give him the benefit of the doubt. But the upshot was there was yet another sort of irritation in the relationship between manager and star.

From Rooney's version of events, it sounds like a bad domestic, like a middle-aged couple who have woken up one morning to realise they hate each other.

The heavyweight problem in the relationship was that Rooney now had two masters, Everton and England, and he was in a prime position to play one off against the other, and his country could always trump his club. In *My Story So Far*, Rooney admits to the tension created by the divided loyalty. He said that he started most games in the 2003–4 season for his club, unlike the season before, but he didn't start scoring for Everton until December.

It was during this period that he started playing for England, in the European Championship qualifiers, and he was performing very well. This led to some 'club versus country problems' which, in Rooney's eyes, became a bit complicated and unpleasant. This difficulty was compounded, it would seem, by Rooney relying on the advice of his agent, Paul Stretford, in preference to the common sense of his team manager. Rooney tells the story in his autobiography of a journey down to London for an England medical when he had a sore knee. He says he was in no condition to play for Everton and, implicitly, England, but was happy to go to London for a check-up to assure the national side that his 'not fit to play' condition was genuine. Rooney, Everton's physio and Moyes were booked on a plane to go down to London for the check-up. Stretford wanted to come too, and had booked himself on the same flight. At the last minute the plan was switched and Moyes drove the Everton party, but not Stretford, to London – according to Rooney, this seemed to be a way of avoiding the agent. Rooney boasts that on the journey down from the north-west he didn't say a word.

When the Everton party got to the hotel, says Rooney, Stretford was already there – the agent had turned Scarlet Pimpernel. The check-up confirmed the Everton diagnosis that Rooney wasn't fit to play, and the unhappy party headed back to Liverpool. Roo thought that this had been a case of muscle-flexing by Moyes. He thought that Moyes had 'overdone it', and the whole episode had shown 'a lack of trust – between the FA and Everton, and both of them and me.' Rooney adds that he found it all trivial but annoying.

One can, however, run exactly the same anecdote and come to a wholly different conclusion, that Moyes was just trying to look after his player, that an agent who was primarily looking after the star's commercial interests may have had no absolute right to attend an England medical, and that spending a whole car journey with a teenager who was in such a monumental sulk that he didn't speak all the way from Liverpool to London might be a pain in the arse.

If it came down to a struggle for Rooney's heart and soul between the two men – Moyes and Stretford – then it is the former who retains an excellent reputation in the football world and the latter does not.

Roo in his book goes on to cite other niggles: that Moyes warned him not to get too close to Duncan Ferguson; that, after one game Everton lost, Moyes said that the team had been beaten because of Roo; and that Roo had been eating 'too many fucking McDonald's'. (Of these crimes, some say, that last one has to be an abomination unto God.)

All of these stories could be told the other way round, that they show just a hard-working and conscientious football manager trying to do his job and get the best out of not just his young star's brilliant though erratic talent but the whole team. For example, at one stage Moyes was clearly concerned about Duncan Ferguson and his application, or the lack of it, to the game. According to Roo's book, Moyes pulled him into his office and warned him to stay away from his old idol. Roo passed on the warning to Ferguson in front of the other players, causing Big Dunc to crack up with Big Laughter.

Rooney is fair to add that there was some kind of battle of wills going on between Moyes and Ferguson. The relationship got so low that Moyes threatened Ferguson with dropping him, that the Scottish manager put the Scottish striker on extra training, but that Ferguson buckled down and improved so dramatically he ended up the captain. The whole story can be read as an exercise in good leadership by Moyes: identifying a problem with Duncan Ferguson, putting pressure on him to improve his game, and then rewarding him fair and square when his performance got markedly better.

In his book, Roo's magnanimous streak allows that, even though he often didn't agree with his manager, the problems may have been generated because of Roo's impatience, inexperience and youth. The consensus of the wider football community sides with Moyes. Most observers sympathised with the Everton manager's attempts to get the best out of Rooney. But Roo was getting footloose and fancy free, and his old boast on the T-shirt underneath his Everton match shirt – 'Once a Blue, Always a Blue' – was beginning to look threadbare, as if he rued the day he ever made it.

Down in the dumps though Roo may have been about his end of the relationship with Moyes, there was something very much to look forward to that summer: Euro 2004. For the tournament, the England team was encamped in a vast hotel on the outskirts of Lisbon called Solplay. However, the Football Association party was dwarfed by the enormous spaces of the otherwise empty hotel – every room had been booked by England lest fans and other undesirables mobbed them – and Rooney in his book laments that the team all felt a bit lost.

England was drawn in Group B with France – the favourites – Croatia and Switzerland. The team played France first and, to begin with, the Three Lions had the lion's share of the play.

Frank Lampard scored in the thirty-eighth minute and later Roo broke through the defence but was brought down by a perfidious Froggy. Becks fluffed the penalty. Still one-up in the seventy-fifth minute, Eriksson took Rooney and the ginger dynamo and later United teammate Paul Scholes off and replaced them with the limited Emile Heskey and Owen Hargreaves – another future Old Trafford chum. Suddenly, the French woke up from their *repos* and knocked two in before the final whistle, causing a mournful demeanour in the England dressing room.

The England v. Switzerland fixture was a wholly different kettle of fish. The bash 'n' brawl stories of the wider Rooney circle a few months back were forgotten, demonstrating, perhaps, the terrifying fickleness of the media. Adoration of the Crocky cyclone was absolute. 'ROO BRITANNIA: LONG TO WAYNE OVER US' – *Daily Mirror*; 'PRICELESS ROONEY IS ENGLAND'S GEM' – *Daily Telegraph*; 'ROONEY HEAD OVER HEELS, WHILE THE SWISS ROLL' – *Independent*; 'ROONEY'S OVER THE MOONEY' – *Daily Star*.

Whole Scandinavian forests were felled in fealty to the eighteen-year-old, and not just for the press in England. 'His accelerations, his desire and his daring make him a rare striker,' said the Parisian version of *The Times*, *Le Monde*. 'The new darling of English football, a matador whose goals have earned him a place in history,' said *A Bola* in Portugal. 'Fantastic, unbelievable, sensational, England celebrated its new king of lions' was the verdict of *Der Tagesspiegel* in Germany.

Simon Barnes of *The Times* described Roo's performance in a
beautifully written piece headlined 'BABY ELEPHANT BRINGS THE HOUSE
DOWN':

> Rooney seems to have modelled his style of play on the baby elephant
> that ran amok in the *Blue Peter* studio. There is the same impossible
> size, and there is the same impossibly young age – Rooney is still only
> 18. There is the same air of not being quite in control, as if he hadn't yet
> got around to counting his limbs. Then there is the same altogether
> unexpected speed, and equally unexpected manoeuvrability. But
> more than anything else, there is the same talent for destruction. Nor
> is it a predictable kind of destructiveness. You can get out of the way of
> a big truck; there's not much you can do about a baby elephant that's
> got your name on it. Nor is there much that a frightened defender can
> do about a rampaging Rooney.
>
> Rooney put the wind up the Swiss last night in the hitherto quiet
> university town of Coimbra. It seems that Sven-Göran Eriksson, the
> England head coach, picks him with the same logic that the Duke of
> Wellington picked his army: I don't know what he does to the enemy
> but he certainly puts the fear of God into me.
>
> He was booked for clattering the keeper in a hefty challenge for
> the ball. He had just given away possession and then immediately
> given away another foul. He looked on the very edge of personal
> control. And that, of course, is when this bullocking sweating man-
> calf generally shows us his best.

Roo scored two out of England's three goals that night. His first goal,
in the twenty-third minute, made him the youngest player to have scored
in the European Championship. After the ball hit the back of the net, Roo
performed a backwards flip, half-man, half-Flipper the Dolphin.

Four days later, England faced Croatia and, yet again, the striker put
two in the back of the net, with the game ending 4–2 in favour of the Three
Lions. The headline writers went into full Orgasmatron mode: 'ROONEY IS
TWO GOOD'. 'ROO CAN STOP HIM NOW'. 'ROO'S A BEAUTY'. 'WHAT A HEROO!'

'WAYNE REIGNS AT THE DOUBLE'. 'WAYNE ON TOP OF THE WORLD'. And that was just the *Daily Star*.

The euphoria can best be summed up by *The Sun*, the leader article of which could not have been more lickspittle and ingratiating:

> OUR HE-ROO: WHAT a Wayne to go! The 18-year-old Lion King led England to triumph last night – and now glory really does beckon for Sven and Co. Brilliant Rooney carries the nation's hopes on his broad shoulders. But he shows no signs of the pressure. Now just three matches stand between England and the cup. Come on lads – we're Roo-ting for you!

Then came the match with the host nation, Portugal. That night the Wezzy was packed and in a hospitable mood. It entertained *The Guardian*'s genial reporter Duncan Campbell.

"'What paper are you from? *The Guardian*? Well, I'll buy the paper in the morning, but I'm a foreman on a building site. Imagine me going in with your paper under my arm – I'll have to hide it in the *Sport*.'"

One local, John Gore, told Campbell: "'Wayne's brilliant. Because he was brought up round here, everyone knows him. He's not big headed. He stops and talks to kids on the street. He's a shy lad, down to earth. It's rough and ready round here but there's good and bad everywhere and Wayne, well he's just brilliant!'"

Another local, Barry Gannon, groaned along with the rest of England when, in the thirtieth minute, Roo clattered into the Portuguese defender Jorge Andrade, and broke the metatarsal bone in the little toe of his right foot. Gannon made light of it: "'Look at the lad's exuberance! Look, he left his boot on the floor but he still went on playing.'"

Roo was stretchered off, to be greeted by a Portuguese medic who jabbed his bum with a needle. For him, Euro 2004 was over. Campbell commented:

> When Rooney went off there was an element of *Hamlet* without the Prince, Troy without Achilles and the World without Wayne. The

Portuguese goal was greeted with collective moans but the noise was nothing compared to the shouts that greeted Sol Campbell's disallowed goal. The sounds from the Western Approaches were loud enough to wake all the residents at the neighbouring West Derby cemetery.

When England lost the penalty shoot-out, Campbell wrote: 'The Western Approaches had turned into the Cruel Sea.' *The Guardian*'s man was allowed to leave the Wezzy wholly intact. Maybe it is not quite as rough as it likes to pretend.

There is something about Rooney's unhinged genius that rises to a challenge and, all things considered, the eighteen-year-old conducted himself magnificently in Portugal. The England manager, normally a master of understatement, said of Roo: 'I don't remember anyone making such an impact since Pelé in the World Cup of 1958.'

Rooney had truly arrived, stamping his way to front of stage in the national pantomime. He had played brilliantly and his injury was no fault of his own. The *Financial Times* noted one by-product of his excellence in a column called 'Stars & Dogs':

> Who shone brightly and who made a mess on the markets this week: Proactive Sports, the sports agency and marketing group, was up 17.5 per cent to 8.4p as its star moved in step with its best-known client, England footballer Wayne Rooney. His performance on Monday against Croatia, building on other strong performances, had investors licking their lips over Proactive's share of the inevitable sponsorship and marketing deals sure to follow and even a slice in the spoils of a potential high-priced transfer. But Rooney's injury against Portugal sent the shares down 7 per cent on Friday, showing that the life of its main asset is precarious.

What the City traders didn't know was that the stock of Proactive's prize asset was about to fall through the bottom of the market, big time. The man the newspapers had worshipped only a few days before was about to have a bucket of shit poured over him.

The second half of 2004 was to prove an extraordinarily painful time for Wayne Rooney, when three of the subterranean pressures on him erupted into public view: his previous use of prostitutes, back when he was sixteen turning seventeen; his feeling that his relationship with his manager was not good, leading to a new determination to leave Everton; and how his agent had ended up in the same room as one of the most terrifying gangsters in Britain.

Calamity, oh, calamity. The run of disasters started immediately in the wake of Euro 2004, when, shortly before going on holiday to the Caribbean, Roo traded in his good name for an exclusive interview and a barrowload of cash from *The Sun*. He may have ended up some £250,000 the richer, but no one had forgotten the Hillsborough disaster and his new paymaster was still the most hated newspaper on Merseyside. Jimmy McGovern, the acclaimed TV writer, responsible for *Cracker* and the drama-documentary *Hillsborough*, summed it up: 'For Wayne Rooney to sell his story to *The Sun* is a disgrace.'

And so said many of Liverpool. The anger in the city seemed only to heighten when *The Sun* ran its full-page apology on 7 July 2004, headlined: '15 YEARS AGO THE SUN MADE A MISTAKE OVER HILLSBOROUGH . . .'

Just how heartfelt was the paper's apology?

Very. In 1993 Kelvin MacKenzie told a House of Commons Select Committee: 'I regret Hillsborough. It was a fundamental mistake.'

Or not very. In 2006 MacKenzie – who by this time had long left *The Sun* – told a fat-cats dinner in Newcastle:

> I was not sorry then and I'm not sorry now. All I did wrong there was tell the truth. There was a surge of Liverpool fans who had been drinking and that is what caused the disaster. The only thing different we did was put it under the headline 'The Truth'. I went on [BBC Radio 4's] *World at One* the next day and apologised. I only did that because Rupert Murdoch told me to. I wasn't sorry then and I'm not sorry now because we told the truth.

A few months on in 2007, MacKenzie popped up on BBC1's *Question*

Time – one of the great dreadnoughts of British democracy – and faced heavy fire from host David Dimbleby. He challenged MacKenzie: 'When you were editor of *The Sun* you've said you apologised to Liverpool because you were told to by Murdoch and you didn't mean it.'

'That's true,' replied MacKenzie. He went on to hedge his unapology a little, but not ever so very much.

The Sun's 2004 apology cleverly appeared to entwine Rooney with the newspaper, a trick that Stretford and Co. at Proactive were quick to disavow:

> Proactive, Wayne and his fiancée Coleen believe that *The Sun*'s repeated apologies for its terrible mistakes in its reporting of the Hillsborough disaster are entirely a matter for that newspaper. We all wish to make it clear that the sentiments expressed in *The Sun* were the views of that newspaper alone and we were not asked to, nor did we, endorse them.

Quick, but not quick enough. It's barely conceivable that his agent would have let Wayne speak to *The Sun* without copy approval or that every line about Wayne's granny and his love of football had been chewed and picked over by Team Rooney to weed out anything difficult. But the Rooney camp had not expected or approved the entwined apology. The damage had been done.

In *My Story So Far*, Roo acknowledges that the affair was a terrible mistake, saying that Paul Stretford took the blame but that he felt at fault too.

Cynics might argue that Stretford may have had an inkling of how the people of Liverpool would react to the *Sun* deal, prior to the interview coming out, but that, as the key decision had already been made to quit Everton, then it was something they felt that they could deal with. But it's always easy to have 20/20 hindsight. What caught out everyone in the deal was the strength of the counter-attack by a city which, for all its faults, is a real community, and one you should not impugn lightly.

One not very interesting aspect of the deal with *The Sun* was that

Coleen had dropped a superfluous 'l' from her name. When she first appeared in the newspapers in the spring of 2003, she was spelt Colleen. Now, definitively, she was Coleen – but you have to be a Coleen anorak to care.

But the big consequence of the buy-up with *The Sun* was that it heralded an open season on Roo from all the other tabloids. Worse for Rooney, any number of people in Liverpool – whores, taxi drivers, gangsters, punters – who had kept their mouths shut about his fun with working girls now had a very good excuse to dob him in. He stood accused of betraying Liverpool for money.

Enter, stage right, Graham Johnson. His previous attempt to nail Roo for whoring had been frustrated by his squeamish editor, Tina Weaver, back when the star was unknown and only sixteen; now, after Roo's display of genius during Euro 2004, he was international property and, at eighteen, an adult, so Johnson was given the green light by the *Sunday Mirror* to hoover up the dirt and then open the hoover bag and fling it all around.

In his book *Football and Gangsters: How Organised Crime Controls the Beautiful Game*, Johnson reveals a little of how he locked on to the skeletons in the Rooney cupboard. He got a call from someone in the game – football, that is – alleging that a blackmail gang were trying to sting Wayne Rooney for Big Money: six figures. The gang had heard that Rooney had once paid for sex with a high-end hooker. The MacGuffin, if Alfred Hitchcock had been writing the screenplay, was that the girl had a twin, also on the game. And twin hookers in a city of virtue like Liverpool wouldn't be that hard to find.

Even better, there was documentary evidence – silly old Roo's note, 'To Charlotte, I shagged u on 28 Dec. Loads of Love, Wayne Rooney', written back in the fag end of 2002, after the encounter in the bathroom with peeling peach-coloured paint.

In his book, Johnson writes that the hooker twins were in danger of being blackmailed by gangsters. However, 'eleventh-hour help was at hand in the form of my good self'. Stepping into the breach, Johnson hit the streets of Liverpool and spoke to another soccer insider, who told him the name of the prostitute who went with Rooney, Charlotte, and the agency, La Femme. The next stage, Johnson said, was for him to turn them over, as it's known in the trade. All of this was happening at exactly the time when Rooney had 'sold his soul' to *The Sun*.

Johnson, with another hack, reported in the *Sunday Mirror* in mid-July 2004 that Wayne Rooney had a 'bombshell announcement' for his club. Rooney, the paper predicted, 'will formally reject Everton's offer of a new contract this week and plunge the club even further into crisis.' The paper added that England's teenage hero of Euro 2004 would return from his Caribbean holiday with Everton ready to set him a deadline of Friday for a decision, but it revealed that Rooney would turn down the £12.5 million package.

This was psychic stuff, delivered to *Sunday Mirror* readers before Roo returned from holiday – and wholly accurate. Meanwhile, the tabloid sleuth was turning over the prozzies. Johnson booked a suite at the Marriott Hotel near Speke, and called La Femme. The twins had quit the escort agency, but he asked for them nicely, and one of them rang back. An appointment was booked for the following night.

When the girls arrived, Johnson put on an act, pretending to be a record company boss. There's no such thing as a good witness if they're drunk, so Johnson ordered in the champagne but not too much. He waffled on about celebs and then popped his question: had the girls ever had a famous client?

'Wayne Rooney,' came Charlotte's reply.

Journalism made simple.

She added: 'He was a knobhead.'

What Charlotte and her sister didn't know was that Johnson had two secret video recorders and two minidisc digital tape recorders at various positions around the room recording every glance, every word.

Johnson went to the toilet and rang *Sunday Mirror* snapper John Gladwyn. He came in and put in a comic masterpiece as a 'flighty, boho, yoga-worshipping PR luvvie', and a cokehead to boot, 'wiping his nose, pretending to be over-alert, jumpy and a bit mad, something like a cross between *Absolutely Fabulous* and a drag queen'.

After some more 'poo, Johnson asked the girls to repeat the famous footballer story. Gladwyn, on hearing their claim, responded by saying that he knew people in the newspapers who would pay good money for a story like that.

Johnson then writes that this is when the 'switch' occurred, 'to use a term favoured by con men everywhere'. The 'switch' means that the party act was dropped, and the girls had a sharp jolt of reality. Johnson and Gladwyn shed their masks and Charlotte and her twin sister were suddenly looking at being on the front page of the *Sunday Mirror*. Which is pretty terrifying, whether you're a call girl or not.

It is worth noting that, as far as Charlotte and her twin sister were concerned, Johnson and Gladwyn did not reveal that they were tabloid journalists until after they had the Rooney story in the bag, on tape. It is not clear from Johnson's book exactly when the journalists confessed to being who they really were, but there is no doubt that the two young women were delighted that their part-time careers as prostitutes were going to be splashed across the front page of a national newspaper.

Or not, as the case may be.

Once Charlotte had admitted that she had slept with Rooney, in the context of what she thought was a bit of a laugh with a music executive and his chum with the very good cocaine-snorting impersonation, then she was kippered. You could argue that Johnson was engaged in a bit of artful entrapment. He concludes the Charlotte episode in his book by saying that the story caused a big sensation, and the *Sunday Mirror* flew Charlotte and her sister off to Spain to keep them away from the rest of Fleet Street. Suffice to say, they didn't stick around in the escort game for much longer. Johnson claims that they 'settled down into college and their day jobs.'

The sleuth concludes that, it was, on reflection, 'probably a bit naughty to deceive the girls'. On the other hand, they were looked after well and the story in the paper caused the gangsters to back off.

It's a public service, journalism.

11

THE MYTH OF THE AULD SLAPPER

The HE-ROO of Euro 2004 was a national disgrace: worse, his relationship with his girl was over. Or, at least, that was how *The Sun* told it the next day, Monday 26 July 2004: 'ROONEY AND COLEEN SPLIT: SHE SLAPS HIM AND LEAVES OVER HOOKER: Tearful Coleen McLoughlin SLAPPED the 18-year-old soccer sensation when she learned about his sordid romp.'

Worse, Coleen 'told friends' – that hoary old familiar – that she told Wayne: 'How dare you? Fuck off!'

On Tuesday, *The Sun* had more: 'COLEEN CHUCKS RING AWAY: £25K ROONEY GEM HURLED TO SQUIRRELS'. The redtop panted that the diamond sparkler may be lost for ever because raging Coleen McLoughlin, 18, hurled it into a densely wooded squirrel sanctuary near the pair's home in Formby, Merseyside.

The scoop caused a rash of metal-detector-wielding treasure hunters to race off to the red squirrel sanctuary, where they were asked to desist by the National Trust. The other bit of bad news for the luckless treasure hunters was that *The Sun*'s squirrel sanctuary story was wholly untrue. (Let's not forget the poor old red squirrels who have never done anyone any harm and are being crowded out of Britain by their bigger, tougher, grey cousins imported from North America. The last thing they needed was their sanctuary being invaded by a bunch of weirdos wearing headphones emitting strange whistling noises while prodding the earth with a metal stick because they were under the mistaken impression that the girlfriend of a millionaire soccer star had chucked her ring away. If I was a red squirrel, I would have been very cross indeed.)

Nor did Coleen leave him.

A tabloid editor broke down in tears and 'told friends' how it works:

> If a celebrity has been caught at it, normally a bloke with his trousers down, shagging someone he should not have been, then he's going to be excruciatingly embarrassed. So long as the basic story's true – he or she is guilty of bonking the wrong person – then you can get away with murder. You can add some extra juicy detail – it may be a load of old cobblers – but you can get away with it. And so we do.

The classic example of a tabloid journo getting away with a little extra detail is the David Mellor exclusive, which hit the headlines in July 1992. Mellor, then the Minister for Fun in John Major's Cabinet, was involved in a kiss 'n' tell scandal in which struggling actress Antonia de Sancha sold her story of her affair with Mellor for £30,000. The publicist Max Clifford added the bit about Mellor bonking Antonia in his Chelsea FC kit. The Cabinet minister was hardly in a position to complain. Likewise, Coleen did not lob her ring into the red squirrel sanctuary. But Rooney was in no position to go to war about it.

Neither Wayne nor Coleen touch on the specifics of the 'Charlotte, I shagged u' story in their autobiographies. They run it into the general mix of the next Roo bonk story from Graham Johnson, which appeared in the *Sunday Mirror* the following month: 'ROO IN A VICE DEN', about his time with the cowgirl and other lovelies in Diva's, back in 2002. This story had the bonus of grainy TV footage of the soccer hero wandering through the brothel.

Pure, unadulterated tabloid gold.

In July 2004 Johnson had got a fresh lead about Rooney, back in 2002 – that he'd been caught on CCTV in Diva's. And someone had kept the tape. Pretty quickly, the Liverpudlian hack suspected that the brothel was, in his words, 'under the "protection" of a mob boss from a notorious crime family'.

The front woman for the brothel was a woman he calls 'Blondie', the money behind it, he says, an anonymous investor, but the people whom everybody didn't want to upset were the gangsters. Johnson negotiated the deal and eventually 'a six-figure sum' – thought to be something around £200,000 – was paid to 'Blondie'. Johnson reruns the original newspaper articles in his book, but then concludes: 'Unfortunately, Blondie was given a hard time by some ruffians and her life was made a misery – an awful consequence which I did genuinely regret.'

What Johnson means is that gangsters threatened and intimidated the poor woman in the hope that she would hand over a cut of the newspaper's cash. Or else.

Rooney was crucified. The *Sunday Mirror*'s headline, 'I CONFESS', set out the soccer star's abject apology: 'Foolish as it now seems...'

Johnson, in his book, says that the admission was a great relief for his team because it appeased the newspaper's lawyers, assuring them that they were doubly safe in publishing the story. Rooney had to plead guilty. He had been caught, red handed, unzipped, twice. He was only an idiotic seventeen-year-old lad at the time, and who among us hasn't done things we were ashamed of when we were that age?

However, Rooney could have held his hands up and fired back. What, to me at least, seems odd is the absolute submission by the Rooney camp. Where was the fight from Rooney, Stretford or Ian 'Mad' Monk? There was no pointing out that the people who ran the brothel had broken virtually every rule in the book: flogging their CCTV tapes to the highest bidder; no mention of the likely connections to organised crime; no mention that the *Sunday Mirror*'s money might have ended up in the hands of organised criminals in order to secure the tapes; no mention of the possibility of blackmail.

'Publish and be damned' was Wellington's terrific response to a sex sting by the nineteenth-century courtesan and blackmailer Harriette Wilson. Why did Team Rooney just put up their hands and meekly accept the slaughter?

In his book Johnson sets out what was going on behind the scenes. Once the deal had been secured with 'Blondie', his editor, Tina Weaver, was negotiating with Monk about how to play the story, convincing the Rooney camp that there was no point in taking out an injunction against it. Johnson's handsome plaudit to Roo's PR man – 'Ian Monk is among the best in the world' – is very kind. But Monk's past record on Fleet Street is not wholly without blemish. Monk – a slab-sized man sporting a bouffant hairdo, looking like a Walnut Whip in human form – has already popped up in this narrative complaining to me about the 'crap' services of his own client's law firm, Peter Carter-Ruck, when the porn baron Richard Desmond brushed against the Gambino crime family.

But there's more. Monk fell from a state of grace in 1996, when he was deputy editor of the *Daily Express*. For reasons best known to itself, the paper was extremely keen to lay its hands on a copy of Allan Starkie's book *Fergie: Her Secret Life*, which critics roughly summarised as a load of old bollocks about a royal trout toe-sucking a bald American. The *Daily Mail* had bought up the British serialisation rights and Monk was charged with doing a spoiler for the *Express*.

The *Express* duly ran a spoiling piece on the travails of the former Duchess of York, containing the gist of the wretched book. Just before the *Mail*'s serialisation – 'the book Fergie tried to ban' – and the *Express*'s counter-attack appeared, a woman telephoned *The Sun*, offering to sell a bootleg copy. She claimed that she was somehow connected to the book's Finnish printers and told Charlie Rae, *The Sun*'s right royal correspondent, she had a copy which she was willing to sell for £5,000. *The Sun* declined and contacted the publisher, Michael O'Mara, to tip him off. O'Mara immediately telephoned the cops, who arranged to meet the 'Finnish' woman at Heathrow and run an undercover sting against her, claiming that they were journalists. Two proof copies of Mr Starkie's book were found in a holdall. They nicked 'Miss Finland' on suspicion of 'theft and handling stolen property' – only to discover that her real identity was Anita Monk, wife of Ian, the deputy editor of the *Express*.

The question that dominated all the milk bars of Fleet Street that night, given that the Fergie book was one of the most closely guarded manuscripts on the planet, was: who had given a bootleg copy to Anita Monk, so that she could sell it on to *The Sun*?

Who could it have been?

Eh?

The Crown Prosecution Service dithered, but later dropped charges against Mrs Monk. The *Express* and their deputy editor parted company. According to *Private Eye*, Monk had nobly told colleagues that he had no idea what his wife was up to and he heaped all the blame on her.

As far as Graham Johnson and the *Sunday Mirror* were concerned, Monk did exactly the right thing in managing the damage of the brothel allegations. He negotiated the capitulation, raised the white flag, sounded the retreat and the circling piranhas closed in. The boy from Croxteth received a savage monstering from all the newspapers that had been hosing him down with treacle only a few weeks before. To make everything worse, it was close season, and he couldn't knock in a few goals to make things better. He couldn't even knock a ball around on the back streets of Crocky because his foot was still in a protective boot after his metatarsal break. And he couldn't be seen in public in Crocky because he would be crucified by Everton fans.

But the worst was yet to come. Rooney's ruin was being tolled.

'DON'T FANCY YOURS MUCH WAYNE – REVEALED: PVC GRAN HE BEDDED IN BROTHEL' was the tabloid front page from hell, running the Wednesday after Johnson's scoop on Sunday. *The Sun*'s Julie Moult had tracked down one of lucky Wayne's conquests and had splashed a photograph of the glamorous lady of the night.

Or not, as the case may be.

The story was not much more than an extended caption, announcing to the world 'the haggard hooker' who dressed in PVC to bonk Wayne Rooney. *Sun* readers were told that the 48-year-old gran – named Trisha but known in the trade as the Auld Slapper – was seen with dyed black hair and a king-sized fag dangling from her mouth; in shapeless tracksuit bottoms, the £45-an-hour prostitute looked anything but tasty. The paper summarised that Trisha had caught the millionaire's eye by squeezing into a PVC catsuit. She rubbed Rooney's face in her boobs, then led him to a back room for sex.

The paper quoted 'an acquaintance' – that's even less reliable than 'a friend' – who said that she was well known in the business as the Auld Slapper. Apparently, in the prime of her youth, Trisha had been 'quite a looker', but Old Father Time was inevitably getting his act together and she had started using that celeb favourite Botox to reduce the wear and tear, to look nice – and because paying punters don't always appreciate vintage editions. 'But at the end of the day,' added our acquaintance, 'she's still a gran and she shouldn't be on the game.'

This was the face that launched a thousand chants – and it summed up something a little bit tacky about Wayne's World. Far more than Johnson's splash, *The Sun*'s follow-up got the biggest laugh in the national panto. The Auld Slapper story hits Britain's schizophrenia about the tabloid press on the nail. We hate and fear them because they're fickle, intrusive and have all the maturity of a spotty adolescent who is about to urinate on the bus shelter. But we love them, too, because every now and then they give us a story that mocks the rich, the comfortable, the bad, the silly or the just plain unlikeable. It seems fundamentally wrong and offensive to many people that someone like Wayne Rooney should have become so rich. But what does he do with his dosh? He spends it on a lady of pleasure whose allure is – how to put this in a gentlemanly way? – hard to capture. The joke reaffirms the great hope of ordinary people everywhere, that there is some righteous order to the world, that the bad will come to a bad end and that good will out. Rooney didn't do anything wrong. He is not a real nasty baddie, but he had made a fool of himself and that was hilarious – and the circle of love–hate schizophrenia about the tabloids is complete.

But what did the lady herself have to say? The story was 'wholly untrue', said the woman *The Sun* said was the Auld Slapper. A year later, she sued for libel. 'GRANDMOTHER IN LIBEL ACTION OVER CLAIM FOOTBALLER PAID HER FOR SEX' was just one of the headlines covering what many expected to be the libel trial of the century. (It's not very old, as centuries go.)

The papers reported the start of the legal battle of Patricia Tierney to clear her name of the charge that she had sex with Rooney at a Liverpool massage parlour. The nation smacked its chops and looked forward to a trial in which the plaintiff, a fifty-year-old grandmother of sixteen, was seeking to get thousands of pounds from *The Sun* because it accused her of sleeping with Wayne Rooney.

The thrust of Tierney's case was that she claimed only to have worked at the massage parlour for three weeks as a part-time receptionist, and she never worked as a prostitute. The law, like the Ritz, is free to rich and poor alike. How could a working-class granny from Liverpool take on the paper with one of the biggest sales on the planet? The answer was 'no win, no fee'.

Mrs Tierney had come to an arrangement with Liverpool solicitor David Kirwan. He wouldn't get any money upfront, but if she were to win, then the wicked paper would not only have to pay his usual fees, but also a handsome 'success fee' on top for taking the risk of getting nothing if he lost. Before the trial came to court, I met up with Kirwan – a short, dapper, posh-ish Scouser – and took him out for dinner at the Frontline Club in London (motto: 'All the women have a past; all the men have no future') and listened to his passionate defence of the woman wronged as 'the Auld Slapper'.

Kirwan later told me that the allegations had destroyed his 'blameless' client's life and caused her grandchildren to be bullied. Earlier, he had set out his client's case to the papers:

> These utterly false and damaging allegations in *The Sun* have had a massive impact on my client's life and that of her family. These dreadful allegations have left her on anti-depressants and barely able to set foot outside of her own home. Mrs Tierney is a married woman, mother of seven children and grandmother of 16. She is not a prostitute and has never been a prostitute, as *The Sun* alleged. The reality is that she worked part-time as a receptionist in the massage parlour for three weeks in August 2003 before leaving for another job. Since the allegations, she and her family have suffered endless abuse and name-calling.

The *Sun* newspaper has destroyed the life of a blameless woman in the reckless pursuit of a totally groundless story. Legal action has commenced against the newspaper and, if the case goes to trial at Liverpool High Court, Wayne Rooney will potentially be called as a witness. Since these allegations were first published in August 2004, Patricia Tierney has been through 12 months of hell. Every time the story is mentioned she is reduced to tears and is prevented from trying to reclaim her life and move on.

It was a moving statement by Kirwan. He clearly believed his client was telling him the truth. Otherwise, he would have been a mug to act on a 'no win, no fee' basis. In January 2007, the case came before Judge Christopher Clarke at Manchester High Court. For the 'DON'T FANCY YOURS MUCH WAYNE' story – and the rest of it – Mrs Tierney was claiming damages for defamation, aggravated damages and exemplary damages. *The Sun*'s counsel, Anthony Hudson, said that, if successful, she would press for £250,000 in damages while her solicitors, David Kirwan's firm, would get their fees of between £250,000 and £500,000 – so *The Sun* would be up to £750,000 poorer. Nice work if you can get it.

Hudson boiled the whole thing down: 'This is a very straightforward case. There is only one issue. Did the claimant work as a prostitute or not? If she did not, she wins. If she did, she loses.'

The bad news for Mrs Tierney was that *The Sun* had done a bit of digging and come up with serious dirt. Back in 2002, a creep had come to Diva's, pretended he was a police officer and demanded sex on the house. The prostitute who dealt with the fake copper was Pat Tierney, then known as Trisha O'Neill, a previous married name. Trisha O'Neill/Pat Tierney had given a seventeen-page statement to Merseyside Police in May 2002, in which she admitted offering sex for £45 a go. She had stated: 'My role was dual. On some days I would work as a receptionist. On other days I would act as a sex worker. My role would be to provide sexual services for clients.' She described her 'working clothes' of a black thong and bra set – and told how on one night she had sex with five men for money.

It was a case of the curse of the black thong.

The moment solicitor David Kirwan and his team of barristers saw the 'black thong' statement, they knew they had trouble. Kirwan told me he confronted his client with the bad news, found her answers unconvincing and the whole team resigned, leaving Mrs Tierney to face the court on her own.

Breaking down in tears in front of the judge, Mrs Tierney asked for time to engage a fresh legal team. She bemoaned her fate and the horrors the case had brought on her: 'It has destroyed my children, my grandchildren, my husband and myself. What I have done, I have had my reasons, but I did not deserve this. If it had not been Rooney, I would not be here.'

To be fair to Roo, he didn't write the 'DON'T FANCY YOURS MUCH WAYNE' article, still less make the 'black thong' statement to the police. Hudson, for *The Sun*, argued that the case should be struck out immediately. Mrs Tierney had deliberately and knowingly engaged in fraudulent conduct, he said.

The judge went away, thought about it and fired both barrels at the Auld Slapper's story. He dismissed the claim, telling Manchester High Court: 'It was a claim conceived in falsehood and continued in deceit. The central plank of the claimant's case – that she was not and never has been a prostitute and only worked as a receptionist – is rotten.'

The paper reported its triumph with sadistic glee: '*SUN*'S COURT VICTORY OVER ROONEY BROTHEL TART', and boasted that it had won a historic legal victory after exposing the prostitute in the Wayne Rooney brothel libel case as a 'LIAR'. It reported that Gran Patricia Tierney, fifty-two, had tried to swindle hundreds of thousands of pounds in damages from the paper, claiming she was just an innocent receptionist. She claimed her life had been ruined by a series of articles identifying her as a hooker known as the Auld Slapper in a Liverpool brothel Rooney used as a teenager. But, the paper said, she left court with a face like thunder after Judge Christopher Clarke heard new evidence proving she was a hooker – and ruled that the case should be struck out.

The Sun reported that its legal manager Tom Crone said that the final bill would be about £750,000. He said Tierney had a no-win, no-fee legal deal, which meant that even though she lost her claim the paper would not be able to recoup a penny in costs as she was in receipt of state benefits. On page eight, a leader stuck the boot in:

> GREEDY tart Patricia Tierney pleasured Wayne Rooney for a few quid in a seedy Liverpool brothel. Then she tried to screw the *Sun* for £750,000, claiming we damaged her reputation by naming her. She insisted she was just a granny helping out at the desk. The case was thrown out because she confessed to police two years earlier that she was a whore. Now she risks jail for contempt of court. Serves her right.

There is something unnecessarily vicious about this leader – smashing the granny who lied – that is troubling. It was right that *The Sun* won the case, but the way they celebrated their victory makes you wonder, yet again, about the nature of the beast.

Thing is, I am tempted to believe her. She was clearly wrong to claim that she had never been a prostitute, but there's no hard evidence that the Auld Slapper ever slept with Wayne Rooney. The point about prostitutes (and rent boys) as witnesses is that they are not reliable. If you are willing to sell your body for £45, then your word can't really be relied upon. If a prostitute tells you 'And, not only did I sleep with Wayne, but so did that grannie over there', that's just hearsay from about the worst possible source. Graham Johnson never put up any serious evidence in his original piece in the *Sunday Mirror* that Mrs Tierney had slept with Rooney; nor did *The Sun* a few days later. But by the time *The Sun* ran the 'DON'T FANCY YOURS MUCH WAYNE' story, Rooney had already been nailed by the 'Charlotte – I shagged u' billet-doux in July 2004 and again by the still from Diva's CCTV tape plastered all over the front page of the *Sunday Mirror* the following month. He'd made a general confession to the *Sunday Mirror* about being a fool and visiting prozzies. That confession made, Rooney's reputation was a wide-open goal, just waiting to be David-Mellored. There was no dividend in Rooney going around denying he'd had sex with 'the Auld Slapper' – no one would believe him.

Or her. I might be quite wrong about this but my view is that if a lady, whoever she is, chooses to say that she has not had sex with Wayne Rooney then, in the absence of compelling evidence to the contrary, we should give her the benefit of the doubt. Otherwise, gallantry in England will be dead.

Of the two – *The Sun* or the Auld Slapper – who do you believe?

You decide.

Meanwhile, the love story of Roo and Coleen was under massive attack. The tabloids seemed ever so keen to promote a divorce – of a kind – between Roo and Coleen. The two families appeared to divide, a little, the Rooneys uneasily defending the fallen soccer hero – 'he was just a lad when this happened' – the McLoughlins tight-lipped but in private seething with anger about his betrayal of 'our Coleen'.

The fault line running between the Rooneys and the McLoughlins heaved. In the eyes of the McLoughlins, Wayne Rooney stood exposed as a scoundrel who didn't know where to put his todger. The Rooneys had to bite their lips. The champion was damaged goods and, yet again, they had to concede the high moral ground to the McLoughlins.

But for the couple themselves, the public humiliation must have been very tough. Coleen in her book recalls being driven to a family get-together and not being able to get out of the car. She watched everyone go in, all her family, but she didn't want to face anyone.

To add to the couple's miseries, as all of Fleet Street's dogs of chaos were snapping at their gates over the whoring stories, Rooney finally decided to make the break with Everton and leave for Manchester United. The reaction was wholly predictable. Graffiti appeared on the walls of Crocky: 'JUDAS', 'ROONEY SCUM' and 'DIE'.

All of that hate, and the man she loved was a national joke for sleeping with a PVC-clad granny, even if he hadn't.

Coleen forgave him his foolishness. In her book, she makes it quite plain that what Wayne did was utterly wrong, but sets out the timeline that the newspapers had kind of buried. Quite simply, Wayne had been visiting the prostitutes two years before the story exploded on to the front pages – before Coleen was properly going out with him. 'The truth is, and

I've never said this before, at that time in our relationship I'd never even slept with Wayne.'

Reflecting on this ghastly experience in her book, she says that not only was she mortified, but the whole experience was surreal, otherworldly. She says that unless you've lived through something like this, it's very difficult to understand, but adds, 'The strangest thing is that even though it was a horrible time it was also the best of times.' She writes, 'The day before the story broke we'd been tipped off' – presumably by Monk or Stretford reacting to calls from the *Sunday Mirror* – 'that it was going to appear.' Coleen's parents and brother and sister were all vacationing in Florida at the time. Such was Coleen's apparent distress that she couldn't face telling Mum and Dad, so she asked her Auntie Tracey, with whom she was staying, to tell them for her. When they heard, 'they wanted to come straight back home from holiday,' she says. But Coleen begged them to stay out; there was, she told them, 'nothing they could do'.

Back in Crocky, meanwhile, graffiti was sprayed 'all over the walls near my mum's house' – the typical nasty stuff, inciting Judas references, threats of violence and revenge and the rest. To add to the intimidating atmosphere, Fleet Street's finest were camped outside the front door of her parents' house. So Coleen and Roo stayed at her auntie's and, together, they found shelter from the hurricane of contempt. She says that, apart from their closest family members, 'no one knew we were there. Wayne would go to training at Manchester United in the back of my Uncle Shaun's little white van, then drive back home in secret.' The hacks had no idea. For once, they'd been 'had' themselves.

This was a pretty impressive achievement by Team Rooney/ McLoughlin. The tabloids would have been hunting in every posh hotel in the north-west, tracking big motors with smoked-glass windows. What they wouldn't have thought of is Roo and Col snuggled up at her auntie's, and him being chauffeured around Merseyside in the back of her uncle's white van.

The hacks got close, once. *The Sun* reported one sighting of the man hiding in the van. The paper said that Rooney vanished after training but surfaced at 1 p.m. in a bizarre incident at an M62 service station.

He emerged from the back of a van and jumped into a Merc driven by Paul Stretford. A surprised motorist told *The Sun*: 'It was weird. I was just having a sandwich and the next second I'm looking at Rooney leaping out the back of a van.'

The millionaire hero who had everything was reduced to being smuggled around the north-west in the back of a van, on the run: the Crocky Pimpernel. It sounds like a bit of a laugh.

There's one other thing. When Fleet Street has done its absolute worst and heaped news of your most embarrassing foolishness upon the nation, you feel rocked, broken, smashed up. You still get up, brush your teeth, smile at the things that make you smile. You'd still run into a burning house to save your loved ones, or the neighbour's cat. You still have it in you to do good. It hurts but you say to yourself: 'I made a mistake, but I'm not that bad.' And that is some kind of comfort.

And another thing. Despite all the crap and, worse, the true stuff that had been spouted about them, Roo and Coleen stuck to each other and made it through to the other side – and that, in my book (which this is), is a small victory for the power of love.

Cue Jennifer Rush.

12

THE HEAVY MOB CAME TOO

Everton's stance on its star player was clear and unequivocal at the start of the 2004–5 season. The Toffees' chief executive Trevor Birch proclaimed: 'The definitive position is that Wayne Rooney is not for sale.'

Well, almost definitive. The cash-strapped club needed the money they would get from selling their golden egg. Besides, the golden egg wanted to run away and there was nothing the club or its manager could do about it. Wayne Rooney had decided to jump ship from Everton that summer. He had been talking to other players in the England dressing room who set out the attractions of the bigger clubs: better money (in fact, much better money), more chance of pots, a bigger machine to deal with the nasty things of life, like tabloid reporters. And there is no doubt that Roo did end his time at Everton miserable and unhappy and in a sulk.

Resentment at slights from David Moyes – real or imagined – oozes from the pages of his autobiography. He says that after his goal-scoring success in his early career at Everton, he began to think there was one person who seemed to be 'a bit upset and envious' of what was happening to him and that was his manager. He adds that he began to suspect that Moyes was unhappy that Rooney was getting such an extraordinary amount of attention.

The Everton manager asked the obvious question – why did Roo want to go? Rooney claims that 'he just wanted to get away from Liverpool'.

And there is another, unstated, big reason that the player might have wanted to leave the Toffees: they hadn't been doing very well that season, and unless the club got its own sugar daddy – and that didn't seem likely at that point – they would be unable to hit the big time.

Roo claimed in his book that the next day the gist of the conversation between Moyes and him appeared in the *Echo*, including stuff about the prostitutes – an allegation that amounted to a gross abuse of trust by the manager to his player and caused him to say that he never wanted to play for Moyes again. Moyes sued and in the summer of 2008 won in the High Court, with Rooney's publishers reportedly paying him £50,000 in damages – which the manager donated to the Everton Former Players' Foundation – and £250,000 in costs.

Rooney's allegation was always absurd. Moyes has a reputation for quiet integrity, and a general wariness of the press. Some managers are gobby; Moyes is not. He weighs his words very carefully and is balanced, thoughtful and restrained in virtually every interview he has given to the press. The libel case raises questions about Rooney's judgement, obviously, but also about that of his number one business adviser, Paul Stretford – yet again.

The move from Everton was seen as a 'money-grubbing' betrayal by loyal fans, which strikes me as being a little unfair. Roo isn't motivated by money, but by playing and winning at football. And I don't doubt that he felt genuine pain at leaving the club that he and his family had supported his whole life. The idea that he was leaving the Toffees just for money must have wounded him deeply – and, worse, he lacked the verbal ability and agility to put across his point of view.

In the end, he texted it.

He was watching Sky Sports on TV with Coleen at her uncle's house when the subject of him leaving Everton came up. Evertonians were texting in, saying that he was a right greedy bastard, a hypocrite, never a 'true blue'. So he felt compelled to text: 'I left because the club was doing my head in – Wayne Rooney.' The Sky presenter asked would the people pretending to be Wayne Rooney stop sending text messages.

In my view Sky's not the brightest media organisation on the planet, although later on, according to *My Story So Far*, they realised the messages really were from Roo because they made a funny, peculiar reference to him: 'We know Wayne Rooney is watching – and we are watching him.'

When this gnomic announcement was made, Roo and Coleen happened to be sitting in their auntie's conservatory with the lights off peering out into the darkness. A thought crossed their minds: were they being watched? The moment of paranoia was ill founded.

But what was real was the passionate, tribal hatred for the outcast; Everton's greatest player for a generation had turned out to be, in Toffee terms, a traitor. Roo, Stretford and, to a much lesser extent, the extended Rooney and McLoughlin families all got it in the neck. Roo is a big boy, but even he was shaken by it: it became truly scary.

Two teams appeared to be in the running for Roo: Newcastle and Manchester United. Despite headlines like 'ROMAN IN FOR ROONSKI' Chelsea never made an approach, Roo says. Newcastle offered £20 million, but their interest always seemed a little half hearted. To cut to the chase, the Hairdryer at Manchester upped his bid to the best part of £30 million, and Roo was moving down the East Lancs Road to Old Trafford, Proactive laughing all the way to the bank as it was entitled to up to £1.5 million for its part in the deal.

The news was greeted in Liverpool with the city's customary wit. In the Everton FC shop someone stuck up a sign: 'SALE: half price on all Rooney stock!'

In late September 2004, Roo, now fully fit, walked on to the sacred-to-some turf at Old Trafford for his debut performance for the Reds against Turkey's Fenerbahçe and answered his critics in the only way he knows how, with a hat-trick.

RIP IT LIKE ROONEY: HIDE THE SCISSORS, MUMS AND DADS!

ENJOY: THE GREATEST DEBUT IN HISTORY

RED BULL ROON

WIN 3 GREAT ROONEY UTD KITS

MAKE WAYNE A NATIONAL TREASURE – *SUN* CAMPAIGN

The Sun, which readers who have been paying attention will have noticed was grubbing around his alleged, non-evidenced fandango with the Auld Slapper only a few weeks before, had switched again.

That's fickle with a capital F.

The red-top's campaign to make Rooney a national treasure was launched with a story by Harry Macadam. *The Sun* sent a letter and application form to the then Secretary of State for Culture, Media and Sport, Tessa Jowell, requesting Wayne be granted national treasure status. If the paper succeeded, he would be declared a 'cultural good of outstanding national importance' – meaning he can never leave Britain to play for a foreign side. The striker would join a string of other national assets saved for ever for the good of the nation. He would be protected beside items like a £12.5 million Joshua Reynolds portrait and a George II silver soup tureen. As government advisers must examine any object before it is made a national treasure, the paper included film footage of Wayne's hat-trick. Sports minister Richard Caborn said: 'Thank you for writing and sending the terrific video.'

Cheeky blighters.

Henry Winter of the *Daily Telegraph* is a measured chap, not one to get carried away. But even he tap-tapped out a paean of praise for the man with golden boots: 'The wrecking ball that is Wayne Rooney swung devastatingly through European defences again last night. Ninety-six days after he limped away from Euro 2004, the English prodigy marked his Manchester United debut with a wonderful hat-trick.' The rest of Fleet Street said the same. The Hairdryer himself kept on calling him the boy, but otherwise thought he was wonderful, as did his teammates, as did the Red Army.

Someone overdid it. Alan Brazil, one of TalkSport's football presenters, proclaimed of Wayne Rooney's hat-trick against Fenerbahçe: 'Three more bombs fell on Turkey last night!' and was promptly sacked by the station's boss – one Kelvin MacKenzie, who had finally discovered the subtle delights of taste and decency.

Off the pitch, however, things weren't quite so rosy. What links Wayne Rooney, the soccer legend, with Tommy Adams, the gangster? The dark side of Wayne's World – the connection with the profession of violence – came out at Warrington Crown Court in September and October 2004, when Hyland and the Bacon brothers stood trial, charged with blackmailing Roo's agent Paul Stretford. (Hyland, Bacon Major and Bacon Minor had gone after Stretford, a living, flesh and blood, human being, not Proactive. You can't get much out of a certificate of incorporation stuck on a wall.)

The real question was: who invited the gangster to the party?

The Crown's case was put by barrister John Hedgecoe. He told the jury that the offence of blackmail is committed if a person with a view to gain for himself or another or with intent to cause loss to another makes any unwarranted demand with menaces, that is to say by intimidation. A demand made with menaces is unwarranted unless the person making it believes a) that he has reasonable ground for making this demand, and b) that the use of menaces, or intimidation, is a proper means of reinforcing the demand.

The jury hanging on his every word, Hedgecoe said that in July 2003 Hyland threatened and intimidated Stretford, demanding that he sign a contract which would, if honoured, result in the payment of thousands of pounds to Hyland or to others in circumstances where Hyland knew that neither he nor anybody else was entitled to have Stretford sign that contract. The Bacon brothers were there as part of a joint enterprise to intimidate Stretford. Christopher Bacon, said Hedgecoe, actually became involved himself, speaking to Stretford in a very menacing manner that was clearly designed to frighten him so that he would sign the contract.

The barrister took the jury back to the start of the story, in December 2000, when young Wayne at the age of fifteen signed a contract with Peter McIntosh's Proform Sports Management Ltd, set to last for two years. The turning point was when Rooney started to play for England youth sides and other agents became interested in managing him, and one of those was Proactive Sports Management Ltd. Wayne played at Everton with a young footballer called Sean Doherty, the son of Mick Doherty, who was then in charge of Everton's youth recruitment, and Wayne's parents got to know Doherty Senior. In September 2001 Mick Doherty moved to

Proactive in a youth recruitment post after his son had left to play for Fulham and he told Wayne's parents about Proactive.

Hedgecoe said: 'On 27 May 2002, Wayne's parents went to a meeting at the Wilmslow office of Proactive where they met representatives of Proactive, including Paul Stretford, the chief executive. Following that meeting the Rooney family decided that they wanted Proactive to look after the interests of Wayne Rooney.'

Nod-nod at the judge and step out of court for a quick existentialist fag break. Proactive was a much bigger, more impressive affair, with scores of professional soccer players on its books. Stretford's Proactive was, if not a great white shark, a pretty big dogfish to McIntosh's sardine. It's not very surprising that the Rooneys were minded to switch to Proactive.

Back in court, the Crown's barrister was cracking on with the story. The Rooneys sent a letter to McIntosh at Proform, telling him they wished to dispense with his services when the existing agreement ended in December 2002. The letter, dated 27 June 2002, signed by Big Wayne and Jeanette Rooney, spelt out the bad news to McIntosh in curious managerialese, as if it had been written by another hand.

> As you are aware the contract between Wayne and yourself expires in December 2002. Following careful consideration we have decided that we will not be renewing this agreement. This is no way a reflection of the work that you have undertaken to date. It is more a review of what we believe are Wayne's requirements going forward. We have therefore made a number of approaches to other football management companies in order to gain an understanding of the services that they offer. We have decided to sign for Proactive Sports Management based in Wilmslow from December, 2002 . . . It only remains for me to thank you for all your support and efforts and to wish you all the best for the future.

You could forgive McIntosh for moaning, 'What future?'

That summer, said Hedgecoe, Mrs Rooney got a phone call from a man called Dave Lockwood who said that he had bought out Proform, and that his company, X8, now represented Wayne. He asked for a meeting with the Rooneys and one took place in October 2002, attended by the Rooneys Senior, Lockwood, John Ebbrell, the former Everton 'Dog of War' – not exactly a name on the sporting nation's lips – and John Hyland. Lockwood and Hyland tried to persuade the Rooneys to let Wayne stay with X8. The meeting only confirmed their decision to go with Proactive, said Hedgecoe.

Stretford and Proactive wanted to get their hands on Roo as quickly as possible, so they decided to offer X8 a lump sum to terminate the contract early. X8 said no, not enough and not the right terms, and the matter went to solicitors. The stand-off between the two camps continued. In November 2002, said Hedgecoe, Stretford was approached by Liverpool legend Kenny Dalglish, an associate of the Proactive company.

Let's pop out of the courtroom for a bit and think about Dalglish. A Scot, not a Scouser, he was raised a spanner throw from W. H. Auden's 'glade of cranes', Glasgow's Govan shipyard. The son of a Protestant engineer, Dalglish, as a boy, was a tribal Glasgow Rangers fan, but cherished a move into big football boots more than his roots. When Rangers' great rivals, Celtic, came knocking at his door, Dalglish ran upstairs to his bedroom and frantically hid the incriminating posters on his wall of his boyhood gods, the Rangers.

In 1977 he was spirited off to Liverpool, for a transfer fee of £440,000, which sounds like small change today but was at that time a record. In his first season, Dalglish scored the winning goal in the European Cup final, against Club Brugge, a Belgian team. Dalglish became perhaps the best player of his generation.

Hedgecoe said that following Dalglish's approach, on 13 November, Stretford flew to Heathrow and attended a meeting at the Le Meridien Hotel. Stretford turned up with Dalglish. Also present were John Hyland, Dave Lockwood of X8, Peter McIntosh of Proform, Ebbrell, Tony Bruce and Tommy Adams.

Hedgecoe told the jury:

> The atmosphere in that room was extremely unfriendly. Hyland
> was very aggressive. He said Stretford was a bully and he did not

like bullies. He said that this was not an ordinary business situation and it was not going to go away. He said that he did not care what the legal situation was; it would not help Stretford in that situation. And he threatened to make problems for another Proactive client, Kevin Campbell, the Everton captain. Hyland then proposed that the solution was for Proactive to manage Wayne Rooney but to pay all the resulting income to X8/Proform. Stretford saw that as a threat rather than a business deal and refused to accede, despite efforts made by Bruce and Adams to persuade him to accept. The meeting then broke up and shortly afterwards Paul Stretford told Mr Thomas Rooney – Wayne Rooney's father – what had taken place.

What doesn't appear to make sense here is what Tommy Adams was up to. Later, the defence in the blackmail trial asserted that Adams was not a neutral but in the Proactive camp. But, if so, why was he pushing Stretford to do a spectacularly masochistic deal with the opposition? One of the frustrations of writing about gangsters is one can't just phone them up and say, 'Excuse me, Mr Gangster, would you kindly explain your behaviour at the meeting of 13 November 2002?' They've ticked the no-publicity box, big time. To be fair to Tommy Adams, there's extremely unreliable gossip – not mentioned in court – that at the 13 November meeting at one very tense moment when Hyland was berating Stretford for making eyes at him, Tommy spoke up and said: 'I don't know about everybody else, but I could murder a cup of tea.' Everybody laughed, but you would, wouldn't you?

But what was Tommy Adams's game, eh?

Hedgecoe's narrative continued. At Hyland's suggestion another meeting took place a week later, on 20 November, this time at the Moss Nook restaurant near Manchester airport. At this meeting only Hyland and Stretford were present. Stretford, clearly under pressure, offered a solution to the problem by suggesting that Proactive should buy out X8/Proform so as to have total control. Hyland agreed enthusiastically and immediately telephoned Tommy Adams. Stretford spoke to Tommy, who was clearly in agreement.

To take another breather from court for a moment or two, it was clear that Tommy Adams was no stand-in spear-carrier in the drama. Hyland was treating Adams as some kind of wigless judge. But what exactly Adams was up to remains, at this point, a bit of a mystery.

One intriguing angle which emerged in legal argument before the blackmail trial proper kicked off was a defence submission to hear the evidence of a minder, sorry, security consultant, an ex-soldier and fireman called Billy Lindfield. Lord Carlile told the judge that Lindfield would testify that he drove Stretford to a meeting with Hyland at the Moss Nook restaurant. 'He drove Mr Stretford there in Mr Stretford's black Mercedes car and he drove him away from there. Mr Lindfield says that on the occasion of the Nook restaurant meeting, Mr Stretford had with him a bag and Mr Stretford told him that there was £250,000 in cash in the bag. Mr Stretford told him that this was money that he hoped to use as a pay-off to John Hyland. It is part of our case that Mr Stretford offered John Hyland cash.'

Lord Carlile tried to persuade the court, even before the trial had kicked off that Hyland and Co. weren't blackmailers. This was just a business dispute, and Stretford had been negotiating all along – and the cash in the bag was possible evidence that he at one stage considered paying Hyland and Co. Judge Hale thanked the defence for its pains, but decided that it did not mean that the trial should not go ahead, and the Crown's case started.

Lindfield's assertion about the cash in the bag was widely reported in the newspapers at the time – quality as well as red top. Stretford has emphatically and consistently denied this story. There was never any cash. The incident never happened – nor could it ever have, because Stretford says he had no way of getting hold of that amount of cash, nor would it have been right or proper to do so. The police checked his bank accounts and found that no such withdrawal had ever taken place.

Back to the prosecution narrative, as told in court. Hedgecoe explained that a few days after the Moss Nook meeting Hyland contacted Stretford again, refusing the offer of a buyout and insisting on a deal in respect of Wayne Rooney. He made further repeated calls to Stretford, who was

now becoming extremely stressed and whose health was suffering. They
met again on 25 November 2002. Once again Hyland was very aggressive.
Stretford agreed to meet Dave Lockwood on 2 December at the Lord
Daresbury Hotel. When that meeting took place Stretford agreed to
pay X8 a lump sum of £25,000 plus a (potentially very much larger)
percentage of commissions earned in the name of Wayne Rooney over
the next three years. Lockwood agreed to put that offer to Hyland. A few
days later Stretford received an abusive call from Hyland refusing the
offer. Hyland continued to phone Stretford and on 12 December 2002, the
night before Wayne Rooney's contract with Proform expired, he made a
very aggressive call to Stretford, insisting upon 50 per cent of all income
from Wayne Rooney's contracts with Proactive.

Hedgecoe told the court that Stretford said he would agree but with
certain caveats. He did not tell Hyland what those were at that time but
he planned that they would involve deduction of Proactive's costs before
paying anything to X8 or Proform or Hyland, and limiting the length of
the contract term to five years or less.

Hedgecoe continued: matters went quiet for some time and Wayne
Rooney signed a new contract with Everton. Hyland then telephoned
Stretford, telling him to attend a meeting at the Novotel hotel at Euston
on 21 March 2003. Present were Stretford, Hyland, Tony Bruce and
Tommy Adams. Stretford began by raising his caveats – not that he would
have called them that: the question of deduction of Proactive's costs, and
limiting the length of the contract. Hyland lost his temper at that point
and demanded 50 per cent of all income over a period of ten years.

The barrister didn't spell it out, but some connoisseurs of how money
works in the beautiful game were speculating back in 2004 that Rooney
could make £100 million over the next ten years or so. So how much
would be the agent's slice of the Wazza action? Several million pounds. If
Rooney helps win the World Cup, then his potato face could win a smart
agent a very great deal of money.

Even with Stretford's caveats in place, we are still talking about Hyland
and X8 getting millions of pounds for doing not a lot. It's nice work if you
can get it. But could they?

Back to the prosecution opening: Hedgecoe told the jury that the others at the meeting – Tony Bruce and Tommy Adams – persuaded Hyland to accept the caveats. (The surreal comedy of convicted drug baron Tommy Adams, widely believed to have been behind a series of gangland wetjobs, allegedly piping up with an obscure Latinism like 'caveat' was lost on Hedgecoe, if not the reporters sitting on the press bench.)

Next, said Hedgecoe, on 31 March 2003, Dave Lockwood of X8 met Stretford at the Lord Daresbury Hotel amid the Jabberwockery and told him that Hyland now refused to accept that staff costs should be deductible under the contract; that's to say Hyland said a big no to one of those caveats.

Stretford disagreed, and Lockwood in that meeting said he would try to sort the problem out. Some time later Stretford received a form of written contract by email. It was from X8's solicitors and purported to be an agreement between a company called IMRA Consultants Ltd and Proactive. Hedgecoe set out the terms: the contract was to run for ten years; payments due from Proactive were to be indemnified personally by Stretford himself; IMRA, under the contract, were to have the right to audit Proactive's accounts and also the right to control any decisions taken over Wayne Rooney's career.

To step away from the courtroom again, this contract would have meant misery for Stretford. By signing this document, he would have handed over effective control of his star asset, Rooney, his company's accounts and his own finances to John Hyland, who had, he felt, threatened him repeatedly.

Hedgecoe took the narrative on: Stretford was angry but he was also frightened. He rang Lockwood and told him to go to hell and to tell Hyland to forget it, and he discussed the matter with colleagues and took some advice. He decided to set up a meeting with Dave Lockwood and to arrange that that meeting would be secretly filmed. He contacted a specialist security company based in Hereford (home of the Special Air Service squadron, and all sorts of private surveillance outfits that go bump in the night; Hedgecoe did not mention Tom Lockhart's name in his opening speech, but it came out in later evidence).

Yet another meeting was arranged at the Lord Daresbury between Stretford and Lockwood. The new security consultant – Lockhart – set up a hidden camera and microphone in the Kingsley suite and briefed Stretford on what was required of him.

The trap was ready.

Lockwood, said Hedgecoe, arrived and the meeting started shortly after 5.30 p.m. on 4 June 2003. After some initial chat Lockwood put a copy of the IMRA contract on the table.

Stretford's plan had been merely to film Lockwood and record the meeting between himself and Lockwood and the demands made by Lockwood on behalf of John Hyland. At about 5.40 p.m. Lockwood received a telephone call and left the room for just over a minute. The prosecution believe that that call was probably made to Lockwood by John Hyland because there is evidence that Lockwood's mobile phone was called at that time by a phone registered in the name of Stephen Hyland, who is John Hyland's brother, and that is a phone to which the defendant had access. That call was timed at 5.40 p.m. and it lasted for 59 seconds. After taking the call, Lockwood returned to the room, and the discussion continued with Stretford indicating to Lockwood that for a number of reasons the terms of the contract were unacceptable to him.

Hedgecoe carried on: then to Stretford's amazement at about 6.07 p.m. the defendant John Hyland suddenly entered the room with the two other co-defendants, neither of them known to Stretford, but clearly recruited to assist Hyland in his plan to intimidate Stretford. What happened next was recorded on tape. Hyland was grossly aggressive and intimidating, said the barrister. He demanded that Stretford sign the contract that was on the table. He shouted at Stretford and repeatedly banged his fist on the table. One of the co-defendants, Anthony Bacon, stood to one side of Stretford. But the other one, Christopher Bacon, leaned over Stretford as he sat at the table, speaking menacingly to Stretford and adding to the general atmosphere of intimidation.

(All of it – including Hyland's charge, 'You scheming little prick', and Chris Bacon's boasts: 'I'm the muscle' and 'If you want to play the gangster bit, bring any man you want into it. Doesn't mind me. . . honestly, that's my game' – had been caught on the secret camera. To be fair, I think that Chris Bacon was only pretending to 'play the gangster', but boasting in England that you are up for playing the 'gangster bit' when you are not gives you some indication of just how thick you have to be to take up cage fighting.)

The barrister went on: Lockwood gave the impression that he had not expected the intrusion by Hyland and the others. He continued to try to persuade Stretford to sign the contract, but Stretford still refused. Eventually, Stretford left the hotel and telephoned the security consultant from his car to tell him what had transpired and then he burst into tears. Stretford has told people that it felt as close as he'd ever come to a real threat of severe harm, or worse.

Later, during the trial proper, Hedgecoe asked Stretford how the situation was affecting his health. The agent began to cry and asked for a moment to compose himself. He said: 'I developed an arthritic nature in my foot' – that's what it says in the court transcript, but obviously an arthritic nature doesn't make sense – 'caused by stress. I had to take medication that I'm now on every day of my life. During the course of this I was going for medical insurance and they found a heart defect.'

(No one has ever said that Stretford has a violent bone in his body. Everyone who has seen the tape has said that the confrontation looked very ugly.)

Hyland was arrested on 3 September 2003, and he kept mum. Chris Bacon was arrested on 23 December and he declined to answer questions, but he read out a prepared statement denying that he had been involved in any intimidation and stating that he was only present to ensure the safety of his friend John Hyland. Anthony Bacon was arrested on 21 January 2004, and he too declined to answer questions but read out a prepared statement, also denying intimidation and stating that he had agreed to attend with Hyland principally because he was concerned for the welfare of his brother, Chris Bacon.

Hedgecoe concluded his opening speech by saying that these three defendants were clearly involved in a very intimidating episode of blackmail in a case where the stakes were potentially enormous.

First up in the witness box was Roo's dad, 'Big Wayne' Rooney. He mumbled his opening answers in such a quiet little boy's voice that the judge had to ask him to speak up. Rooney the Elder didn't look comfortable in court and had barely been at it for a minute when trouble occurred.

> HEDGECOE: About six months or so before Wayne's seventeenth birthday did you and your wife Jeanette start to consider Wayne's future?
> BIG WAYNE: Yes.

Up popped Alex, Lord Carlile, John Hyland's defence Queen's Counsel. A former Liberal MP, now a mover and shaker in the Establishment, a lifelong Burnley FC fan, Carlile is clever, witty and has a twinkle in his voice. In light entertainment terms, Carlile is Bruce Forsyth while poor old Hedgecoe is, perhaps necessarily, more low key: Private Sponge, say, in *Dad's Army*.

Lord Carlile said: 'Please don't lead. This is all in issue, I'm afraid, Your Honour, so I would ask my learned friend not to lead. The circumstances leading to events that followed are not agreed.'

This is first-class legal gamesmanship. 'Leading' in this context means that Carlile was complaining that Hedgecoe was 'leading' the witness, taking him up the exact garden path the prosecution wanted him to go along. The proper way is to ask general questions and the witness will start bubbling the truth, the whole truth and nothing but the truth all on his own. That's the theory. But it was an astute blow by Carlile because watching Big Wayne in court was like watching someone throw biscuits to a dog. He swallowed everything and didn't give very much back. He gave the impression of being pretty unwilling to volunteer information unless it was squeezed out of him. If Hedgecoe couldn't 'lead' a little bit, he was going to struggle.

Court rules don't allow the defence to challenge the prosecution while they are opening the case. It's bad form. But it is open season the moment a witness starts giving his evidence in chief in the box. At his very first opportunity, Carlile's Bruce Forsyth was kicking his legs high in front of the jury – while Hedgecoe's Private Sponge looked on, bleakly. You could almost feel the police slump in their seats, and the twelve good men and women sit up, as if they were thinking to themselves: this jury service could be a bit of a laugh, after Hedgecoe bravely batted on: 'When did the two of you' – Rooney Senior and Jeanette – 'start to consider that position?'

Big Wayne replied: 'About six months of his contract to go, he was looking to [inaudible] . . .'

The prosecution case, almost imperceptibly, had begun to ship water. Hedgecoe moved on to the question of who wrote the kiss-off letter to McIntosh's Proform.

> BIG WAYNE: I don't know.
> HEDGECOE: You don't know.
> BIG WAYNE: We just signed it.

Hedgecoe then turned to the letter written in reply to the kiss-off, by Dave Lockwood.

> HEDGECOE: Did you read that letter?
> BIG WAYNE: I can't really remember now.
> HEDGECOE: You can't really say whether you read it or not?
> BIG WAYNE: Yes.

Roo's father was fast becoming the witness from hell. He couldn't remember much of what he had done to make the switch from old agent to new. He was in defence mode, uneasy, unwilling to open up. An idle observer who had just popped his head into court could have been forgiven for making the mistake of thinking that the man in the box was the defendant.

The moment Carlile's cross-examination kicked off, things got a little livelier. Although this was a trial in which his son's agent was claiming to be the injured party, and therefore one might have expected Rooney

Senior to be more helpful to the prosecution, it soon transpired that the defence got a bit more out of him.

The key, as ever with jury trials, is to ditch legalese and speak in the kind of language that the jury and the witness can understand. It is a simple trick that most lawyers are too up-their-bum to bother with. They talk to the judge and other lawyers in their own etiolated, inspissated argot, sorry, as if they had soup tureen ladles stuck up their bums, leaving the most important people in the courtroom mystified, then bored. The great exception was George Carman, QC, who made seducing juries his life's work. Carlile is in the Carman school of advocates.

> CARLILE: Now we know that everybody knows, I hope, that Wayne plays for Manchester United now but your family are Evertonians, aren't you, really?
> BIG WAYNE: Yes.
> CARLILE: Or at least you were. You probably still are in your heart, Mr Rooney. Don't tell us. And Wayne was an Evertonian from his mother and father's knee, wasn't he?
> BIG WAYNE: Yes.

Carlile got Big Wayne to admit that he'd boxed at bantamweight with John Hyland when they were young, and that McIntosh had been a relatively frequent visitor to the family home, chatting to Jeanette when she was in, and going to matches and events to watch over the Boy Wonder.

More gold stars for the defence, the point being that McIntosh and, in particular, defendant Hyland were not strangers to the Rooney family, but people they had known for years. Slowly the defence strategy began to reveal itself. What Carlile was seeking to demonstrate was that McIntosh and then Hyland's legitimate business interests had been unfairly pushed aside by Stretford and his associates before the original contract ended in December 2002. The legal test was that you could call it blackmail if the pressure to get money was unwarranted. If the pressure was warranted then the judge would have to throw the whole case out.

But getting answers out of Rooney Senior was like getting wine out of a cow. If he wouldn't even begin to talk about what happened, then the defence was going to struggle.

Sitting behind Carlile was Hyland's solicitor, Paul Thomas. The legal convention is that the defence solicitor does not address the court. To the jury, the solicitor looks as though he is paid a lot of money for nothing very much, but that's an illusion. A good defence solicitor is like a swan, serene and silent and pure white above the water, and paddling his scaly black legs like fuck beneath. Thomas had done his homework and it paid off.

Carlile produced a copy of the kiss-off letter from the Rooneys, telling McIntosh's Proform that they were going to move to Stretford's Proactive. It had three signatures on it, the first Jeanette's, the second Big Wayne's and the third Wayne's. The defence barrister slowly led Big Wayne into his own little trap.

CARLILE: Do you accept that this must be a copy of the letter that you sent?

BIG WAYNE: Yes.

CARLILE: Because it's got your signature on it. And it starts: 'Dear Sir/Madam'. I don't think that you were in any doubt whether Peter McIntosh was a sir or a madam, were you, Mr Rooney?

BIG WAYNE: No.

CARLILE: No. He's a man. And if you had been preparing a letter to Mr McIntosh yourself, and there's no criticism at all of you for not doing it yourself, you would have written 'Dear Peter' or 'Dear Mr McIntosh', wouldn't you?

BIG WAYNE: Yes.

CARLILE: This letter was therefore prepared for you and you signed it.

BIG WAYNE: Yes.

CARLILE: And the person who asked you to sign it was who? Mick Doherty or Paul Stretford?

Silence.

CARLILE: Or can't you remember?

BIG WAYNE: Well, it would probably be one of the two but I can't say.

CARLILE: One of the two. Because by 27 June 2002, when that letter was written, Paul Stretford was already involved in becoming Wayne's future agent?

BIG WAYNE: Yes, yes.

Got him. The transcript reveals that the prosecution case had begun to ship water. The defence had got home on the point that Stretford and Co. had not just got the agent's contract from December 2002. They had written the kiss-off letter to their own rivals five months before and the Rooneys had signed it. It all went towards their argument that the original agent's rights had been swept aside. But was it enough to knock out the impression made by the fearful monstering of Stretford by Hyland and the Bacons?

No – or at least, not quite.

So who made the first move to ditch the old agent and bring out the new? The Rooneys? Or Stretford and pals?

Rooney's performances in the FA Youth Cup had been so outstanding, it was obvious to people in the game that he was going to make the Everton first team before very long, and was a player of extraordinary potential. That meant the Rooney family became much more ambitious for their boy and sought a bigger agent. So it was goodbye McIntosh, hello Paul Stretford. Little Wayne was still as far as the law was concerned a minor. In his book, Rooney says that he slept curled up on the sofa while Stretford's point man, Mick Doherty, discussed all the legal ins and outs with his mum and dad. Then they had gone to Stretford's office for further chats. But that's not the full answer. Who made the very first move?

In court, Carlile plucked out the name of one Merseyside footballing great.

CARLILE: Now everybody knows who Kenny Dalglish is, unless they are on another planet or completely uninterested in football. Isn't it right that 'H' [a trader in football intelligence who had been one of the first to spot young Roo's genius] suggested to you that Wayne should move to a top agency and he suggested an agency he described as Kenny Dalglish's agency?

BIG WAYNE: No.

CARLILE: No? Have you ever had a conversation with Paul Stretford or Kenny Dalglish about whether Kenny Dalglish's name should be involved in this case at all?

BIG WAYNE: No.

CARLILE: Not at all? We can take it you have spoken to Paul Stretford about this case, haven't you?

BIG WAYNE: No, not really, no.

CARLILE: 'Not really'?

BIG WAYNE: No.

The court transcript goes on like for this for page after page. Did Dalglish have anything to do with it? Big Wayne stuck doggedly to a line that Dalglish never came to his house, never met him, and that he had no idea that Dalglish was in the Proactive team. And yet Carlile plugged on. Finally, he struck gold, kind of.

CARLILE: Isn't it right that Kenny Dalglish telephoned you to ask if Wayne, young Wayne, was interested in signing up for an agency with which he had a connection?

BIG WAYNE: I have had a phone call off him—

CARLILE: Ah! So Kenny Dalglish rang you, and you are probably aware, aren't you, that Kenny Dalglish has a senior position in Proactive. . . He's the head of recruitment for them, isn't he?

BIG WAYNE: Well, I couldn't tell you, to be honest. He might be. . .

CARLILE: You know he's there in some capacity. Has he ever told you that he owns two million shares in Proactive?

BIG WAYNE: No.

The phone call from Dalglish appears intriguing. The former Liverpool manager wasn't just a neutral in this game but someone with two million shares in the agency he had been promoting with his phone call. Proactive's accounts for spring 2002 boast that their team includes 'Kenny Dalglish, the former Liverpool star and Championship winning manager of Liverpool and Blackburn Rovers, and Mick Doherty, formerly of Everton, who runs the Group's Youth Division, identifying the stars of the future'.

How much were Dalglish's two million shares worth? There is no firm answer to that, other than what the market will pay when the owner decides to sell. Shortly after flotation of the Proactive Group in 2001, the share price peaked at 43p, making a handy £860,000; in 2004 at the time of the trial – and all the terrible publicity – they had crashed to a little under 8p a share, giving Dalglish, if he had been minded to sell, a mere £157,000.

The 2002 accounts for Proactive show that the company had roughly 100 million shares and had a turnover of roughly £4 million, with a profit of £673,000. Proactive, under chief executive, Paul Stretford, although clearly bigger than Proform, was not coining it big time. But if Proactive could get their hands on the Rooney contract, potentially worth as much as £2 million a year, turnover would grow by half. If Proactive got Rooney, one would have expected Dalglish's shares to rocket in price.

Carlile gnawed away at it, like a dog with a bone.

> CARLILE: Has Kenny Dalglish ever been to the house where you were living?
> BIG WAYNE: No.
> CARLILE: Not ever?
> BIG WAYNE: No.

And gnawed and gnawed.

> CARLILE: Was Kenny Dalglish to your knowledge ... ever involved in anything to do with Wayne signing up for Proactive?
> BIG WAYNE: No.
> CARLILE: Were you ever told by Paul Stretford that Kenny Dalglish was going to do some work or get involved in any way in dealing with Wayne's contract with Proactive and his contract with Everton?

BIG WAYNE: No.

CARLILE: *(almost giving up)* No. And you were never at any meeting in which Kenny Dalglish was present?

BIG WAYNE: No.

CARLILE: Would that be right? At any time?

BIG WAYNE: No.

The key defence issue Carlile wanted out in the open – if true – was that the very first opening move came from the Proactive camp. But Big Wayne wasn't playing along with that line.

CARLILE: You had been persuaded by Mr Stretford and his team that they were the right people for Wayne's future?

BIG WAYNE: I wouldn't say 'persuaded'. We went to them.

CARLILE: But that was some time after Kenny Dalglish had telephoned you, of course. And you knew, didn't you, when you went to them, that Kenny Dalglish was associated with them?

BIG WAYNE: No.

CARLILE: You didn't? Well, who did you think Kenny Dalglish was associated with?

BIG WAYNE: *(snottily)* What do you mean, who did I think he was associated with?

CARLILE: Well, which agency did you think was Kenny Dalglish's agency or the one he worked for?

BIG WAYNE: I haven't got a clue.

JUDGE HALE: *(interrupting)* I know you know now. But at the time did you know who Dalglish worked for?

BIG WAYNE: No, no.

CARLILE: Well, what was the point of Kenny Dalglish ringing you? What did he suggest when he rang you?

BIG WAYNE: He wanted to talk to us about going to another agency.

CARLILE: To another agency. [The defence barrister could be forgiven for letting slip the tiniest amount of sarcasm in his next question.] And which other agency did he want to talk to you about going to?

> BIG WAYNE: I don't know.
>
> CARLILE: But was it his agency?
>
> BIG WAYNE: Well, possibly, yes.
>
> CARLILE: Yes. And that turned out to be Proactive, didn't it? Right?

Big Wayne assented. The peer of the realm had finally defeated the unemployed labourer from Croxteth. It had been an epic battle, but crucial. The defence could now use this evidence to support their argument that the very first move in what they saw as the illegitimate poaching of Wayne Rooney from his original agent was made by a man who worked for and held two million shares in the agency that ended up getting him – and all of that went towards the defence argument that Hyland reasonably believed he had a fair point when he demanded compensation for lost income. There is, of course, nothing wrong in approaching a footballer's family and saying 'Can we represent you. . .' and other agencies did so, too. Nevertheless, in the context of this trial, it was a point that helped the defence argument along.

The next step in the defence strategy was to try to convince the jury that Paul Stretford and his team played rough – even dirty – too. The new attack from the defence was going to be that Proactive weren't choirboys, but were mixed up with tricksy folk and a gangster, too. It appears that the aim was to cancel out the very real sense of threat made by Hyland and the Bacons on the video.

The very next day, 5 October 2004, Carlile added into the mix the name of another Liverpool legend, though one not quite so glorious as Kenny Dalglish.

> CARLILE: Now I want to ask you about a man called Kevin Dooley. Kevin Dooley was what?'
>
> BIG WAYNE: Which?
>
> CARLILE: What was he? What did Kevin Dooley do for a living when you first got to meet him?
>
> BIG WAYNE: Solicitor.

When Big Wayne met Kevin Alphonsus Dooley in the summer of 2002 he just happened to be perhaps the biggest crook on the Law Society's books. I can write that without fear of any libel because Dooley had just been condemned by his professional body for an atrocious series of cons against his clients amounting to millions in dishonest frauds and was awaiting sentence. A few weeks later in September 2002 he was struck off.

And because he died in 2004. Dead men don't sue.

Kevin Dooley was the lawyer of choice to Liverpool's soccer stars, gangsters and, funnily enough, at least one former Chief Constable, Sir Kenneth Oxford. His clients numbered former Liverpool players Kenny Dalglish, Robbie Fowler and Graeme Souness, and Everton striker Duncan Ferguson. He also acted for Curtis 'Cocky' Warren, Britain's richest gangster, and enforcer-turned-author Charlie Seiga.

It is fair to say that Dooley was, as crooked lawyers go, crooked. A docker's son, he grew up in the Scotland Road area of Liverpool, leaving school at sixteen and working as a debt collection clerk before qualifying as a solicitor in 1978. Dooley and Co. began in premises on Cherryfield Drive, Kirkby, and Queens Drive, Liverpool, where he employed forty staff. The firm grew and grew like Topsy, with an annual turnover of £1.5 million and profits of £500,000.

But nothing on Planet Dooley was quite as it seemed.

In the early 1990s Dooley had got into bed with a crook called 'Long John' Silver. He promised clients phoney investment returns of 1,400 per cent. Dooley allowed 'Long John' to use his office as a postal address. Dooley's Midland Bank manager warned him in 'no uncertain terms' not to become involved with 'Long John' Silver. (You would have thought the name might be a clue.) The bank manager feared that the proposed transaction was 'specious' – fancy talk for plausible on the surface but wrong in reality – and the bank instrument could be forged. Dooley ignored him and stuck with Silver.

In summer 1996, the Office for the Supervision of Solicitors went through the books of Dooley & Co. in a routine inspection and the business with 'Long John' came to light. The OSS wrote to Dooley warning him that they 'have seen numerous examples of this type of transaction and in every case they [are] either fraudulent per se or part of a larger mechanism designed to facilitate a fraud'. Dooley ignored the OSS and stuck with Silver.

The Sheppard family put £100,000 into one of 'Long John' Silver's schemes and lost their money. Some schemes worked. But in one case, three of Dooley's clients lost $1.4 million – and a judge said he was satisfied 'this money has been stolen'.

In 2000 the OSS raided Dooley's firm. In July 2002 Dooley's case came to the Solicitors Disciplinary Tribunal – and was fully reported in the *Liverpool Echo* and by the BBC. The tribunal heard how Dooley had been involved in nineteen or more money scams promising 'absurd returns' with 'Long John' Silver. Dooley knew that Silver was wanted by police for a series of offences of dishonesty involving a gross breach of trust. Nevertheless, Dooley had continued to allow Silver to use Dooley's firm as his business address.

The prosecuting barrister said that secret tapes made by the police of Dooley at work showed 'not a solicitor conducting a proper practice but something more akin to Fagin and Dodger'. A common feature of the high-yield investment transactions, also known as bank instrument frauds, was that only the intermediaries gained and never the investors. The prosecution alleged that in a clear conflict of interest Dooley repeatedly did not pass a warning from his bank manager, Paul Chadwick, on to clients.

Chadwick told the tribunal: 'I passed on to Mr Dooley that Mr Silver was known to the Midland Bank's fraud department in the hope that would put him on his guard.' Chadwick said: 'Spurious transactions of this nature may be Mafia based.'

That August, shortly after the July 2002 hearing but before the verdict striking off Dooley was announced in September, Dooley was introduced to the Rooneys. Lord Carlile asked Paul Stretford the obvious question: 'Whose idea was it to go to Kevin Dooley?'

Stretford replied: 'We came. . . we came to it as a conclusion that that would be a good person to use for the Rooneys.'

What kind of football agent connects his teenager star with a lawyer like Dooley? Eh?

At the blackmail trial, Wayne Senior opened up a little more. After some heavy lifting by Carlile, he told the court that he was aware Proactive stood to gain up to £1.5 million from the striker's transfer from Everton to Manchester United.

Asked by the judge about the relevance of this line of questioning, Carlile replied:

> What it's got to do with this case is that it is the defence's assertion that Mr Stretford was desperate to get Wayne Rooney as his client because he knew he could milk the cow from both ends. If a solicitor was doing that, he would be struck off without a moment's hesitation.
>
> There is an issue in this case about Paul Stretford's many interests in Wayne Rooney and the ruthless way in which he approached those interests.

Wayne Senior stepped out of the witness box, to be replaced by Stretford himself. Carlile put the boot in: how come Stretford suggested that the Rooney family consult one of the most bent briefs in Britain for legal advice?

> CARLILE: And this was the Mr Dooley who, in August 2002, you knew perfectly well had been up before the Solicitors Disciplinary Tribunal for, to quote the BBC, 'a long-running investment scam worth millions of pounds'?
> STRETFORD: I was not aware of that, no.
> CARLILE: You do regret going to Kevin Dooley with this, don't you?
> STRETFORD: No, I don't regret that.
> CARLILE: He [Dalglish] is a very important part of the setup, isn't he?
> STRETFORD: I think that's questionable whether he's very important.
> CARLILE: Well, isn't he a person you would rely on or have relied on regularly for advice?
> STRETFORD: I have relied on for regular advice.
> CARLILE: Did you stop relying on him for advice after he brought Tommy Adams to a meeting at Le Meridien Hotel in London?

STRETFORD: Did I stop?

CARLILE: Yes . . .

STRETFORD: First and foremost, I didn't know that Kenny Dalglish brought Tommy Adams to a meeting.

It's difficult to work out what Tommy Adams's role was or who had invited him to the party. Carlile tried to get to the bottom of it.

CARLILE: Were you aware that Kenny Dalglish has been approached by the police and asked if he would make a signed statement but has refused to come to this trial in any way whatsoever?

STRETFORD: Yes.

CARLILE: . . .Do you feel let down by him?

STRETFORD: Of course.

CARLILE: . . .Because he arranged to bring to the meeting at Le Meridien Hotel a notorious gangster who had recently finished a sentence of seven and a half years' imprisonment for importing cannabis, who happens to take an interest in sport? That's what it comes to, doesn't it?

STRETFORD: I can't answer for Kenny Dalglish but I'm not aware that he did that, no.

Long before the trial started, Stretford had given a statement to the police setting out his recollection of how the big powwow went on 13 November 2002 at Le Meridien Hotel.

Carlile read much of it out in court. Stretford had told the police:

Tony Bruce picked us up and explained that we were meeting at the Meridien Heathrow Airport Hotel. I expressed my absolute lack of knowledge of what or whom we were going to see. Tony told me not to worry, that a friend of his named Tommy would be able to resolve matters and that everybody could then get on with their lives. I was still apprehensive but chose not to share my concerns.

Carlile goaded Stretford: 'Well, who did you think this Tommy was – Tommy Docherty?' (A much-loved football player and manager of Chelsea and Manchester United, very much of the old school, whose thick Scottish accent used to provide code-breakers watching post-match interviews on BBC *Grandstand* with wondrous amusement.)

The defence barrister kept on at Stretford, asking him why he didn't say: 'Hey, Kenny, who's this Tommy we've got coming? Tommy who?'

Stretford replied: 'I wish I had but I didn't.'

> CARLILE: It's you who brought in the heavy mob, isn't it?'
> STRETFORD: It most certainly was not.
> CARLILE: You just knew he had a terrible reputation... a legend, a sort of Kray-type legend almost.
> STRETFORD: Yes...
> CARLILE: Well, why didn't you make your excuses and leave?
> STRETFORD: Fear, confusion. I just... I didn't. And you're right. It's something that should have... I... I could have done but I didn't...
> CARLILE: You and Kenny and Tommy were the Proactive team, weren't you?
> STRETFORD: No.

The big question is once Stretford was aware that a major gangster was in the room at a matter of vital importance to the future of one of the best footballers in England, why didn't he just walk out? By staying, whatever the reason, Stretford, representing a figure in the public eye, was tarred with the brush of the Adams gang.

So the first impression of the video nasty, that Hyland and the Bacon brothers were the only villains in the panto, had been overtaken by more evidence. Stretford was mixing with some real baddies – and who could be more offside than Kevin Dooley and Tommy Adams?

Carlile went on to read out the bulk of Stretford's statement on what happened at the meeting:

> He [Tommy Adams] explained that he was merely there to arbitrate

and out of courtesy to Kenny would see that nobody got out of hand. He said not to worry. He was sure this matter could be resolved. Kenny looked a little surprised and didn't seem to understand where Tommy was coming from. Tommy explained that someone had been wronged and that the matter needed rectifying. The previous agent, said Tommy, had looked after Rooney since he was young and needed some consideration. Kenny and I both protested that Wayne and his parents were entitled to make their own decisions and that we had behaved entirely appropriately. I also told Tommy that in about a month the agreement ran out anyway. It was made clear to us that the matter needed to be resolved and this was the best way to do it.

Why Dalglish looked a little surprised will remain, like the Mona Lisa's smile, an enigma. Dalglish wasn't telling. His unwillingness to give a statement disappointed Stretford. It is also disappointing because it is well-nigh impossible to understand how Proactive allowed their then employee to get anywhere near Tommy Adams. As for what Tommy Adams thought he was doing, who knows, but he would have been justified in demanding a fee for putting himself out for the parties – that, effectively, is what lawyers do all the time – and that subtle (and potentially expensive) change of role by the gangster would account for the look of surprise on Dalglish's face. And the problem with gangsters is that you can't argue with them. Dalglish's role in this murky affair is hard to fathom, not least because he did not appear in court. The reputation of this once great player was another victim of the time when a gangster brushed against the career of the rising star of British football.

Cynics point out that the gangsters have a liking for 'taxing'. Organised criminals, like the rest of us, are deeply envious of the absurd sums of money society pays the footballers, so if they can cream off a bit of money from an idiot soccer star by sorting out trouble, why not? But in this case, the gangster wasn't planning to 'tax' the footballer direct, but may have wanted to tax his two agents, past and present, who were still squabbling about who owned the star. Was Tommy Adams gunning for a slice of the Rooney bonanza? Eh?

Back at Warrington Crown Court, Carlile was gearing up for his knockout blow. Immediately after he had read out Stretford's version of what Tommy Adams was up to, he started ripping the stuffing out of the prosecution case. To understand Carlile's attack, you need to know the precise FIFA rules against agents poaching talent from their rivals.

Clause IV of FIFA's Code proclaims: 'The players' agent shall . . . respect the contractual relations of his professional colleagues and shall refrain from any action that could entice clients away from other parties.' In other words, no poaching, and, in particular, if a player is under contract with one agent, no contracts with another agent.

> CARLILE: And you were representing to Tommy Adams and others present that up to that point no representation agreement had been entered into between Proactive and Wayne Rooney as you told us earlier this morning?
>
> STRETFORD: Yes.
>
> CARLILE: Would you like to think about that just once more, Mr Stretford? I put it to you that a representation agreement had been entered into between Wayne Rooney and his parents and Proactive well before the end of Mr McIntosh's contract. Is that right or wrong?
>
> STRETFORD: The only representation agreement that was put in place was for his commercial image rights.
>
> CARLILE: That's a lie, isn't it, Mr Stretford.
>
> STRETFORD: Not as far as I am aware, no.

Carlile produced a copy of a Proactive document, signed by Wayne Rooney Junior, Wayne Rooney Senior, Jeanette Rooney and Stretford, and dated January 2003. So what? Rooney's contract with McIntosh's Proform/X8 expired on 12 December 2002, and Stretford was wholly within his rights to offer contracts after that date.

Carlile pointed out that the text proclaimed that this was a 'variation agreement' and said: 'You can't have a variation agreement unless there's an agreement to vary, Mr Stretford, can you?' to which the agent said no, adding, a few moments later, that it was a variation of image rights. They are not covered by FIFA's Clause IV.

The defence barrister said that the variation agreement, signed in January 2003, was from an (earlier) general (or on-pitch, footballing) representation agreement and asked: 'What was the date?'

> STRETFORD: But there was no general representation agreement.
> CARLILE: *(delivering the killer blow)* Then why does it say in this document that there was one dated 17 July 2002?
> STRETFORD: *(at a loss)* I can't answer that.

Game over. The following day, Monday 11 October 2004, Hedgecoe addressed the court.

> Your Honour, Mr Paul Stretford gave evidence last week about the existence or otherwise of contracts entered into between Proactive Ltd and Wayne Rooney prior to the termination of the Proform contract on 11 December 2002. Following the adjournment on Friday last, two representation agreements pre-dating 11 December were disclosed which seriously called into question the evidence of Paul Stretford.

Hedgecoe stated the Crown's position succinctly: 'We do not feel able to rely upon Paul Stretford as a witness in this case.'

Judge Hale summed it up: 'Mr Stretford says there was no footballing contract. That's what he said to Lord Carlile on Friday morning and, 19 September 2002, a contract.'

Even though there was compelling evidence on videotape of Hyland and the Bacons monstering Stretford, the blackmail case collapsed because the Crown could not rely upon the word of its star witness.

In June 2005 the Football Association hit Stretford with nine charges, effectively of bringing the game into disrepute. The FA charged Stretford, one, that he 'failed to protect the interests of Mr Wayne Rooney'; two, that he failed to respect the interests of third parties; three, that he 'did not refrain from actions that could entice clients away from other parties'; four, that he breached FIFA players' agents' rules by agreeing an eight-year deal when the legal maximum is two; five, that he failed to register the 17 July 2002 agreement with the FA; six, that he failed to register the 19 September 2002 agreement with the FA; seven, that he failed to register the 14 December 2002 agreement with the FA; eight, that he made 'a false and/or misleading witness statement to the police' in *R* v. *Hyland, Bacon and Bacon*; nine, that he provided 'false and/or misleading testimony to Warrington Crown Court' in *R* v. *Hyland, Bacon and Bacon*.

Stretford denied the lot and, convinced that he had been wronged, set out to challenge the FA's right to hold a disciplinary hearing against him. Rooney said in a written statement: 'I have informed the FA as to how I came to be represented by Paul Stretford. I was happy then and I still am.'

Len Capeling in the *Liverpool Daily Post* reacted to the FA's charges, some might say, rather sourly.

> Paul Stretford need have no worries. The FA's record in pursuing agents they believe have transgressed is absolutely abysmal. Admittedly, they do have Mr Stretford's bizarre evidence in the High Court to harass him with, but a half-decent brief should ease playful Paul back on to his bed of banknotes. Also on Mr Stretford's team is Wayne Rooney, though some might see that as more of a hindrance. The accused promises a stern rebuttal of all charges. Let wrist-slapping commence.

One can only read this kind of cynical comment in the newspaper and deplore it – but does no one trust the great and the good any more?

After the collapse of the blackmail trial Proform launched a civil suit for damages against Proactive. In the summer of 2006, Judge Hodge ruled that Proform had no chance of success against Proactive because they could not enforce their 2000 contract with the Rooneys because Wayne was a legal minor when it was signed.

In 2006 I rang Lord Carlile, Hyland's QC, and asked him about his client. He took a deep breath and said that Hyland 'is a typical Scouse

character. You should meet him.' Ever cautious, I asked Carlile: 'Do I need
to bring a shotgun?' And he laughed and said no. Then I rang Hyland's
office. A guttural voice with clipped diphthongs answered the phone and
said in Scouse so thick you could butter your bread with it that Mr Hyland
wasn't there. Mr Hyland was in a meeting. I rang off and rang back and
rang off and rang back, and each time I missed him.

Playing phone tag with a man who has been on trial for demanding
money with menaces is no less boring than playing phone tag with your
bank manager. Eventually, I got through to the big man and blurted out
that I had spoken to Lord Carlile and he said that I should get in touch,
and that he, Mr Hyland, was a typical Scouse character.

A long paused followed. The Hood was weighing me up. (The
Thunderbirds theme tune started playing in my head.)

'. . .and Lord Carlile said there was no need for a shotgun.'

A deep, breathy chuckle – one part the Godfather, one part Mr Wheezy,
the squeaky penguin from *Toy Story* who has mislaid his squeak –
reverberated down the line. On and on he laughed. Whatever else people
say about John Hyland, he has a sense of humour. I told him that I was
hanging about outside a pub on Liverpool's Victoria Street, and he said
he would pick me up.

It was always going to be a Mercedes. Not quite brand new, not quite
top of the range. But Hyland wasn't going to be seen dead in a Nissan
Micra.

In the flesh, the Hood's eyes didn't light up bright yellow and he didn't
try to hypnotise me, as he does in *Thunderbirds*. In other respects, he
lived up to my expectations. He circled the city as if he owned it, which
he might well do as far I know. Traffic lights turned green as his Merc
neared. It felt as though the Liver Birds themselves did a little curtsy as
Mr Hyland passed by the Dock Road. Every now and then he would slow
down and wave and shout hello to an acquaintance. Some wore suits,
some did not. They tended to have narrow foreheads, be wary and built
like brick lavatory outhouses – but what do I know? They were probably
all middle managers for the Prudential Assurance Company.

Hyland told me that he used to be a boxer, had fought at Olympic level until he lost to a Korean, and that he knew the Rooneys and the McLoughlins. He said that he had even fought with Wayne's dad in the old days.

'Who won?'

'Don't ask.'

'Go on, who won?'

'I did. Twice.'

We mourned the slow death of boxing.

'It's the only sport that's going backwards. That's the media for you. I told them that they were wrong, but they wouldn't listen.'

I ummed and aahed, hoping that he would deduce from my muttering that I somehow agreed with him.

Near Lime Street he pulled the car over. A sinisterish-looking man (or so I thought, anyway) with a Tesco plastic bag approached the car. This was it, I feared. The man proffered a gift. It could have been an Uzi inside the plastic bag, for all I knew, then I remembered that all of Liverpool wasn't like Croxteth.

'That's me brother,' said Hyland. 'It's my birthday.'

I didn't sing 'Happy Birthday' but we were getting on fine and dandy. Hyland sashayed the Merc through the city centre and we parked with a degree of aplomb outside the Radisson Hotel. He deftly took a laminated sign and plonked it on the dash. 'Valet parking for the Radisson', it proclaimed. I smarted, having got myself a £100 parking fine in London while simply picking up a cat from a friend's. But parking tickets are meant for people like you and me, and not the John Hylands of this world.

He led me into the wide-open prairie of the hotel lobby, where the staff greeted him with the utmost respect, and we met his daughter – who was not just likeable, but lovely – and a used car dealer – who gave me a good tip on when to buy a second-hand Saab soft-top: 'Go for a wet weekend in November when they know that if they sell it, it will be in their Christmas bonus.'

Hyland led the way to the bar. Again, there was no farting about waiting to get served. A flunkey shimmied over at Mach 3 and in no time I was downing a pint. Hyland drank black tea, while daughter and car dealer made small talk. There were so many agendas whizzing around the bar that it made my head dizzy. I wanted to dig as much information out of Hyland as I humanly could without earning his dislike; he wanted to show me who was boss – and yet that he was one of the good guys; and the car dealer almost certainly wanted to sell someone – anyone – a car. Hyland's daughter seemed to be the only one of us who was there for the hell of it.

Amber bubbles winked at the brim of my pint as the small talk washed this way and that. Hyland was beginning to suspect that I didn't know Lord Carlile from Adam, and that he had been conned. He began to clam up. To keep the conversation drifting on, I got on to the subject of Roman Abramovich. I had made a film about the Russian plutocrat and Hyland was fascinated by the story of how an orphan from the cold, cold north had ended up one of Britain's richest men. The best bit, for Hyland, was the story that one of Abramovich's goons had told a friend about the nature of British football.

Abramovich and his friends were honest entrepreneurs, but they worked in what some would describe as a robust business environment. The Great Patriotic Aluminium Wars of the 1990s saw dozens of corpses pile up – managers, lawyers, journalists – before Roman and Co. took over one of the biggest smelters and peace descended. So Hyland was amused to hear that one of the Russians had told friends that 'they were shocked, shocked, shocked at how bent British football is'.

And John Hyland broke into a huge grin, and nodded his head, and started to cackle with laughter, and then he took a phone call, didn't like what he heard, started scowling at me, and I made my excuses and left.

13

'THERE'S NO FUCKING PROBLEM WITH MY FUCKING TEMPER'

Who flung the pizza? Well, there's no doubt that Wayne Rooney was there in the field at the Battle of the Buffet between Manchester United and Arsenal, the greatest conflict involving a slice of pizza hitting the blazer of the manager of Manchester United in recorded human history. But Rooney was on the defending side – and this time, at least, history's finger of blame would be quite wrong to point in his direction.

The battle took place in October 2004 after the Reds smashed Arsenal's historic 49-game unbeaten run, winning 2–0 with a goal by the Crocky Cyclone. United boss Sir Alex Ferguson was reportedly splattered with pizza, soup, water and sandwiches during the confrontation – forcing him to change into a tracksuit for his post-match TV interview. Witnesses told the papers how it kicked off, with United striker Ruud van Nistelrooy tapping Arsenal boss Arsène Wenger on the shoulder and teasing him about the result.

Wenger turned on Fergie, remonstrating with him, jabbing away at the Scotsman and, reportedly, making critical remarks about Wayne Rooney. The players got stuck in but security men broke the whole thing up and Roo writes it down in his book as not much, saying the battle itself was nothing really, just handbags at five paces with a bit of pizza thrown in.

Submission and Wayne Rooney do not go together like, say, gin and tonic. And yet Rooney in *My Story So Far* is deeply, almost morbidly submissive towards Sir Alex Ferguson. It's so Uriah Heepish it's slightly creepy.

The contrast with how Rooney refers to David Moyes is quite remarkable. Moyes is always 'Moyesy', which is the kind of thing that players call each other, not their managers. You can't imagine Rooney calling his United manager 'Fergie' – and he doesn't. It's always 'The Boss'.

In the 'Rooney report' at the back of the book he is asked the question, who is his most admired manager? You're ahead of me: yes, it's Sir Alex Ferguson. Rooney says that's not because he's the boss of Manchester United, but because he's the best. Cereal-packet psychologists might speculate that Rooney has always been looking for a strong authority figure and in the Boss he has found it. But there's something interesting about Ferguson, too. For a man with the reputation of ferocity, he appears to have a weakness, a kind of 'Dat's My Boy' complex (after the dog in the *Tom and Jerry* cartoons who adores his daft puppy). The Scottish hard man seems to like to have at least one wayward player on his books at any one time. Over the years Ferguson has protected Bryan Robson, Roy Keane and now Rooney with a fatherly indulgence – 'Dat's my boy.'

Rooney has found in Ferguson something he needs; and Ferguson has found something in Rooney that he needs to protect. The odd thing is that, almost from the word go at Old Trafford, Rooney did not change. He still scored goals, but he still got into too many stupid rows on, and sometimes off, the ball. He was still getting headlines for all the wrong reasons. He was doing what he did worst: losing it extremely badly when losing – and it happened both when he was playing for his new club team and when he was representing his country.

England flopped against Spain in November 2004, in Madrid. It was supposed to be a friendly but the Spanish supporters behaved abominably to England's black players, booing every time they got the ball. The best response would have been for England to have knocked Spain into a cocked hat – but they were pretty useless, conceded an early goal and then wandered around like a bunch of old ladies in search of a teashop with doilies. Frustrated and angry at the lacklustre performance of his own teammates, Roo let his own emotions rule him. His aggression was out of control. Most observers were surprised at the leniency of the Greek referee Georgios Kasnaferis. Rooney should have had a yellow card for a violent and stupid tackle on the Spanish winger Joaquín Sánchez Rodríguez and a red card for the idiotic shoving of Spanish goalkeeper Iker Casillas in the back. Sven-Göran Eriksson took stock and pulled off Rooney a few minutes before half-time.

In anger at this very public humiliation, Roo ripped off his black armband, *in memoriam* for Emlyn Hughes, the Liverpool and England legend, who had died a few days before the friendly, and appeared to treat the Swedish manager to a chorus of 'fuck off's. No one doubted that Roo meant no disrespect to Hughes, but it reinforced the public image of him as a hot-headed thug. The *Daily Mail* spoke for Middle England: 'LOONEY ROONEY LETS THE COUNTRY DOWN'. In his book Roo concedes that his behaviour was 'not nice'.

Meanwhile, up the East Lancs Road, Everton were defying all predictions. They had lost their Boy Wonder to the team with more dosh, and all the smart money had been on the Toffees taking the drop at the end of the 2004–5 season. It didn't quite turn out like that. On the contrary, Everton made a blistering start to the season, winning match after match against far more moneyed opponents. It was almost as if Rooney's genius had been some kind of curse that had inhibited the lesser but real enough talents of the rest of the team. Moyes, too, seemed liberated, no longer having to spend oceans of his time worrying about how to keep his best player while the sharks with bigger chequebooks circled. There must also have been a 'let's show Roo' factor: that Everton was a football team, not a one-man band. At Christmas 2004, Everton were second in the Premier League. The *Sunday Mirror* commented that without the Boy Wonder, the Toffees were going from strength to strength and were real contenders for a Champions League spot. Moyes, said the paper, had developed a tightly knit, well-organised, feisty outfit who played great football and were hard to beat. Yet, with the possible exception of free-scoring Aussie midfielder Tim Cahill, there were no standout players on the Blue half of Merseyside.

The *Independent on Sunday* quoted Everton's chairman, Bill Kenwright, on Moyes the miracle-maker: you knew the manager was a one-off within three minutes of talking to him. That feeling about a person had only happened to Kenwright once before in his life and that was when he was very young and started 'big' school and he sat on the bus on the way to school next to someone special. He went home and told his mum about it. That lad was Paul McCartney.

Moyes, without Rooney, was doing very well.

Boxing Day, yet again, was taken at face value by Rooney when United met Bolton Wanderers.

'ROONEY SLAP CASTS UGLY SHADOW ON UNITED WIN' – *Independent*.

'WAYNE FURY' – *Daily Mail*.

'ROONEY'S VIDEO NASTY' – *Daily Express*.

The Reds won 2–0, but the England star had pushed his hand into Bolton defender Tal Ben Haim's face during the win at Old Trafford. For an ex-boxer, it wasn't much of a slap, but in the modern game it wasn't on. The Israeli went down as if he had been pole-axed by a rampaging brontosaurus wielding a pickaxe handle, which was a little bit theatrical. Neither the referee nor the linesmen saw it, but Roo got a suspension afterwards when the video evidence was reviewed. In his book, Roo wasn't particularly meek about the incident. He says that he was fouled by Tal Ben Haim who also gave him a mouthful, so he gave him a push. Rooney said Ben Haim went down like a bag of shite, as if he knocked him for six with an uppercut. Point is: a football pitch is not a boxing ring.

In February 2005, Roo's reputation sank lower when Manchester United played Arsenal. The *Daily Star* headlined the story 'THERE'S NO F***ING PROBLEM WITH MY F***ING TEMPER!' The paper reported that Rooney was filmed swearing twenty times in a minute, helping out its readers with the maths: that's spitting out the F-word every three seconds. Challenged that he had a short fuse, he replied: 'Nothing really. I don't think there is a problem with my temperament. My record shows that.'

His record showed the opposite. After he was given a yellow card for bad behaviour, he was shown swearing at referee Graham Poll like a machine gun, firing 'Fuck off' – or something very much like that phrase – at him every 2.7 seconds. The referee took aside his captain, Roy Keane, and his fellow England teammate, Gary Neville, to ask Rooney to calm down. Poll told Keane: 'I can't keep warning him.'

Kev Mitchell, for my money one of the best sportswriters in Britain, and by no means a stuffed shirt, was deeply unimpressed by Rooney's attitude to reasonable authority. He asked himself what effect bad behaviour in Premier League matches might possibly have on the ordinary, amateur game and wrote up his shocking findings in *The Observer*.

> Ben Youard is a 34-year-old maths teacher from Islington in north London who, like thousands of players up and down the country, enjoys recreational football. Except on one rather remarkable day. . .
>
> 'I was playing in a match in the Invicta Sports League in south London,' he recalls. 'The opposition were all in their early twenties and they had a centre-back who was particularly aggressive – kicking people, making late tackles, all that. Somebody made a bad tackle on him, and he completely lost it with the other player. The referee had to pull them apart and, when the game restarted, the guy went off to the sideline to his bag, pulled a gun out and started waving it at the referee saying, "Next time anyone does that to me, I'm going blow their head off." His teammates calmed him down and made him put the gun away. The game was abandoned immediately and all of the opposing team, apart from the gunman, pleaded with the referee not to report them to the FA. They said the nutter was just a ringer who didn't normally play for them. That's the excuse that all teams use when there's a bad incident like that.'

'The most enlightening part of Ben's story,' reflected Mitchell, 'is contained in the final phrase: ". . .when there's a bad incident like that".'

Like pulling a gun after losing a tackle.

Away from football, Rooney's good name continued to be under attack.

In April 2005 a few pals and their girlfriends, Coleen included, went round to Rio Ferdinand's house. The blokes slipped off down the pub and the girls caught up with the errant men in a club in Alderley Edge. Roo freely admits that he and Coleen had a bit of a row and then, because Coleen had a photo shoot in Cyprus to fly off to early next morning, they left before the others. In his autobiography, Roo tells how *The Sun* and its Sunday sister paper the *News of the World* falsely alleged that this minor tiff was much worse. He said they used headlines like 'CRAZED ROONEY THUMPS COLEEN' and 'YOU BRUTE'. The *News of the World*, Rooney said, piled in, accusing him of a 'violent and nasty assault' on her. It was said he had slapped her across the face, punched her in the ribs and then told her to 'f*** off home'. Rooney said it was all rubbish – he had not touched her in any way.

Roo sued and, in April 2006, *The Sun* and the *News of the World* crumbled and the case was settled on the steps of the High Court. Roo got an apology and collected damages of around £100,000, plus all costs, and gave it all away to three charities, Alder Hey Children's Hospital, SOS Children and Claire House, a rest home for sick kids, where Coleen's sister Rosie goes every now and then. The apologies were terse, but grovelling.

The Sun ate humble pie. The paper wrote that it had on 12 April 2005 published a front-page article under the headline 'CRAZED ROONEY THUMPS COLEEN'. The article, *The Sun* said, alleged that Wayne Rooney had slapped his fiancée across the face and that he had to be calmed down and restrained by teammates. They now accepted that these allegations were false. They sincerely apologised for the embarrassment caused by the article. They agreed to pay substantial damages as a mark of regret and Mr Rooney's costs. The paper ran a leader, entitled 'WIN IT LADS', which said that they were pleased to have reached a settlement with Wayne Rooney and looked forward to welcoming the England team back with the World Cup. The *News of the World* also issued an abject apology.

At the end of the season in May 2005, Manchester United hadn't done all that brilliantly. They came third in the Premier League, lost to Arsenal in the FA Cup Final and didn't progress into the juicy bits of the

European Champions League. Wayne's old mates in Crocky looked down on United's misfortune with charity: 'Ha ha ha.'

But Roo did manage to sign off the season with a beauty of a goal, yet another of his out-of-space shots caught on a volley and powered in from somewhere on the far side of Jupiter. It was against Newcastle at Old Trafford on 24 April. Roo had just been arguing with the referee – the usual – and he himself admits in his book that he wasn't really looking for the ball when it seemed to fall out of the sky. He whacked it out of frustration and anger at the ref – and it flew in. It was voted Goal of the Season on TV.

This is as concise an exposition of how Rooney's demons and genius are intertwined as we will ever get.

Meanwhile, Everton – one of the poorest sides in the Premiership, widely expected to come a cropper and go down to the Championship – came fourth, exactly one place behind Man United, and above their great rivals Liverpool. The *Sunday Times* gave David Moyes a mock *Blue Peter* Award for making a Champions League football team out of the footballing equivalent of sticky-back plastic, washing-up-liquid bottles and Lee Carsley – the Irish international who had played a blinder for the Toffees.

By their own wholly ridiculous standards, the summer of 2005 passed *relatively* quietly for Roo and Coleen. One could almost say that the press had got a bit bored with them. The Hairdryer, being a sharp-witted old owl, took Manchester United to Japan for some pre-season friendly games, which proved too far away or too expensive for the tabloids to bother the squad.

Still, Roo remained an easy target on a soft news day. Professor Oliver Hoener of the University of Mainz in Germany had spent years studying videos of matches and interviewing top players. He concluded: 'Mindlessness is a good quality for a striker and good decisions have nothing to do with intelligence, which is why players such as Wayne Rooney show so much genius on the pitch.'

The Sun took aim at the open goal and scored: 'PROFESSOR: SECRET

OF GREAT SOCCER IS DON'T THINK (MUST BE WHY ROONEY IS SUCH A SUPERSTAR).'

They illustrated the professor's musings with a graphic of Roo looking particularly thick with a large white blank where his brain might be, apart from a single small question mark. The paper filled out the story with two quotes from soccer greats, illustrating the professor's observation, one from Brazilian star Ronaldo, 'We lost because we didn't win,' and one from the Wales legend Ian Rush, who said after his time at Juventus: 'I couldn't settle in Italy. It was like living in a foreign country.'

Roo isn't the only footballer in the world who says daft things.

Coleen, meanwhile, reinvented herself yet again. She had been written off as a money-grubbing chav by the handbag-wielding howitzers of Fleet Street. Responding to that, she turned on her heels and walloped the lot of them by suddenly appearing in *Vogue* magazine, looking extraordinarily beautiful.

The overpaid bitch queens of Fleet Street scrabbled around, aghast. They opened and closed their mouths, but they had nothing to say. Coleen had stuffed them. The *Vogue* interview was by Justine Picardie, a sympathetic and intelligent writer. She didn't pass off Coleen as the female pope, but she took her as she found her: soft spoken, disarmingly young, 'very vulnerable'. Justine never used the word, but the one that was implied throughout the piece was that Coleen was *nice*. Justine noted that Coleen didn't bring along any security to the *Vogue* shoot but her 'immensely likeable mum', Colette, and her aunt, Tracey, who saw Wayne and Coleen through the nightmare of the prostitutes. In her piece, she quoted Angela Carter, who, in 1967, set out the nature of public taste: 'a capricious goddess, goddess of mirrors, weather-cocks and barometers, whom the Elizabethans called mutability'. Justine concludes her piece offering Coleen one piece of advice that it would be a shame if she changed too much.

> 'Oh, I know,' says Coleen. 'If I lose weight from around my face, I don't
> look like me. And I do want to be *me*. . .' Her big hazel eyes flick away
> from her notebook for a moment, and she glances at her reflection,

almost furtively, in the mirror opposite. And then, quickly, she smooths back a stray lock of hair, and you can see that she is steadying herself, steeling herself – not just for the *Vogue* photographer, but for the unseen future, too, whatever it may bring.

The contrast with the usual snotty crap in the tabloids about Coleen was a breath of fresh air.

For the start of the 2005–6 season, Manchester United had brand new owners, the Glazer family, headed by geriatric boss Malcolm Glazer, who his critics say has a striking resemblance to Noddy's friend Big Ears – he who sits on the red-and-white spotted toadstool in the Enid Blyton books. *Forbes* magazine puts his wealth at roughly $2.2 billion, and worries about the family's 'massive debt load' which, the rich man's magazine says, 'continues to hamper profitability despite rising revenues'. Some followers of the beautiful game have a downer on the Glazers. In the view of the critics, the Florida-based family borrowed heavily to buy their very nice Mancunian cow and are now milking it for every cent they can get. The business is now run by the sons, Malcolm, in his eighties, having suffered from a series of strokes. They're shrewd and savvy, the Glazers, taking a very, very low profile, leaving all the public talking to Sir Alex Ferguson. Five years on in 2010, the Glazers offered a £500 million bond to help ease their debt repayments. It was doubly oversubscribed.

The Glazers appear to have bought a very nice milking cow indeed. None of the Glazers appear to have taken a salary from Man United, true, but the bond prospectus did report that from July 2006, in five chunks, £10 million was paid in 'management and administration fees' to companies affiliated to the Glazers. Under the terms of the 2010 bond, the family is entitled to be paid up to £6 million by Man United in management fees. The prospectus also revealed that each of Malcolm Glazer's five sons and one daughter personally borrowed about £1.66 million from the club, a total of £10 million.

At least, some say, Rooney scores goals.

His aim at the start of the 2005–6 season was to win the World Cup

for England in the summer of 2006 and bag some pots for Manchester
United. But he could not shake his demons off. The start of the new
season saw a series of goals – he found the back of the net in his first three
games, celebrating another great goal against Newcastle by swearing,
'You fucking beauty', which caused offence when it was picked up by the
superb hearing technology of the TV soundmen – and then a series of
shaming performances: yellow cards, a red card and an industrial amount
of swearing at rival players, referees, his captain. . .

The international fixture list featured a game against minnows
Northern Ireland. The Irishmen ate the big fish and spat it out, closing
the game 1–0 up against the Three Lions.

Rooney disgraced himself in the first half. He was booked for a foul on
Keith Gillespie and reacted by kicking the ball in the general direction
of another Irishman, David Healy. For this total want of sportsmanship,
Rooney picked up a yellow card.

Rooney reacted to this censure by sarcastically applauding the Swiss
referee, Massimo Busacca. The England captain, David Beckham, had to
step in to prevent the colour of the card going down the light spectrum.
Rooney then appeared to start swearing, 'Fuck off' at his captain. *The
People* ran their version of the exchange between Roo and Becks.

> BECKS: F****** calm it down NOW. . . get yourself sorted and do the
> job we need.
> ROO: That's total b*******. I'm doing my f****** best, what more do
> you want?

Not happy bunnies.

The row carried on at half-time when Roo said of Beckham that he was
a 'flash bastard'. The two men squared up, dangerously, as Becks allegedly
told Rooney that he was 'out of order'.

No apology was forthcoming. Instead, according to Joe Lovejoy, football
correspondent of the *Sunday Times,* Roo told Becks to 'get stuffed'. The
News of the World alleged that the actual language used by Roo by way
of reply was somewhat more robust: 'Fuck off, you cunt.' Rio Ferdinand,

Roo's friend and Man United teammate, stepped in to calm things down. He too was told to 'fuck off'.

England assistant coach Steve McClaren entered the fray and he got a 'fuck off' too. It was only when Sven arrived to read the Riot Act that the striker recovered his composure. At the start of the second half, Roo and his captain publicly shook hands.

For the rest of the game a meek and docile creature calling itself Wayne Rooney wafted around the pitch, behaved himself and performed like one of the ladies on the perfume counter at Harrods while the England team fell apart and let the Northern Irish walk all over them. 'You're not very good,' the Northern Irish fans sang at the end – and they were being polite.

The more thoughtful sports writers had a pretty compelling explanation for Roo's almighty sulk in the second half. He hates playing right up front, alone, and likes coming through the defence from the centre – but that role was reserved exclusively for David Beckham. The fundamental problem for England was that it seemed as though the rather wonderful and stable friendship built between Beckham and Eriksson had ossified. The team strategy had been built around Becks from the early Eriksson years. In 2001, it worked beautifully, never better, when England defeated Germany 5–1 at Munich. But as time had rolled by and the 2006 World Cup neared, the captain was no longer the world-beater he had once been. Worse, the strategy showed a lack of mental suppleness on the part of the manager.

Rooney was in some ways a victim of Eriksson's lack of flexibility. Paul Wilson in *The Observer* set out the argument in a piece headlined: 'ENGLAND'S COACH IS UNDER FIRE, BUT RESENTMENT BUILDING AGAINST THEIR OVERINDULGED CAPTAIN IS THE REAL PROBLEM'.

An Arsenal blogger was less polite: 'England are just a bunch of brain-dead Sky-famous journeymen, mismanaged by a Swedish con man who can make even Wayne Rooney look bad. Sven is not a motivator or a tactician, he's a groupie. One day he and Becks will get married and go to live in Tuscany.'

So, atrociously behaved as he was, some people who knew about football agreed that Roo did have something genuine to moan about. And, to be fair to the teenager, Roo appeared to be genuinely contrite about his behaviour. Until he did it again, the following week when Manchester United drew with Villarreal of Spain, 0–0. After a miserable sequence of three quick fouls, he got into bother with the referee, no-nonsense Dane Milton Nielsen. Ian Ladyman in the *Daily Mail* felt sympathy for Rooney, that he was a little unfortunate to have been booked for a trivial trip on Villarreal captain Quique Álvarez in the sixty-fourth minute. But Rooney compounded the fault by sarcastically applauding Nielsen, almost clipping the official on the nose. Ladyman noted that no referee in Europe would stand for such insolence and, inevitably, Nielsen turned, produced a second yellow card and then flourished the red. Quique Álvarez had appeared to dive under Rooney's challenge. But Rooney's reaction to being booked – clapping his hands right in Nielsen's face – was worse than stupid. Ferguson didn't even look at Rooney as the striker left the field, which spoke volumes for his feelings.

At this stage, Roo's career record could be summarised by the fact that he had been booked and/or sent off on almost as many occasions as he had scored goals – thirty-two yellow and two red cards making a total of thirty-four versus thirty-seven goals.

The Sun's headline writers put the boot in, wholly predictably, trembling before 'THE DARK SIDE OF THE ROON', 'WAYNIAC' and 'WAYNE LOONEY'. The paper followed that up with 'OVER-REACTION MAN: 30CM ROONEY DOLL CAN KICK, PUNCH AND SULK. You've heard of Action Man – now here's Over-Reaction Man, a toy figure of hot-headed Wayne Rooney.'

The strange thing is that despite all the slapping Roo suffered from papers like the *News of the World*, he still seemed to be happy to talk to them. In December 2005, the paper reports that Rooney told the *News of the World* there was a feeling they should win the World Cup for Sven. All the players liked him and respected him, he respected them, and, more importantly, he trusted them. Rooney went on to bury the hatchet with his captain, Beckham. He told the paper that David had been a great friend to him, a great captain and a terrific player. He explained that he was very frustrated when so much was made of their argument during the Northern Ireland game. Arguments happen on and off the pitch, he said, but they happen because you try to help one another and because you care: it was blown up out of all proportion. Rooney said that the next day they were on the phone talking, speaking in the dressing room afterwards and everything was sorted out.

What's striking about this stuff is that he is amiably being quoted in a newspaper that only the other day had alleged that he had told the England captain to 'fuck off, you cunt' and a newspaper that he was suing for alleging, falsely as the paper conceded on the steps of the High Court in April 2006, that he had thumped Coleen at a nightclub. The explanation is simple. Plastered over Roo's chest in the *News of the World* interview is a T-shirt depicting 'The Real Thing' – advertising the world's number-one carbonated sugary drink which makes fat people fatter and rots teeth. On the inside page, the real deal is spelt out: 'SPORT OF THE WORLD – WE GET THE INTERVIEW THEY ALL WANTED' and in much smaller type: 'In association with Coca-Cola'.

Roo gave the interview to a big paper as part of his sponsorship deal with Coca-Cola. Once you get into bed with a corporate major, they call the shots. If you don't play along, you don't get the dosh. It is not impossible that Roo might have preferred not to talk to the *News of the World* while he was suing it for libel, but that is part of the reality of being a celebrity.

It's not as nice as it looks.

14

ENGLAND'S GLORY?

The England football team has some of the finest and most expensive players in the world. There is only one problem. They fall to pieces when they leave this green and pleasant land and go somewhere, anywhere, called Abroad. If only the World Cup could be played in Wembley every time, then we would show the Continentalists. Perhaps, like Dingle, it's something to do with the water.

Abroad was a bad place to go if you were part of the Three Lions in 2006. The first victim of Abroad was not a player but the manager. In January the increasingly unloved England boss took a few days off from his busy preparations for the World Cup with a business trip to explore working with an Arab sheikh on a sports project in Dubai. Sven and his agent, Athole Still, were put up in Dubai's seven-star Burj al-Arab hotel, knocked back £900 worth of vintage champagne, guzzled crab cakes and lobster, and went for a trip around the bay in the seventy-foot gin palace *Eternity*.

Fool, Sven, fool. Had the meeting been in a pub in Skeggy, then he might have suspected that he was walking into an elephant trap. The ostentatious display of wealth was illusory and the Arab sheikh was fake. If Sven had ripped off his mask, he would have revealed Mazher Mahmood, the investigations editor of the *News of the World*. The enormously elaborate sting – estimated to have cost around £100,000 –

caught out Sven freely admitting that he was off the moment the World Cup was over, and there was a fair bit of tittle-tattle about the players. Sven shared with his new-found friend the belief that Aston Villa might be up for grabs. He mused about getting David Beckham away from Real Madrid, said that Michael Owen liked the money but wasn't very happy at Newcastle, and thought that Rio Ferdinand could be lazy at times. On Rooney, the *News of the World* reported the following exchange: so, what was Rooney like? the man from the *News of the World* asked. Was he a good boy? Sven replied implying that Rooney's problem was his temper, he came from a poor family, very rough, his father was a boxer and he could have been a boxer as well. Then, turning to the other players in his side, their reporter asked who were the other stars? Sven answered: Michael Owen, but he said that you couldn't compare the two – the one who was coming was Wayne Rooney. Sven's agent, Athole Still, interjected that he would never be a Beckham, not in terms of the brand, but the manager said as a player Rooney might be – implying that he was as good as Beckham.

This wasn't quite the muck the *News of the Screws* was digging for. You could get that level of intelligence on Rooney – best player, rough family – from a regular at the Wezzy for a pint of beer and a packet of crisps, not £100,000.

The sting did have the effect of undermining the England manager, and would have caused some unease between him and his star players. None of that would have remotely bothered the boss of the *News of the World*, Rupert Murdoch. He's from Abroad.

Sven's remark about the Rooney family being a bit rough was not wildly inaccurate. To the tune of 'Winter Wonderland', guess who was caught singing this ditty?

One Harold Shipman,
There's only one Harold Shipman.
Scousers say thanks
Cos he only kills Mancs,
Walking in a Shipman wonderland.

The *Sunday People* had discovered that Wayne's kid brother Graham, then eighteen, had been filmed on the internet singing the praises of serial-killer GP Harold Shipman – responsible for the murder of almost 300 elderly patients with morphine injections – because his victims were Mancunians, not Liverpudlians. After the song, Graham smirks directly at the camera and chants: 'Harold Shipman killed your nan, he's a Scouser.'

The paper pointed out that Wayne knows nothing about his brother's sick joke.

The uneasy tension between the Rooney and McLoughlin clans was outed in a most peculiar way by the *Daily Mail* when they printed an untrue story about Coleen's twentieth-birthday party in early April 2006. Rooney says in *My Story So Far* that the paper had alleged that the two families had to be kept apart in separate rooms in case they all started fighting. The paper had referred back to the 'Battle of Coleen's 18th Birthday' when fists flew – though, as Rooney reveals, the media had got it wrong and that the punch-up had in fact been his family v. the bouncers, not the Rooneys v. the McLoughlins. Rooney, in his autobiography, said there was actual proof, which they could show quickly, that the story was completely untrue – because his family hadn't even been at the party. The *Mail* printed an immediate correction. But the interesting bit of this particular mangled yarn is not that the *Daily Mail* got it wrong, but that Roo's family had not been invited to or didn't choose to go to Coleen's party. In the normal way, wouldn't you expect at least a few members of the boyfriend's family to turn up to his girlfriend's bash?

As the tempo for the run-up to the World Cup heightened, Roo's troubles off the pitch continued to grab the headlines: 'ROO'S £770K BETS DEBT: MICHAEL OWEN SET UP ENGLAND GAMBLING RING . . . NOW BOOKIES ARE CHASING WAYNE'.

The *Sunday Mirror*'s Rupert Hamer was a proper reporter in Fleet Street's finest traditions. (He was killed in Afghanistan in January 2010 by a Taliban bomb.) Hamer's story on Rooney's gambling was solid and worth telling. The paper charged that Roo had run up secret gambling debts, as part of a ring that included England teammates Michael Owen, John Terry, Frank Lampard and Rio Ferdinand. Hamer reported that what started as a light-hearted 'school' run by racing fan Michael Owen had spiralled out of control and had caused friction and bad feeling in the camp just two months before the World Cup.

The *Sunday Mirror* said that Rooney, along with Lampard, Terry and Ferdinand, had been placing bets on credit with one of Owen's business partners, Stephen Smith, who ran a private bookmakers, Goldchip Ltd. The paper reported that while other players had enjoyed some success, Rooney found himself losing tens of thousands of pounds on horses, dogs and football matches he wasn't involved in.

The paper quoted an anonymous source alleging that the boys would contact Smith and place huge bets. Rooney, being young and naïve, started with hundreds of pounds which soon became thousands of pounds and then became tens of thousands of pounds. By Christmas he realised he was in trouble and was being chased to settle his account. He started placing bigger sums to try to recoup some of his losses but he just found himself in more debt. His people were furious that someone so young was allowed so much credit. He had no idea what he was getting into. They thought it was very irresponsible of the bookies. Rooney, in his book, confesses much. He admits that he got into gambling 'out of boredom'.

It's a real curse for our topflight soccer players. They are so cocooned from the big, bad, nasty world out there, they end up living very boring lives. They can't go out and meet the public, they can't drink before a game, they can't do anything dodgy lest they get photographed by the paparazzi, so they end up spending hours upon hours in hotel rooms on their own. Gambling is an obvious and seductive distraction, and its charms proved too great for Rooney to resist.

He gambled while at Everton and ended up fifty grand in the red. That's not pocket change, even for a Premiership star. Coleen discovered it, and Rooney stayed away from the bookies for a year. But then he says someone in the England dressing room passed on the number of a private bookmaker. Rooney goes out of his way to say that this player was not his England teammate Michael Owen, but he, Owen, did use the same bookie, called Mike.

It was all done by phone texts – no receipts, no bills, no letters, no final demands. All you had to do was to text 'Mike' your bet and he would place it.

Like every other loser, he started winning at first. He won big money, totting up £51,000, which was handed over to Rooney in cash, not by cheque, by a young lad who visited the training ground. Then he started to lose money big time, but because there was no paperwork the boy from Crocky had no idea how much he was in the red. The guillotine came down one night in February 2006, before Man United were to play Blackburn.

This time the text from Mike was grim. It said that Roo had to do something about his balance, but in the meantime, could he pay back the £51,000 that he'd been given in cash for his early winnings.

Rooney rang Stretford, who began to investigate. When the story broke, so did the rest of Fleet Street. The *Daily Mail*'s Paul Hayward did some digging and discovered that 'Mike' worked for Goldchip Ltd, whose boss Stephen Smith was a 57-year-old former shoe salesman who had got out of footwear and into soccer. He had befriended Terry Owen, Michael's father, when the two were at Bradford City, Owen as a player and Smith as commercial manager. Smith had become head of Owen Promotions, which handled the player's property portfolio and some, but not all, commercial tie-ups. Goldchip was set up to provide secure anonymous betting for the footballers. Hayward reported that the firm was designed to provide a secure, independent connection between players and layers. Thus a bookie taking a bet via Smith's company would not know the identity of the gambler.

But the former toiler in the British Shoe Corporation had no bookie's licence for much of the time Goldchip was taking Rooney's bets. He was acting as an agent for another bookie. It all looked a little too informal. When the *Sunday Mirror* story broke, much of the comment attacked Rooney for being a moron but some targeted Goldchip for taking bets with no paperwork, with no bookie's licence of their own, and for exploiting a rich but, ahem, not very bright sportsman.

Goldchip was, however, in the clear as the company had been authorised to receive bets as an agent to a bookmaker until the proper licence came through. The former shoe salesman (Smith) and the dodgy agent (Stretford) sat down and hammered out a deal, the precise details of which have never been made public.

A statement from Goldchip Ltd read:

> Following recent press stories, Goldchip is pleased to state that outstanding issues between the company and Wayne Rooney have now been fully resolved as a result of talks between Stephen Smith and Paul Stretford of Proactive Sports Management. The matter is now closed and there will be no further comment.

Proactive was keen to dampen down talk of Rooney falling out with Owen over the gambling debt: 'Any suggestions of a rift or a dispute between Wayne and Michael are completely without foundation as far as Wayne is concerned. Wayne and Michael remain the best of pals.'

And that was as it should be, because the best of pals were about to go into battle for the World Cup. Three–nil down against Chelsea in the fag-end of a not too great season for a club with the celestial expectations of Manchester United, and Roo goes for gold in the Blues' penalty area in the seventy-eighth minute. Their fullback, Portuguese Paulo Ferreira, catches the Crocky Cyclone in a fair tackle and he falls. Something pops, and England's great hope goes down with a broken metatarsal bone. He may be out of the World Cup 2006 for good.

This was no joke. The moment Roo broke his foot somehow managed to be even more unfunny to some than much of *Rio Ferdinand's World Cup Wind-Ups*. In this programme, Roo's Manchester United teammate Rio set out to be the successor to the Two Ronnies. It didn't quite work out as funny as planned. Ally Ross was particularly harsh in the *News of the World*, describing Ferdinand as a slack-gobbed, finger-clicking halfwit, who clearly fancied himself as Britain's version of *Punk'd* star Ashton Kutcher. He wrote that Rio had even equipped himself with a naff catchphrase: 'You've been Merked.' The uncomic highlight of the ha-di-bleedin'-ha show, wrote Ross, was 'mute gimp Wayne Rooney' killing a youngster's pet dog.

Roo and Coleen came out of the sting rather sweetly. Rooney was invited to visit a vet's and then asked to hold a drip in the air for a dog on the operating table, listening to a life-support machine go beep-beep. At one point, the vet who ran the animal sanctuary asked for £40,000, otherwise all the animals would get it. Roo's instant response was eloquent. He didn't say, 'No, that's too much,' but looked wary and muttered something about asking Paul – Stretford, his agent. With Roo, you see what you get: he's a street footballer who, it seems, can't mumble his way out of a paper bag.

Everyone exits the room, leaving Rooney alone with the youngster's pet dog on life support. Then, to Rooney's horror, the beep-beep machine flatlines. He's killed the dog. Only the viewer knows the dead dog in question is, in fact, stuffed. Oh, all right: it did make me laugh. So the prank worked, kind of.

Roo's silence was that of someone who, then at least, did not seem at ease as a public speaker and, also, a man who cares about animals and other people's feelings. He appeared to be worried stiff that he may have killed the stuffed dog, and that the little boy who owned the dog would be terribly upset. In the background, Coleen kept on creasing up with laughter for the whole event. When Rio finally popped in, Roo didn't blow his top but smiled mildly.

He'd been had, but he was big enough to be amused by it. One came away from watching the show thinking that Coleen has an irrepressible sense of humour and that Roo is, shockingly, not quite the beast he's made out to be in the headlines but rather, off the pitch, a very ordinary bloke.

But the image puppeteers had a very different game to play. The most striking image in the run-up to the World Cup didn't represent a shy man trying to care for someone else's sick pet, but Wayne Rooney, naked from the waist up, his mouth wide open in a lion's roar, and a great smear of blood-like red paint running from the top of his forehead down to his tummy button, and across from one clenched fist to the other. The Nike ad made Roo a living, breathing St George Cross in blood: a bold and stark image that *The Sun* put on its front page. The not-so-subtle association between the rawness of Roo's game and bloody battle was made and Roo (and his agent) were duly rewarded. But there is always a downside. Some of the people who would have looked at that image would have been World Cup referees. Did they buy into the Roo–blood association too deeply? It was only an ad for a sportswear and boot company, you might say. But the power of the image was strong: it said that Wayne Rooney was a blood-red warrior, and, having seen it, you could be forgiven for not giving him the benefit of the doubt when a rival player accused him of a vicious foul. But that was never going to happen, was it?

For a long time it looked as though Roo would never go Abroad, in particular, Germany. Sitting around on a broken foot while everybody else was playing football in preparation for the World Cup was agony piled on agony for Roo. To begin with, he couldn't even drive because his air-boot restricted control of the foot pedals. One of the best stories in his autobiography is the gentle joshing between him and Kona Hislop, one of Stretford's people at Proactive, who had to drive to Manchester United's training ground every morning so that Roo could spend time in an oxygen tent to accelerate his recovery. Kona's brother, Shaka, was the former West Ham goalkeeper who was preparing for one last hurrah with Trinidad and Tobago, who were also in the World Cup. The two men spent the drive to and from the training ground yakking away, with Roo worrying whether he would ever play and Kona gently teasing him about T&T getting to the final.

If you want a quick explanation of why football is a force for good in international relations, most of the time, you can't do much better than Wazza and Kona. The soccer star applied his mind to recovering from a broken metatarsal bone faster than anyone else in recorded history, and he succeeded. He is not a lazy genius, but someone who works ferociously hard at getting fit. For effort, you've got to give Roo ten out of ten.

The docs looked at the bone, wondered at the miracle of it healing in record time, and declared Roo fit. The headlines proclaimed 'THE BIG MAN IS BACK', sourced to something Roo is alleged to have said on his arrival in the England dressing room. In his book Roo, convincingly, denies this nonsense. He is not the type to grandstand with boastful phrases. That's not his style. But the gist of the sentiment was true enough, and the sigh of relief from England fans was huge and heartfelt.

When England's soccer team went to Germany, the Wags came too. The English language is the greatest linguistic road crash of all time – Anglo-Saxon smashes into Danish Norse and then grinds into French – generating three times as many words as its nearest rival. (Shakespeare, our greatest writer, had a vocabulary of 24,000; Verlaine, France's greatest man with the pen, a mere 8,000.) But 'Wags' is not, perhaps, English at its best. It comes from a contraction of 'wives and girlfriends'. The players were holed up in an exclusive spa hotel on the edge of Baden-Baden, the Wags at a hotel in town, muddled together with the press. Every time the Wags went shopping, had a drink or a laugh, the snappers were there, to capture it all. If you are followed around 24/7, eventually someone will capture an embarrassing moment. I know from personal experience. It's an industrial process – and it worked.

The image of a witches' brew of mindless airheads on a gigantic shopping-spree-cum-drinking-binge was presented to a gobsmacked nation. It was as mildly unfair as it was mildly true. They did shop, they did drink and they did have a laugh. Most of the papers went big on Posh's dietary habits. Coleen came across – to summarise thousands of words in one – as normal.

The copy off the pitch was better than the copy on. England went into the tournament second favourite, with some world-beating players and, in Sven, one of the smoothest-talking managers of the modern age. And yet England never quite came into its stride, never swaggered, never established its quality. The football was thin stuff, with the team scraping home by embarrassingly small margins against the international equivalents of Tranmere Rovers.

England won the first game against Paraguay 1–0, which Roo sat out on the subs' bench. For the second, against Trinidad and Tobago, he came on in the fifty-second minute, but looked rusty. England won 2–0, but against this level of competition a world-beating team should have scored seven goals. Beckham looked old, Rooney – no reflection on him –

like an athlete who hadn't exercised for six weeks; only Liverpool's Peter Crouch was showing real flair. England drew 2–2 with Sweden to get into the last sixteen.

There seemed to be an absence of inspiration in the England camp and that, as far as the press were concerned, was Sven's fault. Just before the Ecuador game, Rooney found himself next to Beckham. The story later came out that he told his captain that he was going to score from a free kick today. Becks asked him how he knew that.

'Because,' Roo replied, 'your free kicks have been shit in training all week.' And lo, it came to pass that Beckham scored from a superb free kick on the hour. Psychic Rooney gave Becks as big a hug as you could imagine. Rooney played better in this game, but the team as a whole was still firing on two cylinders.

Foreboding spread. Were England up to winning the World Cup? Somehow, it didn't feel right.

I went to Germany for the Ecuador game. It was boring. Much more interesting were the echoes of war between Britain and Germany. I am of the generation that missed the war but loved the replays, perhaps too much. The definitive text is, of course, 'The Germans', that episode of *Fawlty Towers* in which a German guest orders a prawn cocktail and Basil, in John Cleese's brilliant satire on the British hospitality industry, whispers to Polly through his teeth: 'Don't mention the war. . . So it's all forgotten now and let's hear no more about it. So that's two eggs mayonnaise, a prawn Goebbels, a Hermann Goering and four Colditz salads.'

My abiding memory after the Ecuador game was watching an England fan wearing a red Three Lions shirt slowly walk up an escalator to street level. He was so profoundly drunk he had pooed himself, great long brown stains trailing down his legs and the stink proclaimed his presence from thirty feet away. A group of England fans found this sight so impressive that they took out their camera-phones and snapped away. This mass act of ghoulishness at a fellow man's humiliation, made possible with the very latest 21st-century technology, was quietly sickening.

A police car turned up. Having been reared on *Biggles*, *Dad's Army* and stories of the ruthless Hun, I fully expected something nasty from the

German cops. The police officer went to the boot of his Mercedes estate police car and opened it. The back of the car was full of the most up-to-date German police control methods. What would he pull out? A riot stick? An electric cattle prod? Instead, he got a blanket out and wrapped it around the pooey Englishman like a grandmother looking after a toddler who's made a mistake.

England's glory? England's poo, more like.

Come out of Gelsenkirchen train station on 1 July, ahead of England's quarter-final with Portugal, and you were greeted with a roiling sea of white and red, shouting about somewhere called 'INGERLAND', flying blow-up plastic Spitfires, humming *The Dam Busters* theme tune and drinking as if the End of the World was coming in two minutes' time. Around the corner, giant German riot cops clad in ribbed black like enormous beetles waited and waited. They could, they really could – but only if someone gave them the order. But no one gave the order because it wasn't that kind of occasion, and Germany isn't that kind of country any more, and the England fans were, if not angels, only Angles who had taken the boat.

The bit that made me laugh out loud, parodying the whole war thing, was a group of lads from a pub in Leicestershire, all of them wearing T-shirts emblazoned with the legend 'DON'T TELL 'EM YOUR NAME, PIKE'.

To people who don't get the reference, one of the funniest episodes of *Dad's Army* ever was when the team of Walmington-on-Sea heroes capture a sinister Nazi U-boat captain. The Nazi broils with menace and asks for the name of the snotty-nosed mummy's boy in the unit, to include in a list of people to be investigated once the Germans invade. At which suggestion Captain Mainwaring, played by the late great Arthur Lowe, snaps what was on the T-shirt. It was an old joke, from which all the anger had been spent. The Second World War felt a very, very long time ago, and only had reality in an elderly TV comedy.

The game itself was like an elderly TV comedy too. England spluttered and backfired against Portugal until the hour mark, when Rooney was powering up the pitch and he won a ball against three Portuguese players. They swam after him, but he twisted and turned, fighting to keep control of the ball. One player banged into him from the side, one player banged into him from behind, and he clattered to a full stop and came down like an oak tree, his back foot seeking stability but finding the testicles of Portugal's Ricardo Carvalho. Roo stood up, saw his Manchester United teammate Ronnie goading the referee into booking him, and looked up to see the red card held high above him.

He shouldn't have gone Abroad, see?

England lost on penalties, as they had in Euro 2004. In the spill-over event at Gelsenkirchen for people like us who had failed, miserably, to get tickets for the game proper, the mass of INGERLAND fans slumped to the ground. For some reason I remained standing but felt like a general of a dead army. All around, people lay on the grass, as if they had been mown down in battle. And then they stood up again, and hugged their mates, and drank some more, and phoned their dads and mums back home.

It seems trite and too obvious, but it would be wrong not to say it: we were all of us a part of the power of football to do good, to channel nations' warlike instincts into the harmless activity of kicking a ball around. If you disagree, ask my dad's generation. When the game was over back then, some of his mates – far too many – and some of the people on the other side – far too many – didn't get up again. Football isn't war and anyone who tells you different hasn't been to one.

Wayne Rooney could have been damned as a national disgrace, but he wasn't. I've looked at the evidence again and again, and my own view is that Roo is innocent. The problem is not his behaviour at Gelsenkirchen, but his whole history: his clatterings of the past, the obscenities shouted at Beckham, on and off the pitch, the ugly history of yellow and red cards, even his bloody image flogging Nike trainers told against him. With that history, if you were a neutral referee, who would you find for: the man with the bad reputation or the defender with the mangled testicles?

The man who tipped it against Roo, the nation believed, was his club teammate, Ronnie, who urged the ref to discipline Crocky's Own, and then winked at his bench when he was sent off. That wink lost the Portuguese an awful lot of friends back in England.

Rooney, almost alone, has done his utmost to express his disappointment at Cristiano in measured terms. In a statement he said:

'I bear no ill feeling to Cristiano but am disappointed that he chose to get involved. I suppose I do, though, have to remember that on that particular occasion we were not teammates.'

The Scouser's camp has been so leaky in the past, and any human frailty by its hero ends up plastered on the front pages so damn quickly that I, for one, suspect that Roo's conduct at Gelsenkirchen has been, if not forgotten, forgiven. It helps that Portugal got knocked out and didn't win the World Cup either.

Perhaps the best epitaph for Rooney's role in the failed 2006 World Cup campaign came from the world's least emotional man, Sven-Göran Eriksson: 'You, more than me, need Wayne Rooney in the next few years,' he pleaded with the press, 'so, please, pay attention, don't kill him, I beg you.'

Well said, that Swede.

Coleen's twenty-first birthday celebration in April 2007 was a festival of yucky tat. *Hello!* paid good money for exclusive rights to the photographs and proclaimed the event in their curiously pompous headline-writing style: 'COLEEN'S BIRTHDAY EXTRAVAGANZA: IT'S THE BEST PARTY I COULD EVER IMAGINE . . . ALL THE FUN OF THE FAIR . . . WAYNE'S AMAZING DIAMOND LOVE TOKEN . . . THE GLAMOROUS GUESTS AND STAR PERFORMERS'.

The photographs in *Hello!* tell the story of Rooney and Coleen as they would like the world to see it: a sweet one of them together; her sitting in a towelling robe getting her lips done by some beauty therapist bloke with sticky-up blond hair; her leaning against a wall, looking at the camera with Bette Davis eyes; the cake, decorated with a blue handbag and pink shoes, circled by dozens of mini-cakes emblazoned with a photograph of Coleen pouting at the camera.

Narcissism made edible.

The party arena, pre-bunfight, bathed in an alien pink glow; two ladies on stilts looking like leggy ostriches; three of her mates, dressed to the nines; Coleen having a laugh; Crouchy and Rooney; Coleen and her adopted sister in a wheelchair; a close-up of the ten-carat yellow-diamond Chopard ring, a minor asteroid; Coleen showing off the ring to guests; people messing about at a funfair; assorted snaps of footballers and Wags; one of Wayne, Coleen and their brothers together; one of Rooney, Coleen and her mum and dad and one of Rooney, Coleen and his mum and dad – two separate photographic sittings for the Rooney and McLoughlin parents.

Maybe they ran out of chairs.

The tabloids got excited when Wayne's cousin Natalie Rooney flashed a boob at the cameras.

No one was punched, no one was knocked flat, and the police weren't called. What kind of Rooney party is that?

15

'WITH THIS BLING I THEE WED'

St Tropez is a lah-di-dah place in the south of France full of absurdly expensive motor cars and little dogs that go yap and poo on the pavements. It's the French version of Blackpool, although the pork pies are not, as they say, *moins cher.* In June 2007 Wayne and Coleen were snapped by the *Daily Mirror* having a laugh by the pool in a St Tropez resort, with Roo doing a pretty impressive backflip. They were splitting time between the beach and a private yacht.

As you do.

He'd had another good footballing year, the same mixture of rage and sweet shots on the pitch, but, perhaps thanks to Coleen, rather less nonsense off it. After the failure of the World Cup, the 2006–7 season had opened grimly with Rooney being sent off in a friendly match against Porto in August 2006 after elbowing Porto defender Pepe. Match referee Ruud Bossen wrote a 23-page report justifying the decision and Rooney got a three-match ban. A letter of protest was written to the FA, citing the lack of punishment handed down to other players who were sent off in friendlies. Rooney also threatened to withdraw his permission for the FA to use his image rights if they did not revoke the ban, but the FA had no power to make such a decision and Rooney was left with egg on his face, on the sidelines.

Then, boringly, he stopped scoring goals for ten matches until, typical for Rooney, he came back with a hat-trick against Bolton Wanderers. The Scouser retained his composure about Ronnie Cristiano. It's almost as if he was in training to be the next dean of the diplomatic corps. As the season came to a close, Roo had scored the same number of goals as Ronnie – twenty-three in all competitions for Manchester United. But it was the Portuguese who walked away with both the PFA Player and the PFA Young Player of the Year Awards. That would eat at a lesser man.

A few days after St Tropez, Wayne and Coleen and several England teammates were off to Las Vegas to watch boxer Ricky Hatton knock seven shades of something or other out of his opponent. Quite a few of their other stars had left their partners back in Blighty, but not Wayne. Coleen was with him for all the fun, snapped by the *Sunday Mirror* going down an escalator with her back turned to the flat bit where you get off, at five o'clock in the morning. One can't help but think, studying the picture, that if that's a story, I'm a vampire sex cult virgin.

In August 2007 a new season started badly, yet again, when Rooney fractured his dreaded metatarsal after colliding with Michael Duberry of Reading. He got better fast and started scoring goals for Man United again, but the papers were twitting him for his failure at the international level. Looking forward to Euro 2008, the *Daily Telegraph*'s Henry Winter noted, coldly, that 'the last time Wayne Rooney scored a competitive goal for England he was an Everton player. Three years of hurt have followed.'

Things didn't get that much better.

The boring Swede had been replaced by an even duller Englishman. Steve McClaren lacked sparkle, verve, panache. The tabloids had it in for him as England's attempt on Euro 2008 stuttered and fizzled, a firework that went out not long after the blue touch had been lit. The end for England's hopes came in November 2007, when England crashed out to the pesky Croats.

David Beckham – the cynosure of the multimillionaire soccer star, with his, some say, space alien wife, global fame, fleet of cars, mansions and string of endorsements – insisted that the England superstars had not been spoilt by wealth and fame: 'I can assure you it doesn't matter how many cars or houses you've got, when you lose a game like this you're hurting as a player, just like the fans.'

A few days later there came news that would bring a smile to the heart of every teacher in Crocky: 'MAN U STAR GOES BRAINY – EDUCATING ROONEY' screamed *The Sun*. 'Wayne Rooney is going all intellectual', it claimed, 'by studying for his GCSE exams in English and Maths.' The paper illustrated the piece with a faked but nevertheless amusing photograph of Wazza in a top hat, wearing a monocle and carrying a cane.

He didn't need any fancy credentials to get into Moscow in May 2008. In fact, nobody did, not even a Russian visa. The Russian authorities woke up one morning to realise that they were hosting the UEFA Champions League in the Luzhniki Stadium between Chelsea and Man United and very few of the fans were going to get a visa in time. So – and this goes to show the power of the beautiful game – one of the most authoritarian governments in Europe waived its own visa rules. All you had to do to get into Moscow was show that you had a ticket for the game.

Isn't football wonderful?

Manchester United had just pipped Chelsea to the Premier League by two points so that match in Moscow was a chance for the Londoners to get one back over the Red Army, or for the Mancunians to rub Chelsea's nose in it. I was on the other side of the world in Shanghai, making a programme about China's abuse of human rights in the run-up to the Olympics – nice skyscrapers, too much torture, not a lot of free speech and don't mention the Dalai Lama – but we found an English pub with a telly and watched the great battle, surrounded by a sea of Chinese Man United fans. Tranmere Rovers not being in the final, I was neutral but, given the overwhelming backing for United in the pub, I found myself yelling on Chelsea – a mistake. It was a great, edgy, nervy game with Rooney playing powerfully. When it came to penalties I had to look away into my beer. The moment the Chinese crowd went nuts it was clear that Chelsea had lost.

In July 2008 the FA's Disciplinary Committee, which had heard the matter behind closed doors, delivered its verdict on Paul Stretford. In a statement the FA said: 'The commission found that Mr Stretford did encourage Mr Rooney and his parents to enter into a representation agreement with Proactive Sports Management Limited on 17 July 2002 although he knew Mr Rooney was still then under contract with Pro-Form.'

In all, the committee found Stretford guilty on seven out of nine charges. The latter were broken down into sub-charges, some of which were found to be proved and others unproved. If only one sub-charge in a charge was found to be proved, then that was still bad news for Stretford.

On charge one, that Stretford had 'failed to protect the interests of Mr Wayne Rooney' – proved; two, that he failed to respect the interests of third parties – proved; three, that he 'did not refrain from actions that could entice clients away from other parties' – not proved; four, that he breached FIFA Players' Agents rules by agreeing an eight-year deal when the legal maximum is two – proved; five, that he failed to register the 17 July 2002 agreement with the FA – proved; six, that he failed to register the 19 September 2002 with the FA – not proved; seven, that he failed to register the 14 December 2002 agreement with the FA – proved; eight, that he made 'a false and/or misleading witness statement to the police' in *R* v. *Hyland, Bacon and Bacon* – proved.

The ninth charge was that Stretford had provided 'false and/or misleading testimony to Warrington Crown Court' in *R* v. *Hyland, Bacon and Bacon* and was broken down into eight sub-charges. The committee found that

> Stretford's conduct had been improper and/or had brought the game into disrepute – specifically with regard to all or any of the following: a) The date at which Mr Stretford/Proactive entered into contracts of representation with Mr Wayne Rooney; Proved. b) The number of contracts of representation entered into between Mr Stretford/Proactive and Mr Wayne Rooney; Proved. c) The fact that he had misled the Court regarding the existence of the representation contracts dated 17 July 2002 and 19 September 2002 and the nature of those agreements; Proved. d) The fact that he had told the Court that he had taken over the representation of Mr Wayne Rooney on 13

December 2002; Proved. e) The fact that he had told the Court that the contracts prior to the 14 December 2002 agreement related only to image rights; Proved. f) The fact that he had claimed in his evidence in the Crown Court that he had not heard of the 17 July 2002 agreement, nor had he been aware of the terms of that agreement; Proved. g) The fact that he had told the Court that he had not 'muscled in' to make Mr Wayne Rooney breach his representation contract with Pro-Form. Proved.'

To paraphrase Lady Bracknell in Oscar Wilde's *The Importance of Being Earnest*, to mislead a jury once may be regarded as a misfortune; to mislead a jury twice looks like carelessness; to mislead a jury eight times looks dodgy.

The Disciplinary Committee left out the kitchen sink, but you get the drift. Stretford was fined £300,000 and banned effectively for nine months.

Stretford was not a happy bunny.

He put out a statement, proclaiming:

I believe the verdicts of the disciplinary panel against me are a travesty of the facts heard by its members during the hearing. I will be lodging an immediate appeal against the verdicts and continue to maintain my complete innocence of the charges brought against me. These charges came about as a result of my appearance at a criminal trial as a witness for the prosecution against men accused of blackmailing me with menaces. In pursuing their case against me, the FA seems almost wilfully to have cast me as the accused in the trial rather than a prosecution witness acting properly in the interests of justice.

Stretford appealed and lost. One year on, in the summer of 2009, he bit the bullet and accepted the nine-month ban and the fine of £300,000.

The fine might seem a lot of money to you and me, but Stretford's car of choice is an Aston Martin – which retails at around £140,000 a pop – so we're looking at him taking a hit worth, to him, two cars and a bit.

Not that much then. The prophecy of the *Liverpool Daily Post* – 'let wrist-slapping commence' – seems on the money. Nevertheless, we are looking at an imperishable stain on Stretford's record. Having given 'false and misleading' evidence won't go down very well in court if the dodgy agent ever seeks to sue anyone who may care to write a book called *Rooney's Gold* – some might say.

In the autumn of 2008 the agency that Stretford created and Stretford fell out with each other. They parted company. Proactive claims Stretford was sacked for 'gross misconduct'. Stretford maintains he terminated his own contract. Writs flew. Rooney stuck by Stretford through thick and thin. When the ban finished in the spring of 2010, Stretford popped up again as Rooney's officially credited agent. In truth, he had never gone away. The two men have a great bond, perhaps because they have been through so many scrapes together. When all the dust has settled down, if you want Wayne Rooney to sponsor your spanking new toaster or pop drink or supermarket, you call Paul Stretford.

The upside of England being knocked out of Euro 2008 was that Wayne and Coleen could get hitched that summer. *The Sun* put it nicely: 'Always look on the bright side of wife.'

Wayne's stag do was in Ibiza, the Gomorrah of the Mediterranean. It set him back a reported £250,000 to fly out fifteen mates to the island where anything goes. But very little did. Did 'Fear of the Curse of the Honey-trappers' hang over his every move? Or had Wayne become a completely different man? Who knows?

What was obvious is that just one photograph showing Wayne chatting up a girl would imperil Coleen's big day. So Wayne and pals were mightily well chaperoned. On the stag were his dad, Wayne Senior, Coleen's dad, Tony McLoughlin, his best man, Shaun Molloy – Coleen's uncle – and Paul Stretford.

The party booked into a £20,000 villa, larked about the pool, drank the odd shandy and then Wayne was made to parade in a Borat-style Y-shaped mankini. It's a pity there are no snaps of this costume in the public domain because it would show Wayne's more feminine side.

The next day they boarded a boat and headed for the nearby island of Formentera. One of the lads wore a leopard-skin thong and Rooney was reported to jest that he was 'fucking caked'. They ate a curry.

On the razzle back on Ibiza, girls were *verboten*. The *Daily Mirror*'s Emily Nash and Louisa Pilbeam – almost certainly former head and deputy head girl at Roedean respectively – reported:

> One pal confided to us: 'We've been roped off in VIP areas where Wayne's security have completely banned girls. They can't let any of them anywhere near him in case someone takes a photo. The single lads are all gutted at seeing all these stunning girls coming towards us but not being allowed in. Coleen's not worried at all because she knows everyone keeping an eye on him.'

They added that they saw the England hero politely snub a female fan as she tried to chat to him in a bar. Another member of the Wazza party told her: 'It's nothing personal, but he can't be seen talking to girls.'

Coleen had three staggette or hen parties: a trip to Miami with her mates, one whole day in a spa in Manchester's posh Lowry Hotel with her mum and Wayne's too, and then a quick hop with a few pals to the Canaries to top up her tan.

The wedding invitation was ever so coy: 'Colette and Tony McLoughlin would be delighted if you could join them in celebrating the marriage of their daughter Coleen to Mr Wayne Rooney – to be held at a destination in Europe.' Invitees were asked to form up at John Lennon airport on 10 June.

Skeggy?

No, Portofino, a pretty port in the top left armpit of Italy, once the holiday home of Aubrey Herbert, the half-blind English aristo who was offered the throne of Albania, twice, but that's not important right now.

The wedding cost a cool £3 million, no, make that £5 million. The two figures were bandied about in the papers but reportedly either £1.5 million or £2.5 million of that cost was defrayed by *OK!* magazine, which bought the rights to the wedding snaps. The deal was a brilliant coup for the

Express group newspaper baron and titty TV pornography entrepreneur Richard Desmond. Once you know some of the history of the Desmond empire, the saccharine prose style of his *OK!* magazine seems almost a parody: the bride wore 'a cream strapless organza dress with embroidered bodice and a cascade skirt by Marchesa, and a pair of towering white Christian Louboutin shoes with crystal-encrusted heels . . . the registrar's table was dressed simply with drifts of white hydrangeas and roses. . .'

Don't mention the zapped testicles.

Very tasteful were *OK!*'s snaps too: bride and groom being radiantly happy on the front page; bride looking pretty gorgeous in the gardens of the Villa Durazzo, their two hands showing off wedding bands reportedly worth half a million quid – 'with this bling I thee wed'; a huge half-page picture of roses and a smaller one of the happy couple and their mums and dads. Roon's mum, Jeanette, had reportedly shed seven stone for the wedding and she looks in fine trim; Wayne Senior – oh, it pains to write this – looks like a defendant who has been found not guilty; and Colette and Tony McLoughlin are all smiles.

There are snaps of the couple signing the paperwork, with Coleen wiping away a tear; more grins from bride, groom, best man Shaun Molloy and maid of honour Claire Rooney; bride and groom having a quick snog; pre-do snaps of the girls in curlers and the boys in dressing gowns drinking bubbly; a quartet – violins, double bass – playing the theme to *Z Cars* (oh, I made that up); Coleen in wedding dress standing against two windows, overlooked by a medieval-ish painting featuring two bishops or similar divines holding crooks; Roo, his brothers Graeme and John and Coleen's brothers Joe and Tony; the bride walking along a pillared pathway, attended by her costumiers, her father and, at the back, a bald-headed gent who could be security; a sweet picture of Coleen's wheelchair-bound adopted sister Rosie; a lovely snap of bride and groom with his childhood hero, Duncan Ferguson, and his partner; bride and groom plighting their troth before God in the Church of San Girolamo; petals being thrown like confetti; the couple releasing doves into the air. There's more but, frankly, just typing this stuff up makes me sick.

'I THEE WET' was *The Sun*'s miserablist headline. The copy rained on their parade, announcing with unrestrained glee that 'Big-spending Wayne Rooney and Coleen McLoughlin . . . couldn't buy fine weather.' After three scorching days of 80°F temperatures, the heavens had opened and Coleen, who had spent the night on a luxury yacht, walked off the boat with a brolly held over her head. But a local Italian proverb saved Coleen's bacon: *Sposa bagnata, sposa fortunata* – 'a soaked bride is a loaded bride'.

Or something like that.

The wedding party took place with the sixty guests, Desmond's *OK!* panted, 'seated at beautifully dressed round tables, each adorned in crisp ivory linen, complemented with ivory coloured chairs and a satin sash around the back, secured with a pretty diamanté bow.'

What about the zapped testicles? Shh! Tuxedo-clad waiters served out a mouth-watering first course of fish and chips with a pint of Guinness for each guest, er, sorry, handmade Tuscan pâté or king prawns on a bed of lettuce. Next up pork pies, er, sorry, flambéed chicken or sea bass with rock salt, washed down with Laurent-Perrier Rosé 'poo or the local plonk, Vino Nobile di Montepulciano. For pudding, they had a tower of profiteroles.

The cake was not from Eccles.

The entertainment was Westlife, the Irish boyband, who had been hired for a reported £400,000. Wayne joined in and showed his true talent, singing 'Swear it all over again'. At midnight on the dot Queen's 'Somebody to Love' burst out of the loudspeakers, then came the fireworks.

The next day they all went for a ride on a big yacht and drank more champagne.

It did not sink.

16

WORLD CUP WONDER BOY

Sometime in 2009 something clicked inside Wayne Rooney's head and he became a boringly reliable goal-scoring machine. He'd always been exceptional but uneven, brilliant but unruly. In the 2009–10 season he just scored goal after goal after goal. Perhaps the new factor in his life was Fabio Capello, the stone-faced Italian brought in to give England a chance of doing something right in the World Cup. Rooney has said of the Italian that he is 'like a strict father'. As with Ferguson, Rooney seems to prosper under a strict, no-nonsense boss. Capello's advice to him was simple – don't hang about in the centre, go up front and score goals. And that Rooney has proceeded to do. In the best form of his life, he smashed in the only goal of the opening game of the season against Birmingham City thus bumping up his tally at United to ninety-nine. He got his century and one for luck two weeks later when he scored twice in a 5–0 away win at Wigan (not so) Athletic. In November, he scored his first hat-trick for three years in a 4–1 slaughter of Portsmouth. He saw out the Old Year by helping to demolish Hull, winning Man of the Match, and three days later grabbed another goal in United's repeat 5–0 thrashing of Wigan, this time at home. On fire, in January 2010 Rooney scored all four goals in Manchester United's 4–0 win over Hull.

Goal after goal after goal: goals against Arsenal, AC Milan and Aston Villa – and that's just against clubs starting with the letter A. (Did anyone mention Manchester City? It doesn't begin with A.)

Goals with the boot and goals with the head.

But something else wasn't happening, too. There were no miserable headlines in the tabloids about Rooney shaming Coleen and texting or bonking X or Y or Z. The temptations are still out there – they always will be for a multimillionaire England player – but New Rooney is not coming out to play. It's as if his passion for the game, his diehard will to win, is more important to him than messing about with people he shouldn't be messing about with. In a season when England's captain, John Terry, was stripped of his post because he had had an affair with lingerie model Vanessa Perroncel, the former partner of his then England teammate Wayne Bridge, and Ashley Cole split up with Cheryl over a battery of embarrassing allegations about him texting naked snaps of himself to Page Three girls, Rooney's name hasn't been mentioned on the front pages once. Except for scoring goals.

So what's caused Old Rooney – the boy who used to frequent Diva's – to mutate to New Rooney, the squeaky-clean goal machine? Well, his love for Coleen, obviously. A new maturity, both on and off the pitch.

And everybody go: WAAAAAAAAAAAAAAAAAAA!

Kai Rooney was born in November 2009, a bouncing baby boy. *The Mirror* won the battle of the headline puns with 'GA GA GOO ROO', with *The Sun* offering 'IT'S ANOTHER GREAT DRIBBLE FROM...' and *The People* 'ON THE BAWL'. Whatever the headlines, it's clear from the snaps that Wayne and Coleen love their lad. They have even dressed him up in an Everton strip – a fact that might cause a chin or two to wobble over the gazpacho soup and heart-shaped croutons at Manchester United's commercial department.

Meanwhile, the long, long battle over who gets to represent Wayne Rooney dragged its way into Court 44 of Manchester's Mercantile Court. It was mid-February 2010. The rump of Proactive, now part of Formation Group, was suing Wayne and Coleen for not paying its claimed cut – a cool £4.3 million. After the split in October 2008 between Proactive and Paul Stretford, the Rooneys had stuck with the agent. They stopped paying Proactive commissions of up to 20 per cent on multimillion-pound contracts signed by them with outfits like Coca-Cola and Nike. Proactive wanted their share of the dosh – past and future.

The lawyers flabbered out on the court benches like so many pin-striped elephant seals on an Antarctic beach, dreaming of fish or fees or whatever lawyers dream of. Above the judge, the Lion and the Unicorn did their thing. (It always amuses me that the symbols of the Crown and British justice are an animal that doesn't live here and goes round biting the heads off people and a mythical beast from fairy tales with a boner on its bonce. Spot on.) After a bit a fat man in a big black shirt walked in and sat down next to a solicitor who looked like Ant or Dec with specs. He was Wayne Rooney Senior.

Enter Paul Stretford, heavyish frame but not porky, with an energy about him. He walked past me on the way to the witness box and smiled pleasantly. His voice was soft, his manner a bit nervy, a dogfish out of water. Ian Mill, QC, Proactive's silk, poked him a bit to little effect, then his silk, Paul Chaisty, QC, asked him about the blackmail trial. Suddenly, Stretford froze, stopped talking and started to – I use this word figuratively – melt. The brief told him to take his time.

Was this bad am-dram? 'Saucy Worcester – thou too? Forsooth?' Was the agent hamming it up a bit? Or had his memory been jogged to think back to the worst time in his life? Who knows? He sipped water and recovered his composure.

The lawyers took him through the nuances of the two footballing agreements signed by the Rooneys with Proactive (then run by Stretford) in the summer of 2002, when the star was still contracted to Peter Mac. Then Mill started asking about the late Kevin Dooley, another embarrassing question.

Soon Stretford left the witness stand and his place was taken by Wayne Rooney. In the flesh he's smaller than you imagine, lithe, muscular, with a boxer's animality that draws you to him and repels you at the same time. Rooney comes complete with an edge of danger. 'Mute gimp' was how one snotty hack described him for his performance in *Rio Ferdinand's World Cup Wind-Ups*. The gimp has gone. Instead, Rooney gave the oath in a strong voice and knocked back a series of legal jousts with not swagger but self-confidence. He wasn't a natural in court – who is? – but he wasn't afraid to speak his mind and to refine his evidence when needed. He is no Cicero, but he's better than Beckham.

As he gave his evidence, some of the dealings of Planet Rooney came out. Sir Alex Ferguson restricts his sponsorships to five, lest they get in the way of his day job. He was only doing four out of five – Nike (£1 million a year, according to court papers filed in 2009), Coca-Cola (£600,000 over four years), EA Sports computer games (£200,000 a year) and Tiger beer. 'To be honest, I'm probably doing the max,' Rooney said in thickish Scouse. 'My wife has just had a baby. I need time to spend with them and I need time with my family as well. It could change but not at the minute.'

Rooney clearly sided with Stretford in his dispute with Proactive, but didn't seem to grip the key point at the heart of Proactive's case – that if the sponsorship deals were signed with Proactive, then they get the commissions, not the man who happened to be holding the pen at the time of the signing ceremony, Stretford.

At one point, the two briefs and the judge needed to know how much Rooney earned from Man United. Rooney fished out a piece of paper from his pocket and folded it and it was passed around the three legal bods.

In the lift on the way down to lunch I said: 'I wonder what was written on the paper. More than I get...'

'More than this whole lift gets...' said someone else.

'More than this entire building...' said a third, which was probably over the top because we are talking about a mass of lawyers' earnings, after all.

Next up was Jeanette Rooney, who looks hugely better after she has shed stones in weight. She's the feisty one in the family: feisty, ferocious and fun, blonde hair, eyes of black granite. One of the briefs started yakking on about Peter Mac and she closed that down: 'He was a schoolboy agent.'

It is fair to say it hasn't been all plain sailing with Paul Stretford, the agent they ended up with – the Rooneys' meeting with Dooley, the crooked lawyer about to get struck off for his relationship with 'Long John' Silver, the eight-year contract (only six years too long), the brushes with the gangster, the collapse of the blackmail trial because the Crown couldn't rely on the agent's word, the fine and the ban from the FA and, in the spring of 2010, a civil case in which details of the Rooneys' finances were outed in open court for the world and his wife to hear. The Rooneys will not spare their financial blushes if millions of pounds are at stake. Is Paul Stretford worth all the baggage he comes with? That's a question that only Wayne and Coleen can answer. After the split with Proactive, Stretford co-founded Triple S Sports & Entertainment Group. According to Ian Monk's PR agency, Triple S's clients include Wayne and Coleen.

At the time of going to press, the judge had still not delivered his verdict on Proactive versus the Rooneys.

Fancy the ladies in leopard skin, do ya? If so, top totty in a big-cat-spotted beach gown graced the cover of *Hello!* magazine in April 2010, bearing the legend: 'OPENING THE DOORS TO THEIR STUNNING NEW HOME IN BARBADOS COLEEN ROONEY INVITES US INTO HER AND WAYNE'S LIFE – OUR BEAUTIFUL BABY BOY – MY ROMANTIC HUSBAND – WHY I'M PROUD OF MY CURVES.'

Coleen, sporting ear-rings the size of industrial egg-whisks and the aforesaid spotted number, was snapped dangling her pins in the pool at the couple's new pad in the West Indies. (Readers who have been paying close attention will have spotted that the Rooneys, after the Wedding of the Millennium, dumped Richard Desmond's *OK!* magazine for *Hello!*) And that's just for starters. There's acres of snaps of Coleen on her own in her pad by the Caribbean, her eyes smoking at the camera in a bedroom wearing a fireman's yellow smock with buttons down the middle; slinky Coleen wrestling with a curtain, one high heel angled to show off her ankle at its best, revealing enough leg to cause a riot in, er, north Tehran; Coleen in the kitchen looking foxy juggling oranges in a dress that looks like a fist fight in a hydrangea bush. (That's someone else's joke, but I love it.)

The birth of a new baby, the romantic soft spots of a man, the curves of a woman's body – these are private matters, some say. Then they should read Coleen's interview with *Hello!* It's grimly saccharine stuff, self-intruding and intrusive.

> *HELLO!*: Is Wayne romantic?
> COLEEN: Not gooey romantic ... He's a man's man.

That's enough of that.

HELLO!: Did you speak to Toni Terry or Cheryl Cole about their marriage problems?

COLEEN: I've met Toni many times before when we've been away with England and she's an absolutely lovely girl . . . Cheryl is just so nice and doing so well.

On her and Wayne: 'what's nice is that we have a balanced relationship.' What's nice about Stalin and Yezhov is they had a balanced relationship. All right, all right, I am not for a moment comparing Wayne and Coleen with Stalin and fellow mass-murderer and NKVD chum Nikolai Yezhov. But the two Soviet killers were once pictured happy as Larry at the opening of the White Sea Canal – and when Yezhov was butchered on Stalin's orders in 1940, he was literally airbrushed out of the picture.

There's no serious harm in Coleen's interview with *Hello!* and if you like reading stuff like this, then good luck to you. But the images and the words of 'COLEEN ROONEY INVITES US INTO HER AND WAYNE'S LIFE' are so airbrushed they are very far from reflecting real life.

What seems to me objectionable is the way that lawyers for the Rooneys bang on about the couple's right to privacy and yet the couple are happy to take a heavily airbrushed version of their lives to market. Celebrities are only human and Wayne and Coleen are not bad people, far from it. But having your cake and eating it is not a human right, at least, not yet.

Free speech is.

On the pitch in the spring of 2010 as the season winds up to a close, Ferguson's policy of playing Rooney virtually non-stop has secured a great, goal-scoring run for the Crocky cyclone. Wayne has been on such terrific form that, as an England fan, one prays that he won't be felled by some stupid tackle and go clattering down – a knee, an ankle, a leg. England fans are already moaning that Sir Alex Ferguson has been playing him every match, to which the obvious retort is that watching Rooney boil in frustration on the sidelines is the best possible way of igniting his anger – and we don't want that at all.

In the end it was the ankle, whilst playing Bayern Munich in the Champions League Quarter Final first leg at the Allianz Arena. In the last breath of the game, Rooney slumped to the ground, his ankle twisted. He missed the crucial Premier League match with Chelsea. United, without their talisman, lost to the nancy boys from the King's Road – not my description but that of the Stretford End. Man United look set to be pipped to the post for the Premiership. But they're not quite finished yet.

Ferguson, ever wily, played Rooney's injury big. He wouldn't be fit for the return match with Bayern Munich.

So it was with some surprise that, standing in the Stretford End, surrounded by a sea of green and gold scarves – two of the loan-rich Glazers popped in, but seemed to be very quiet about it – I saw Wayne Rooney step out onto Old Trafford. The big man was back, and for forty-odd minutes, he played beautifully, electrifying the entire game, creating play, making havoc with Bayern's defence, so that United were 3–0 up. It couldn't last and it didn't. A couple of tackles, a twist and turn too fast, and Wayne was limping, desperate to do his bit, but physically, at the end of a long season, not up to it. The Germans clawed back one and it was the end of the first half.

But such is Ferguson's faith in Rooney that there he was back again for the start of the second half, while fitter, lesser strikers strained at the leash. Not a sensible gamble. Rooney stuttered and limped some more. Rafael da Silva got a red card, and down to ten men it was miserable to watch. Rooney was taken off and then the Germans took the rump of Manchester United apart. Without Rooney, in that game, Manchester United looked like Tranmere on a bad day. Eventually, Arjen Robben banged in a cracking volley and it was *auf Wiedersehen* Europe, United going down 4–4 on aggregate on away goals.

With Roonaldo gone and Rooney injured, the Red Devils don't look very scary. For Manchester United, if there's no serious money for new talent around, then there may be trouble ahead.

That leaves the World Cup. By then, Rooney will be back at full fitness, bursting to have a go for the greatest prize in football.

To watch Rooney's astonishing work rate on the pitch is a thing to behold. And then you remember Brian Stimpson, the psychotic head teacher played by John Cleese in the film *Clockwise*, who barks: 'It's not the despair; I can cope with the despair' – and then, gaining some measure of mental composure, some sense of self-knowledge – 'it's the hope.'

Come the World Cup, let's hope he kicks the ball. (And not the balls of another player.)

Let's hope he's on fire. (But not arrested for arson.)

Let's hope he does himself and everyone in the Wezzy and the rest of us proud.

That's the thing about our favourite lion. You never know whether he will roar for England or bite your legs off.

Or both.

But as I said at the beginning, that's the way we like our lions, rough, not smooth.

INDEX